D1321715

EMQs for
Medical Students
Volume 1

PASTEST
Dedicated to your success

EMQs for
Medical Students
Volume 1

Adam Feather
Paola Domizio
Benjamin C T Field
Charles H Knowles
John S P Lumley

PASTEST
Dedicated to your success

© 2001 PasTest Ltd

Egerton Court
Parkgate Estate
Knutsford
Cheshire, WA16 8DX

Telephone: 01565 752000

First edition 2001

ISBN: 1 901198 65 0

A catalogue record for this book is available from the British Library.

The information contained within this book was obtained by the authors from reliable sources. However, while every effort has been made to ensure its accuracy, no responsibility for loss, damage or injury occasioned to any person acting or refraining from action as a result of information contained herein can be accepted by the publisher or the authors.

PasTest Revision Books and Intensive Courses
PasTest has been established in the field of postgraduate medical education since 1972, providing revision books and intensive study courses for doctors preparing for their professional examinations. Books and courses are available for the following specialties:
Undergraduate exams, MRCP Part 1 and Part 2, MRCPCH Part 1 and Part 2, MRCOG, DRCOG, MRCGP, MRCPsych, DCH, FRCA, MRCS and PLAB.

For further details contact:

PasTest Ltd, Freepost, Knutsford, Cheshire, WA16 7BR
Tel: 01565 752000   Fax: 01565 650264
Email: enquiries@pastest.co.uk   Web site: www. pastest.co.uk

---

Typeset by Saxon Graphics Ltd
Printed by Bell and Bain Ltd, Glasgow

Contents

Contributors

Adam Feather MRCP
Specialist Registrar in Elderly Care
Care of the Elderly Department
Newham General Hospital
Plaistow
London

Paola Domizio BSc MB BS FRCPath ILTM
Senior Lecturer in Histopathology
Department of Histopathology
Barts and the London, Queen Mary's School of Medicine
West Smithfield
London

Benjamin C T Field MB BS BMedSci MRCP
Specialist Registrar in Endocrinology and Diabetes
Department of Medicine
Charing Cross Hospital
London

Charles H Knowles MBBChir PhD FRCS
Specialist Registrar in Surgery, North East Thames
Honorary Lecturer in Surgery
Academic Department of Surgery
Royal London Hospital
and
Clinical Lecturer in Academic Surgery
University of London

John S P Lumley MS FRCS
Professor of Surgery and Honorary Consultant Surgeon
St Bartholomew's Hospital, London
Member of Council, Royal College of Surgeons of England
Past World President, International College of Surgeons

Preface

The problems of equating a medical examination to a training programme are compounded when candidates are being assessed from different programmes, and sometimes from different continents, with varying linguistic skills. Nevertheless, standard-setting bodies have a responsibility to examine at an appropriate level, to ensure the delivery of optimal medical care to the community they represent.

The emphasis of the final examination should be to ensure the candidate's fitness to practise. Recent developments in examination systems have been to divide them into their component parts, with an emphasis on the objective assessment of each section. Thus, every qualifying doctor should have proven competencies in written knowledge and clinical skills, and be able to communicate, examine and relate to patients.

This text is devoted to the extended matching question (EMQ), a newer technique that is being used alongside or replacing the MCQ. It has been used in North America since the mid-1990s, and after its introduction into the UK by the Royal College of General Practitioners in the MRCGP examination, it has gained favour with a number of other Royal colleges and medical schools.

There is always a danger that the technique is being examined as much as the medical information, and whatever system is used, it is essential that the candidate is fully aware of, exposed to and practised in the chosen technique for any examination.

This pair of texts is intended to address this problem. They have been prepared for the final medical examination and the material is drawn from all parts of the undergraduate curriculum. They also serve as an introduction to EMQs for students early in their clinical course and provide suitable revision material for postgraduates entering this form of examination in every discipline. They will be helpful to examiners not versed in preparing EMQs, both from a stylistic and content point of view. It is advisable to use teams of examiners and students to assess new questions, as opinions can vary on correct responses, especially those involving clinical management. The authors will not be surprised, or offended, if some of their own responses are challenged over time. In general, EMQs are more focused than MCQs and they are a welcome extension of this style of examination.

Introduction

Traditional final and postgraduate examinations consisted of a written essay paper, a clinical of long and short cases and a viva. Although these methods provided excellent doctors for most of the last century, when they were assessed by objective measurements their reliability, reproducibility and validity came into question. Another problem with each of these methods, was the limited amount of a curriculum that could be assessed in a single diet of an examination. It could thus be a lottery as to whether candidates were asked well known or unfamiliar material and whether examiners were asking obscure details of their own speciality.

Continuous assessment of a course ensures matching of the training and assessment of its content. However, this is only possible for internal examinations.

Many techniques have been introduced to extend the area covered by a single examination and to standardise its marking system. The objective structured clinical examination (OSCE) has so far proved the most reproducible and reliable of the new systems. The written paper has received a great deal of attention: although the traditional free response essay allows a candidate to demonstrate extensive knowledge, it covers an extremely small area of the course. When questions are set around the core of the curriculum, as is appropriate in a valid and reliable examination, these questions are easily spotted. Also, poor organisation of facts and illegible handwriting can contribute to failure as much as a lack of basic knowledge. Short answers and short essay questions widen the area of assessment, and also reduce the reliance on technique. The MCQ has retained an important place in medical examinations for thirty years. The technique allows examination across a wide field, but clinical options are rarely totally right or wrong and well-constructed questions, even when set by a group of examiners, can still mislead well-prepared candidates.

The extended matching question (EMQ) is able to cover a wide area of the curriculum and assess the candidate's knowledge of clinically relevant information. It also goes beyond a simple recall of factual information, and assesses a candidate's ability to interpret data drawn from realistic, often existing, clinical problems.

Each EMQ has a theme, a list of options, an introductory statement and a series of stems or vignettes. A quick look at any of the subsequent questions will provide an idea of its format. The chosen themes cover a wide range of topics that are all relevant and important to clinical practice. They include the anatomy of tissues and organs, symptoms, abnormal signs, normal and abnormal investigations and specific diseases. They are organised by system and are listed in the contents at the beginning of each volume.

All options are feasible answers and are clustered around the chosen theme. They usually provide an extensive cover of the topic, and serve as revision aids, but are not necessarily all-inclusive. The larger the number of options, the less likely a correct answer can be obtained by chance, elimination or exclusion. However, the number also relates to the topic, the design of the question and the maximum number of feasible alternatives. Rare conditions are occasionally included, both as options and correct answers, providing a broad exposure to the field. The chosen number of options is between eight and twelve, although this may be extended from five to twenty, depending on the topic. The options are listed alphabetically, unless a more appropriate order exists.

The introductory statement must be carefully read, as it tells the reader what is expected of them. Usually one option has to be chosen to answer each stem or vignette. The stems or vignettes determine the standard of a question, and must be pitched at the appropriate level for any examination. At an undergraduate level, vignettes are rich in uninterpreted symptoms, signs and investigations, but in more advanced examinations a clinical summary may be given without the need to sort out basic information. Key diagnostic criteria may be deliberately excluded to avoid making an answer too easy, or to stimulate the reader to think more deeply around a topic.

The vignettes must be sufficiently detailed to only match the intended option from the list. However, in a few cases, where this increases understanding and clinical reasoning, more than one option has been identified: this is stated clearly within the introductory statement. Options provide a whole range of alternatives, including isolated facts, encouraging recognition and recall, but emphasis is given to clinical decision-making and interpretation of material, focusing on clinical scenarios. The number of vignettes is generally five, but this varies in different sections.

The second half of each book gives the answers to each question, together with an extended explanation, providing an overview of the topic and a revision aid for each theme. It is not necessarily comprehensive, but should identify gaps and direct further reading.

The time allowed for an EMQ examination differs from that of MCQs as each vignette can be quite complex, reflecting clinical practice, and time is needed to consider all options. In general, 120—160 vignettes can be answered in two hours, and not more than 200 should be included in a three-hour examination. The scoring is one mark for each correct answer: if more than one option is correct, a mark or a proportion of the mark can be scored. There is no negative marking in EMQ assessment.

Six practice examinations are listed at the end of the book, drawing questions from across the syllabus: each is intended as a two-hour examination. Questions are taken from both texts. For those not yet fortunate enough to have bought or acquired both volumes, there is a clear distinction between the two halves of each examination, and they can be answered independently.

QUESTIONS

CHAPTER 1

General Pathology

1. THEME: PATHOLOGICAL PROCESSES

A Apoptosis
B Atrophy
C Dysplasia
D Embolism
E Fibrosis
F Hyperplasia
G Hypertrophy
H Infarction
I Metaplasia
J Metastasis
K Necrosis
L Thrombosis

For each of the patients listed below choose the most appropriate pathological process from the above list.

1. A 45-year-old man presents with 'acid heartburn'. An endoscopy is performed at which the lower oesophageal mucosa appears red and velvety. A biopsy taken from this area shows glandular epithelium.

2. A 75-year-old man presents with symptoms of urinary outflow obstruction. Investigations show an enlarged prostate gland.

3. A 21-year-old woman suffers a fractured left femur in a road traffic accident. She requires traction and is bed-bound for several weeks. On removal of the traction, the left leg is weak and the left quadriceps are visibly wasted.

4. A 32-year-old woman who is taking the oral contraceptive pill boards a flight from London to San Francisco. On arrival her right leg feels uncomfortable. The following day her right calf is swollen and tender.

5. A 40-year-old woman has a cervical biopsy following an abnormal cervical smear. The biopsy shows lack of maturation throughout the whole thickness of the epithelium.

6. A 65-year-old man with long-standing hypertension develops cardiac failure. A chest X-ray shows enlargement of the heart and an echocardiogram shows a thickened left ventricular free wall.

2. THEME: CELLS OF THE IMMUNE SYSTEM

A   Cytotoxic T-lymphocyte
B   Dendritic cell
C   Helper T-lymphocyte
D   Langerhans' cell
E   Macrophage
F   Mast cell
G   Memory B cell
H   Natural killer cell
I   Plasma cell
J   Stem cell
K   Virgin B-lymphocyte
L   Virgin T-lymphocyte

For each of the descriptions below, select the cell type from the above list.

1. An antibody-producing cell with an eccentric nucleus, a 'clock-face' pattern of nuclear chromatin and a perinuclear halo.

2. An antigen presenting cell that is important in determining the response to antigen by virgin T-lymphocytes.

3. A cell bearing CD3 and CD4 molecules on its surface.

4. A phagocytic cell containing lysozyme.

5. A cell bearing CD8 that recognises processed antigen in association with class 1 MHC molecules.

6. A type of lymphocyte that bears CD56 on its surface and can attack tumour cells and virally infected cells without the need for prior sensitisation.

3. THEME: COMPONENTS OF ANTIGENS AND ANTIBODIES

A   Epitope
B   Fab fragment
C   Fc fragment
D   Hapten
E   Heavy chain
F   HLA
G   IgA
H   IgE
I   IgG
J   Light chain
K   Superantigen
L   Variable region

For each of the descriptions below, choose the component of antigen or antibody from the above list.

1. The part of an antigen that binds to an antibody.

2. The part of an immunoglobulin molecule responsible for antigen binding.

3. An immunoglobulin involved in mast cell degranulation.

4. A molecule that must bind to a carrier protein before it can elicit an immune response.

5. A group of molecules, coded for on chromosome 6, responsible for rejection reactions.

6. An antigen that can activate T-lymphocytes without being processed by antigen-presenting cells.

4. THEME: TECHNIQUES IN MOLECULAR MEDICINE

A   DNA fingerprinting
B   DNA sequencing
C   Hybridisation
D   Linkage analysis
E   Northern blotting
F   Polymerase chain reaction (PCR)
G   Southern blotting
H   Transfection
I   Transformation
J   Western blotting

The following are all brief descriptions of common molecular techniques utilised in medical research. Please select the technique which best fits each description from the above list.

1. The insertion of a gene or genes into mammalian cells.

2. A term used for the *in vitro* formation of base pairs between nucleic acids. It is usually used to probe for the presence of a specific sequence of DNA or RNA.

3. A method to separate and detect proteins using a denaturing sodium dodecyl sulphate (SDS)/polyacrylamide gel.

4. An *in vitro* technique designed to isolate and amplify small, specific segments of DNA between 10^5 and 10^8 from insignificant quantities of template (less than 1 μg) in a short space of time.

5. A method which investigates the possibility that a gene of interest is close to, and therefore often inherited with, a known genetic marker.

5. THEME: TYPES OF INFLAMMATION

A Acute suppurative
B Basophil-rich
C Caseating granulomatous
D Chronic
E Eosinophil-rich
F Fibrinous
G Histiocytic
H Non-caseating granulomatous

For each disease listed below, please select the type of inflammation characteristic of the disease from the above list.

1. Tuberculosis ☐

2. *Helicobacter pylori* associated gastritis ☐

3. Rheumatic pericarditis ☐

4. Sarcoidosis ☐

5. Bacterial meningitis ☐

6. Hookworm infection ☐

6. THEME: MEDIATORS OF ACUTE INFLAMMATION

A Arachidonic acid
B C3b
C E- selectin
D Factor XII
E Histamine
F Intercellular cell adhesion molecule 1 (ICAM-1)
G Interferon-gamma
H Interleukin 1 (IL-1)
I Lysozyme
J Plasminogen activator
K Prostaglandin E2
L Superoxide anion

For each of the descriptions below, select the correct inflammatory mediator from the above list.

1. A substance involved in the opsonisation of bacteria.

2. A substance released from mast cells that leads to increased vascular permeability.

3. A molecule important in oxygen-dependent bacterial killing.

4. A member of the immunoglobulin gene superfamily expressed on endothelial cells.

5. A multifunctional peptide that induces expression of adhesion molecules on vascular endothelium and acts as an endogenous pyrogen.

6. An enzyme that attacks the cell wall of some bacterial species.

7. THEME: INFECTIOUS DISEASES

A   Actinomycosis
B   Amoebiasis
C   Aspergillosis
D   Candidiasis
E   Cryptosporidiosis
F   Falciparum malaria
G   Giardiasis
H   Leishmaniasis
I   Pneumocystis pneumonia
J   Schistosomiasis
K   Strongyloidiasis
L   Toxoplasmosis

For each of the patients below, select the most likely disease from the above list.

1. A 35-year-old man presents with abdominal pain and bloody diarrhoea one month after returning from holiday to India. Colonoscopy shows multiple flask-shaped ulcers throughout the colon. Biopsy of the ulcerated areas shows PAS-positive trophozoites with ingested red cells in the ulcer slough.

2. A neonate presents soon after birth with jaundice and an enlarged liver. He is also found to have hydrocephalus and choroidoretinitis. A skull X-ray shows foci of calcification.

3. A 35-year-old woman who is receiving chemotherapy for high grade lymphoma develops shortness of breath accompanied by a dry cough. Chest X-ray shows bilateral reticulonodular shadowing. Sputum culture is negative. Transbronchial biopsy shows alveoli filled with a foamy eosinophilic material and numerous boat-shaped organisms staining positively with a silver stain.

4. A 48-year-old Egyptian man presents with a six month history of haematuria. Cystoscopy shows a polypoid mass in the bladder. Biopsy of the mass shows granulomatous chronic inflammation around clusters of parasite ova.

5. A 30-year-old English journalist who is working in Africa develops fever and rigors. On examination she has hepatosplenomegaly. Examination of a blood film shows parasitised red blood cells.

continued . . .

11

6. A 32-year-old man with AIDS presents with a two week history of dysphagia. Endoscopy shows white plaques on the oesophageal mucosa. Biopsy of the plaques shows fungal hyphae and yeast forms on the mucosal surface.

8. THEME: BACTERIAL INFECTIONS

A   Campylobacter jejuni
B   Chlamydia trachomatis
C   Clostridium difficile
D   Clostridium perfringens
E   Escherichia coli
F   Haemophilus influenzae
G   Listeria monocytogenes
H   Neisseria meningitidis
I   Salmonella typhi
J   Staphylococcus aureus
K   Streptococcus pneumoniae
L   Streptococcus pyogenes

The patients below have all presented with infections. Select the bacterium which is the most likely cause from the above list.

1. A 21-year-old medical student presents with a twelve hour history of severe headache, photophobia and pyrexia. Clinical examination shows a petechial rash over the trunk. CSF analysis shows numerous neutrophils and Gram-negative cocci.

2. A 32-year-old woman presents with dysuria and frequency for two days. Gram stain of a midstream urine specimen shows neutrophils, erythrocytes and Gram-negative bacilli. Urine culture shows >10 organisms per ml. The colonies are lactose fermenting.

3. An 84-year-old man being treated for a chest infection on the care-of-the-elderly ward develops increasingly severe diarrhoea. Sigmoidoscopy shows white plaques on the mucosal surface. Faecal analysis isolates a toxin that is cytopathic in cell culture.

4. A 57-year-old vagrant woman presents with a one week history of productive cough, pyrexia and worsening shortness of breath. A chest X-ray shows consolidation of the left lower lobe. Gram stain of the sputum shows many neutrophils and Gram-positive diplococci. Sputum culture shows alpha-haemolytic, draughtsman-shaped colonies.

5. A 12-year-old boy develops a wound infection after a right hemicolectomy for Crohn's disease. Gram stain of the exuded pus shows clusters of Gram-positive cocci. Culture shows coagulase-positive golden yellow colonies.

6. A 45-year-old woman develops diarrhoea and abdominal pain two days after eating fried chicken in a restaurant. Gram stain of the faeces shows Gram-negative, motile, spiral-shaped rods. Faecal culture shows oxidase-positive colonies.

9. THEME: PATHOGENIC VIRUSES

A   Coxsackie virus
B   Cytomegalovirus
C   Epstein-Barr virus
D   Hepatitis C virus
E   Herpes simplex virus type 2
F   Herpes zoster virus
G   Human papilloma virus
H   Measles virus
I   Parainfluenza virus
J   Parvovirus
K   Rhinovirus
L   Rotavirus

For each disease listed below, select the virus most likely to cause the disease.

1. Genital warts

2. Infectious mononucleosis

3. Croup

4. Aseptic meningitis

5. Diarrhoea in children

6. Subacute sclerosing panencephalitis

10. THEME: TYPES OF AMYLOID PROTEIN

A   AA amyloid
B   AL amyloid
C   Atrial natriuretic factor
D   Beta amyloid protein
E   Beta-2 microglobulin
F   Calcitonin
G   Islet amyloid polypeptide
H   Transthyretin

For each of the diseases below select the type of amyloid protein deposited in each disease from the above list.

1.   Plasma cell myeloma   ☐

2.   Alzheimer's disease   ☐

3.   Rheumatoid arthritis   ☐

4.   Type 2 diabetes mellitus   ☐

5.   Medullary carcinoma of the thyroid   ☐

11. THEME: TYPES OF EPITHELIUM

A   Pseudostratified ciliated columnar
B   Simple columnar
C   Simple cuboidal
D   Simple squamous
E   Stratified cuboidal
F   Stratified squamous, keratinising
G   Stratified squamous, non-keratinising
H   Transitional cell

For each of the tissues or organs below, select the type of epithelium found in each from the above list.

1. Bladder

2. Ectocervix

3. Trachea

4. Pericardium

5. Skin

12. THEME: ENVIRONMENTAL CARCINOGENS

A   Aflatoxin B1
B   Arsenic
C   Asbestos
D   Beta-naphthylamine
E   Betel nut
F   Cigarette smoke
G   Cyclophosphamide
H   Ionising radiation
I   Nitrosamines
J   Polychlorinated biphenyls
K   Ultraviolet light
L   Vinyl chloride

For each of the tumours below, select the most likely causative carcinogen from the above list of options.

1. Malignant melanoma of the skin

2. Squamous cell carcinoma of the lung

3. Transitional cell carcinoma of the bladder

4. Hepatocellular carcinoma

5. Adenocarcinoma of the stomach

6. Papillary carcinoma of the thyroid

13. THEME: VIRAL AND MICROBIAL CARCINOGENS

A *Aspergillus flavus*
B *Clonorchis sinensis*
C Epstein-Barr virus
D *Helicobacter pylori*
E Hepatitis B virus
F Human herpesvirus type 8
G Human papillomavirus
H Human T-cell leukaemia virus type 1
I Rous sarcoma virus
J *Schistosoma haematobium*

For each of the malignancies below, select the viral or microbial carcinogen associated with the malignancy from the above list.

1. Squamous cell carcinoma of the cervix

2. Primary gastric lymphoma

3. Kaposi's sarcoma

4. Hepatocellular carcinoma

5. Burkitt's lymphoma

14. THEME: GENE ABNORMALITIES IN NEOPLASIA

A Amplification of n-myc
B Deletion of APC
C Deletion of Rb
D Mutation in BRCA1
E Mutation in K-ras
F Mutation in NF-2
G Mutation in p53
H Overexpression of bcl-2
I Translocation t(8:14)
J Translocation t(9:22)

For each of the neoplasms below, select the associated gene abnormality from the above list.

1. Follicular lymphoma

2. Familial carcinoma of the breast

3. Chronic myeloid leukaemia

4. Retinoblastoma

5. Adenomas in familial adenomatous polyposis

15. THEME: NEOPLASMS

A Adenocarcinoma
B Adenoma
C Burkitt's lymphoma
D Fibroadenoma
E Lipoma
F Melanoma
G Myeloma
H Neurofibroma
I Osteosarcoma
J Squamous cell carcinoma
K Squamous cell papilloma
L Transitional cell carcinoma

For each of the patients below, select the neoplasm they are likely to have from the above list.

1. A 65-year-old man, a lifelong heavy smoker, presents with a six week history of cough and haemoptysis. Investigations show a mass at the hilum of the left lung. Sputum cytology shows highly atypical keratinised cells.

2. A 40-year-old woman presents with a 3 cm mobile lump in the subcutaneous tissue of her abdominal wall. Excision of the mass shows a well-circumscribed soft yellow mass.

3. A 14-year-old boy presents with a two week history of swelling around the left knee joint. X-ray of the knee shows a partly calcified lytic lesion in the distal femur that lifts the periosteum.

4. A 72-year-old man presents with painless haematuria. A mid-stream urine specimen shows no bacterial growth. Cystoscopy shows a friable mass near the left ureteric orifice.

5. A 42-year-old woman presents with a recent onset of bright red rectal bleeding. Flexible sigmoidoscopy shows a pedunculated 1 cm polyp in the rectum.

6. A 53-year-old man presents with a two month history of dyspepsia and weight loss. Endoscopy shows a large ulcerated mass on the lesser curve in the antrum. Biopsy of the lesion shows signet ring cells.

16. THEME: EPONYMOUS CELLS

A Clara cell
B Kupffer cell
C Langerhans' cell
D Langhans' cell
E Leydig cell
F Paneth cell
G Purkinje cell
H Reed-Sternberg cell
I Schwann cell
J Sertoli cell

For each description below, select the cell that the description applies to from the above list.

1. A multinucleate giant cell found in tuberculous granulomas ☐

2. A cell that produces myelin in the peripheral nervous system ☐

3. A supporting cell found inside testicular tubules ☐

4. A neoplastic cell diagnostic of Hodgkin's disease ☐

5. A cell found in the sinusoids of the liver ☐

17. THEME: VITAMIN DEFICIENCY

A   Folate
B   Nicotinic acid (niacin)
C   Vitamin A
D   Vitamin B1 (thiamine)
E   Vitamin B6 (pyridoxine)
F   Vitamin B12 (cobalamin)
G   Vitamin C
H   Vitamin D
I   Vitamin E
J   Vitamin K

For each of the patients listed below, select the most likely vitamin deficiency from the above list.

1. A 46-year-old man, a long-standing chronic alcoholic, presents with peripheral neuropathy and worsening loss of memory. On examination, he also has ataxia, nystagmus and mild pedal oedema. He is admitted to hospital for investigation where the nurses notice he is confabulating.

2. A 39-year-old woman presents with dyspepsia and shortness of breath on exercise. Blood tests show a severe anaemia, which on investigation is found to be megaloblastic. Gastric biopsies taken at endoscopy show severe atrophic gastritis, predominantly in the corpus. Anti-parietal cell antibodies are detected in the serum.

3. A 52-year-old man with long-standing chronic pancreatitis and consequent steatorrhoea presents with recurrent epistaxis, malaena and haematuria. On examination he also has numerous bruises on his arms and shins.

4. A 76-year-old woman who lives alone is visited by social services after a worried neighbour says he has not seen her for several months. On questioning she admits that she has hardly left her flat for four months as she has become increasingly agoraphobic. She has been surviving on tinned soup and crackers. Her GP is called to examine her and finds she has swollen, bleeding gums, and bruises over her shins. Her skin shows a hyperkeratotic papular rash and petechial haemorrhages.

5. A 3-year-old Indian boy whose parents are strict vegans is taken to his GP with a cough. On examination of the chest, he is found to have anterior protrusion of the sternum. The GP also notices that he has lumbar lordosis and bowing of the legs.

CHAPTER 2

Head and neck

1. THEME: PHARMACOLOGY OF THE EYE

A   Antazoline
B   Atropine
C   Brimonidine
D   Carbachol
E   Fluorescein
F   Hypromellose
G   Phenylephrine
H   Pilocarpine
I   Timolol
J   Tropicamide

The patients below have presented with eye disorders. Choose the most appropriate drug from the above list.

1. A 40-year-old woman presents to her GP with dry itchy eyes, dry mouth and bilateral parotid enlargement. Schirmer's test is positive.

2. A 64-year-old woman in otherwise excellent health is referred by her optician to Ophthalmology outpatients. The optician has noticed cupping of the optic disc and enlargement of the blind spot. Tonometry confirms the diagnosis of chronic simple (open angle) glaucoma.

3. A 19-year-old woman presents to her GP with conjunctivitis. This has occurred in early summer for the last five years, each time lasting for about six weeks.

4. A 58-year-old man with poorly-controlled type II diabetes mellitus attends his diabetes clinic appointment and complains of deteriorating vision. A short-acting mydriatic is required to assist fundoscopy.

5. A 15-year-old boy presents to the A&E Department with a painful red eye having run through a plate glass door. A detailed corneal examination is performed with the aid of an ocular diagnostic preparation.

2. THEME: RED EYE

A   Acute (closed angle) glaucoma
B   Acute iritis
C   Bacterial conjunctivitis
D   Herpes simplex keratitis
E   Herpes zoster ophthalmicus
F   Keratoconjunctivitis sicca
G   Pterygium
H   Scleritis
I   Seasonal allergic conjunctivitis
J   Subconjunctival haemorrhage

The patients below have presented with red eye. Choose the most appropriate diagnosis from the above list.

1. A 27-year-old nurse presents to the A&E Department with blurring vision and pain in her left eye. Examination of the cornea with fluorescein reveals a dendritic ulcer.

2. An 18-year-old man presents to his GP with a gritty feeling in his eyes. His younger siblings are also suffering similarly. On examination the conjunctivae are red and swollen with a discharge which is crusting the eyelashes.

3. A 61-year-old woman presents to her GP with severe pain and loss of vision in her right eye which began four hours previously. She notices haloes around lights. Examination reveals ciliary vessel hyperaemia with an oval, partially dilated, unreactive pupil.

4. A 52-year-old oil worker, recently returned from the Gulf, presents to his GP having noticed an obstruction to vision in his left eye. Examination reveals a thickened ingrowth of conjunctiva with prominent vessels which has extended to overlie the cornea.

5. A 28-year-old man with ankylosing spondylitis presents to his GP with pain and blurring of vision in his left eye. Examination reveals ciliary vessel hyperaemia, a small pupil and a hypopyon.

3. THEME: AUDITORY PAIN AND DEAFNESS

A   Acoustic neuroma
B   Acute middle-ear effusion
C   Acute suppurative otitis media
D   Barotraumatic otitis media
E   Cholesteatoma
F   Chronic serous middle ear effusion
G   Foreign body in the ear
H   Otitis externa
I   Otosclerosis
J   Wax

The patients below have all presented with otalgia, discharge from the ear or deafness. Select the most appropriate diagnosis from the above list.

1. A 32-year-old man presents with deafness and discomfort in his left ear on return from a recent summer holiday in Majorca. He perceives the onset of his disturbance to have followed bathing in the hotel swimming pool.

2. A 26-year-old man presents with a short history of severe pain made worse by jaw movements and discharge from the right ear. On examination, he has pus in the external auditory meatus and the skin of the external auditory meatus is erythematous, swollen and tender.

3. A 60-year-old man presents with deafness and a feeling of pressure in the left ear. Examination reveals retraction of the tympanic membrane. Rinne's test is negative on the left. Weber's test lateralises to the left side. Posterior rhinoscopy reveals a large exophytic tumour.

4. A 45-year-old man presents with a one year history of foul-smelling purulent discharge from the left ear and increasing deafness. On examination after removal of the discharge, an attic perforation is visualised which is occupied by a greyish substance. Radiography reveals a sclerotic mastoid.

5. A 20-year-old woman presents with a one year history of tinnitus and deafness in both ears. The deafness is worse on the right side and is less marked in places with background noise. The patient's father has worn a hearing aid since his late teens. On examination, the tympanic membranes are normal. Rinne's test is negative bilaterally and Weber's test lateralises to the right side.

continued . . .

6. A 45-year-old woman presents with left-sided deafness of approximately five years duration. Clinical examination reveals an absent left corneal reflex and some evidence of ataxia on balance testing. □

4. THEME: ANATOMY OF THE NOSE AND PARANASAL AIR SINUSES

A   Bulla ethmoidalis
B   Ethmoid sinus
C   Eustachian tube
D   Frontal sinus
E   Inferior concha
F   Maxillary sinus
G   Middle concha
H   Sphenoid sinus
I   Superior concha
J   Vestibule

For each of the descriptions below, choose the most appropriate structure from the above list.

1. A posterior relation to the supraciliary arch. □

2. Is related inferiorly to the molar teeth. □

3. Is a medial relation of the orbit. □

4. Is an inferior relation of the pituitary gland. □

5. Is a medial relation of the nasolacrimal duct. □

5. THEME: EPISTAXIS

A Allergic rhinitis
B Drug induced
C Foreign body
D Leukaemia
E Malignant neoplasm
F Osler-Weber-Rendu disease
G Pyogenic granuloma
H Thrombocytopenic purpura
I Trauma
J Wegener's granuloma

The patients below have all presented with epistaxis. Please select the most appropriate diagnosis from the above list.

1. A 3-year-old child presents with bleeding from one side of the nose. His mother had noticed a foul-smelling discharge from the nose on that side for some months. This had only temporarily responded to courses of antibiotics. Examination of the nostrils shows an inflamed mucous membrane and a blood-stained mucopurulent discharge.

2. A 21-year-old-man presents with unilateral epistaxis. He says he has not been feeling well for some weeks (malaise, fatigue, breathlessness). On examination he is clinically anaemic (out of proportion to the quantity of blood loss described). Full blood count: Hb 7.1 g/dl, WCC 21.2 x 10^9/l (immature myeloblasts).

3. An elderly man presents with epistaxis. He has recently had open heart surgery with placement of a prosthetic mitral valve.

4. A young woman presents with epistaxis. On anterior rhinoscopy she has a smooth swollen red mass with contact bleeding.

5. A middle-aged man presents with a long history of repeated and heavy epistaxes. On examination of his nose the mucous membrane has several red spots on both sides. Inspection of his face and skin reveals similar cutaneous red spots, that are dilated capillaries.

6. THEME: ANATOMY OF THE LARYNX

A Arytenoid cartilage
B Cricoid cartilage
C Cricothyroid membrane
D Epiglottis
E External laryngeal nerve
F Hyoid bone
G Inferior thyroid artery
H Recurrent laryngeal nerve
I Thyroid cartilage
J Thyrohyoid membrane

For each of the descriptions below, please choose the most appropriate structure from the above list.

1. Forms the only complete cartilaginous ring within the respiratory passages.

2. Gives the anterior attachment of the vocal chord.

3. Is a medial relation to the piriform fossa.

4. Innervates the cricothyroid muscle.

5. Gives posterior attachment to the quadrangular membrane.

7. THEME: HOARSENESS

A   Acute viral/bacterial laryngitis
B   Candidiasis of the larynx
C   Carcinoma of the bronchus
D   Chronic laryngitis
E   Laryngeal carcinoma
F   Laryngeal papilloma
G   Myxoedema
H   Sicca syndrome
I   Singer's nodules
J   Tuberculous laryngitis

The patients below have all presented with hoarseness. Please select the most appropriate diagnosis from the above list.

1. A 34-year-old man presents with a two month history of hoarseness, following a cold that has not resolved. He smokes ten cigarettes a day and only drinks socially. He works as a market trader. On mirror examination of the larynx both cords are slightly red but there are small swellings one-third of the way back on each cord.

2. An 8-year-old boy presents with hoarseness, but is otherwise well. On mirror examination of the larynx he has two pedunculated swellings on the vocal cords.

3. A 60-year-old man, who smokes 20 cigarettes a day, presents having been hoarse for several weeks. On mirror examination of the larynx the left vocal cord is lying near the midline and does not move. There is no other apparent abnormality in the larynx.

4. A 60-year-old man, who smokes 20 cigarettes a day, presents having been hoarse for several weeks. On mirror examination of the larynx there is a white mass on the right vocal cord. The cord moves normally.

5. A 60-year-old man, who smokes 20 cigarettes a day, presents having been hoarse for several weeks. He has been short of breath and wheezing for some time. He has been prescribed a steroid inhaler by his GP for COPD. On examination the throat is red with white patches. The larynx and vocal cords appear red and beefy. The cords, however, move normally.

8. THEME: UPPER AIRWAYS OBSTRUCTION

A   Acute epiglottitis
B   Bilateral recurrent laryngeal nerve paralysis
C   Carcinoma of the larynx
D   Coma
E   Fracture of the larynx
F   Fracture of the mandible
G   Inhaled foreign body
H   Inhalation or ingestion of irritants
I   Ludwig's angina
J   Papilloma of the larynx

The patients below have all presented with stridor or breathlessness. Please select the most appropriate diagnosis from the above list.

1. An 8-year-old child presents with stridor. His mother says that he has had many operations on his larynx to remove growths, but that they have always come back.

2. A young man has been brought into casualty semiconscious, having been beaten up. His face is grossly swollen, when he tries to lie on his back his breathing immediately becomes stertorous and he becomes cyanosed.

3. A 4-year-old child is admitted with a history of rapidly increasing stridor. She was well six hours previously but developed a sore throat, followed by vomiting and stridor. On admission, she is dyspnoeic, pale, anxious and has a temperature of 39.5°C.

4. A middle-aged man has been admitted to the medical ward with breathlessness and a tentative diagnosis of chronic obstructive airways disease with an infective exacerbation. He has been a lifelong smoker. On examination he is apyrexial. His wheeze is inspiratory rather than expiratory, and there is indrawing of the suprasternal notch and supraclavicular region. On further questioning he says that he has become increasingly hoarse over the past year.

5. On recovering from a subtotal thyroidectomy, a middle-aged woman develops hoarseness and stridor.

6. A child is brought to the surgery with intermittent attacks of wheezing. These had been present since he choked after falling over whilst running around and eating at the same time. He is observed in one of these attacks and the features are those of stridor.

9. THEME: ANATOMY OF THE PHARYNGEAL MUSCLES

A   Inferior constrictor
B   Levator palati
C   Middle constrictor
D   Palatoglossus
E   Palatopharyngeus
F   Pharyngobasilar fascia
G   Salpingopharyngeus
H   Stylopharyngeus
I   Superior constrictor
J   Tensor palati

Please choose the most appropriate muscle from the above list to match the following descriptions:

1. Is attached to the stylohyoid ligament and the lessor horn of the hyoid bone.

2. Underlies the posterior pillar of the fauces.

3. Is attached to the oblique line on the thyroid cartilage.

4. Is innervated by the ninth cranial nerve.

5. Has a common raphé of origin with the buccinator muscle.

10. THEME: VESSELS OF THE NECK

A   Common carotid artery
B   External jugular vein
C   Facial artery
D   Internal carotid artery
E   Internal jugular vein
F   Maxillary artery
G   Subclavian artery
H   Superficial temporal artery
I   Thoracic duct
J   Vertebral artery

For each of the descriptions below, select the most appropriate vessel from the above list.

1. Posterior relation of the internal jugular vein in the root of the neck.

2. Is crossed from lateral to medial by the 12ᵗʰ cranial nerve.

3. Divides at the level of the upper border of the thyroid cartilage.

4. Is palpable over the body of the mandible.

5. Passes over the sternomastoid muscle.

11. THEME: NECK LUMPS

A   Branchial cyst
B   Cervical rib
C   Cystic hygroma
D   Lymphoma
E   Metastatic carcinoma
F   Multinodular goitre
G   Pharyngeal pouch
H   Sternomastoid tumour
I   Thyroglossal cyst
J   Tonsillitis

The patients below have all presented with a palpable lump in the neck. Please select the most appropriate diagnosis from the above list.

1. A 20-year-old woman presents with an asymptomatic painless lump in the midline just beneath her chin. The lump is smooth, spherical, approximately 2 cm in diameter, non-tender and fluctuant to palpation. The lump moves on swallowing and on tongue protrusion.

2. An 80-year-old man presents with a history of recurrent sore throats, halitosis and regurgitation. Recently he has been seen by his GP for a chronic cough and has also noticed some difficulty swallowing. On examination he has a 5–10 cm indistinct mass behind the sternomastoid muscle below the thyroid cartilage. The lump is soft, smooth and compressible on palpation.

3. A 64-year-old man presents with an asymptomatic slowly growing painless lump in the posterior triangle of the neck above the clavicle. Direct questioning reveals a three month history of malaise, weight loss, pruritus and episodic night sweats. The lump is 3 cm in diameter, hard and non-tender.

4. A 25-year-old woman presents with a painless swelling in the upper lateral part of the left side of her neck. On examination a 7 cm ovoid, smooth, non-tender, fluctuant swelling is palpable lying deep to, and protruding anteriorly from, the upper-third of the sternomastoid muscle.

5. A 72-year-old man presents with an asymptomatic slowly growing painless lump in the neck. On examination he has a hard 2 cm mass lying laterally in the anterior triangle of the neck, deep to the upper third of the left sternomastoid muscle. You notice that the patient has dysphonia.

12. THEME: TUMOURS OF THE HEAD AND NECK

A   Acoustic neuroma
B   Adenoid cystic carcinoma
C   Ameloblastoma
D   Carotid body tumour
E   Nasopharyngeal carcinoma
F   Olfactory neuroblastoma
G   Pleomorphic adenoma
H   Squamous cell carcinoma
I   Squamous cell papilloma
J   Warthin's tumour

For each of the patients below, select the most likely head and neck tumour from the above list.

1. A 42-year-old woman presents with a smooth swelling just in front of the right ear. Ultrasound examination shows a mass arising from the right parotid gland. At surgery, the mass is found to be encapsulated and has a lobulated, rather gelatinous cut surface. Histology shows a benign mixed tumour with both epithelial and connective tissue elements.

2. A 65-year-old man, a life-long heavy smoker, presents with a slowly growing painful ulcer in the floor of his mouth. On inspection, the mucosa around the ulcer is thickened and white. Cytological examination of scrapings from the lesion shows malignant cells with focal keratinisation.

3. A 53-year-old woman presents with tinnitus and increasing deafness in the left ear. CT scan shows a well-circumscribed 2.5 cm mass at the left cerebellopontine angle. Histology of the excised mass shows a benign tumour of neural origin.

4. A 34-year-old Chinese man presents with left nasal obstruction and hearing loss in the left ear. On examination he is also found to have an enlarged lymph node in the left side of the neck. CT scan shows a mass in the left nasopharynx. Biopsy of the mass shows an undifferentiated malignant tumour with a heavy lymphocytic infiltrate. The tumour cells express Epstein-Barr virus-related antigens.

5. A 32-year-old man presents with a painful swelling of the right mandible. X-ray shows a circumscribed lytic lesion 5 cm in diameter. Histology of the excised mass shows a tumour containing odontogenic epithelium resembling normal enamel organ.

CHAPTER **3**

Neurology and Psychiatry

1. THEME: CRANIAL NERVE ANATOMY

A   Abducent nerve
B   Accessory nerve
C   Facial nerve
D   Glossopharyngeal nerve
E   Hypoglossal nerve
F   Oculomotor nerve
G   Trigeminal nerve
H   Trochlear nerve
I   Vagus nerve
J   Vestibulocochlear nerve

For each of the statements below, select the most appropriate cranial nerve from the above list.

1. The afferent pathway of the gag reflex. ☐

2. Damage is accompanied by the inability to whistle. ☐

3. Is required for a normal cough. ☐

4. Is needed to look down and out. ☐

5. Facilitates looking under a table. ☐

2. THEME: SPINAL CORD AND PATHWAYS

A   Dorsal grey column
B   Dorsal spinocerebellar tract
C   Dorsolateral tract
D   Fasciculus gracilis
E   Fasciculus proprius
F   Lateral corticospinal tract
G   Substantia gelatinosa
H   Ventral corticospinal tract
I   Ventral grey column
J   Ventral spinothalamic tract

Please identify the most appropriate pathway from the above list to match the following descriptions.

1. Carries fibres that synapse in the upper medulla and decussate to form the medial lemniscus.

2. Carries fibres that decussate in the medullary pyramid.

3. Carries ascending neurones responding to cutaneous pain and temperature stimulation.

4. Carries predominantly ipsilateral ascending proprioceptive fibres from the thoracic nucleus.

5. Lies between the dorsal root and the dorsal grey matter.

3. THEME: VISUAL DEFECTS I

A   Amaurosis fugax
B   Bitemporal hemianopia
C   Central scotoma
D   Cortical blindness
E   Diplopia to left gaze
F   Diplopia to right gaze
G   Left homonymous hemianopia
H   Hypermetropia
I   Myopia
J   Tunnel vision

The following patients have all presented with visual defects. Please choose the most appropriate diagnosis from the above list.

1. A 51-year-old diabetic man presents to his GP with a one hour history of 'blindness' in the left eye. He describes how a 'black curtain' suddenly descended over the vision in his left eye whilst he was watching television the previous evening. His vision is now normal and pulse, blood pressure, BM, visual acuity and fundoscopy are normal.

2. A 59-year-old woman with known hypertension presents in the A&E Department with loss of vision. Neurological examination, including fundoscopy, is unremarkable other than blindness in both eyes. The patient has little or no insight into the problem and falls trying to leave the Department.

3. A 38-year-old woman presents to her GP with headaches, visual problems and strangely that 'her shoes and gloves no longer fit her'. On examination she is clinically acromegalic and has the classical visual defect associated with an enlarging pituitary tumour.

4. A 51-year-old man presents to his GP with a six hour history of blurring of his vision. On examination he has an obvious left sixth nerve palsy.

5. A 26-year-old woman presents to her GP with parasthesiae in her hands associated with painful eyes and blurring of her vision. Examination confirms signs of an early peripheral sensory neuropathy and loss of central vision in the right eye.

4. THEME: VISUAL DEFECTS II

A   Abducens nerve palsy
B   Cataract
C   Diabetic background retinopathy
D   Diabetic proliferative retinopathy
E   Occipital infarct
F   Oculomotor nerve palsy
G   Optic atrophy
H   Pituitary tumour
I   Retrobulbar neuritis
J   Vitreous haemorrhage

The following patients have all presented with visual defects. Please choose the most appropriate diagnosis from the above list.

1. A 36-year-old man with known nephropathy and peripheral sensory neuropathy presents in outpatients with worsening visual problems. On examination his visual acuity has fallen to 6/24 in both eyes and fundoscopy reveals maculopathy, retinal haemorrhages, exudates and neovascularisation around the disc.

2. A 47-year-old woman presents to her GP with sudden onset of pain in the right eye associated with a headache. On examination she has a complete ptosis of the right eye associated with a fixed, dilated pupil which is facing 'down and out'.

3. An 89-year-old woman presents to her GP with worsening vision particularly in the right eye. On examination she is clinically in sinus rhythm at 88/min, BP 130/85 mmHg, and BM 4.7 mmol/l. Visual acuity is markedly reduced in both eyes, but more so on the right, and fundoscopy is impossible due to 'defects' in the anterior chambers.

4. A 25-year-old man presents to his GP with a three day history of blurred vision. On examination he looks well and his visual acuity is reduced in both eyes but eye examination including fundoscopy is otherwise unremarkable. Subsequent investigation shows marked delay in visual evoked responses (VER).

5. A 29-year-old known alcohol abuser presents to his GP with reduced vision in both eyes. On examination he has several stigmata of chronic liver disease and smells of ethanol. His visual acuity is reduced in both eyes and fundoscopy reveals pale discs, with no associated retinopathy.

5. THEME: PUPILLARY ABNORMALITIES

A Argyll Robertson pupil
B Brain stem death
C Cataract
D Gunn's pupil
E Holmes-Adie pupil
F Horner's syndrome
G Iridectomy
H Oculomotor palsy
I Opiate overdose
J Pontine stroke

The following patients have all presented with abnormal pupils. Please choose the most appropriate diagnosis from the above list.

1. A 49-year-old man with long-standing diabetes mellitus presents for his annual diabetic review in outpatients. On examination of his eyes it is noted that his pupils are small and irregular and accommodate but do not react to light. VDRL is negative.

2. A 53-year-old chronic smoker presents to his GP with increasing shortness of breath associated with pain and paraesthesiae along the radial border of his left forearm. On examination he has marked wasting of the web space between the thumb and index finger of his left hand, a sunken left eye with a pinpoint pupil and signs of a left pleural effusion.

3. A 16-year-old schoolgirl is noted to have asymmetrical pupils at a routine medical. The left pupil is size 4/8 and reacts normally to light. The right pupil is size 6/8, and is slow to accommodate and react to light. Visual acuity in both eyes is normal.

4. A 23-year-old man is brought into the A&E Department by ambulance. His GCS is 3/15 and he has fixed, pinpoint pupils. He improves with intravenous naloxone.

5. A 46-year-old woman presents to her GP with headaches behind her right eye. On examination of her pupils the left pupillary responses to direct and consensual light are normal. The right pupil reacts very slowly to direct light, consensual reaction is normal but the pupil dilates slightly as the light is swung back from the left pupil towards the right.

6. THEME: CRANIAL NERVE LESIONS

A Abducens nerve
B Facial nerve
C Glossopharyngeal nerve
D Hypoglossal nerve
E Oculomotor nerve
F Olfactory nerve
G Trigeminal nerve
H Trochlear nerve
I Vagus nerve
J Vestibulocochlear nerve

The following patients have all presented with cranial nerve lesions. Please choose the most appropriate affected nerve(s) from the above list. The answers may require more than ONE selection and options may be used more than once.

1. A 32-year-old woman presents to her GP with a twelve hour history of weakness with drooping of the left side of her face. On examination she has lost the wrinkles on the left side of her forehead and has an obvious droop to the left side of her mouth.

2. An 81-year-old man presents to his GP with shooting pains in the right side of his face. The pain is reproduced by tapping on the right side of his maxilla.

3. A 72-year-old woman presents to her GP with weakness and wasting of her upper limbs associated with difficulty in swallowing, nasal regurgitation and speech problems. On examination she has bilateral loss of the gag reflex and aspirates on teaspoons of water. She is also noted to have a spastic, wasted tongue.

4. A 64-year-old woman presents to the A&E Department with a four week history of a dull headache worse in the mornings and exacerbated by coughing. She has a large mass in the right breast and is noted to be unable to abduct the left eye.

5. A 42-year-old man presents to the A&E Department with a six week history of dizziness, vomiting and left-sided tinnitus. On examination he has nystagmus to the left, associated with loss of the left corneal reflex, left facial droop and neural deafness.

7. THEME: FACIAL NERVE PALSY

A   Bell's palsy
B   Cerebello-pontine angle tumour
C   Lyme disease
D   Mononeuritis multiplex
E   Myasthenia gravis
F   Parotid tumour
G   Pontine demyelination
H   Pontine haemorrhage
I   Ramsay Hunt syndrome
J   Sarcoidosis

The following patients have all presented with a facial nerve palsy. Please choose the most appropriate diagnosis of their palsy from the above list.

1. A 31-year-old woman with neurofibromatosis presents to her GP with vertigo, left-sided tinnitus, visual blurring and a left facial droop. On examination she has nystagmus to the left, associated with a left Vth, VIth and VIIth nerve palsy.

2. A 26-year-old woman presents to her GP with a left-sided facial palsy. Several days previously she had woken with a right-sided facial weakness but this had resolved over 2–3 days. She has also developed pain and swelling in her parotid glands associated with fever and painful 'red eyes'. Subsequent investigations confirm bilateral hilar lymphadenopathy on CXR and hypercalcaemia.

3. An 82-year-old man presents to the A&E Department with a left facial palsy associated with pain around his left ear. On examination he has an obvious left facial palsy with loss of the wrinkles of his forehead associated with vesicles in the left external auditory meatus.

4. A 24-year-old woman presents to her GP with a two month history of pain and blurring of her vision now associated with a right-sided facial palsy and facial spasm. Subsequent investigations reveal delayed visual evoked potentials.

5. A 61-year-old man with known type II diabetes mellitus presents in the outpatient clinic for his annual review. In the last few months he has developed paraesthesiae and numbness in his right ring and little fingers, a right-sided foot drop and a left-sided facial weakness.

8. THEME: HEAD INJURY

A   Basal skull fracture
B   Depressed skull fracture
C   Diffuse axonal injury
D   Extradural haematoma
E   GCS 4
F   GCS 8
G   GCS 11
H   GCS 13
I   Subarachnoid haemorrhage
J   Subdural haematoma

The patients below have all sustained head injuries. Please select the most appropriate clinical description from the above list.

1. A 36-year-old man was the unrestrained driver of a car. On impact he was thrown against the windscreen. On examination he has bruising to the face and chest and has several obvious limb deformities. He opens his eyes to, and withdraws from pain. He is groaning and no words are discernible.

2. A 23-year-old male intravenous drug abuser falls from a window whilst trying to evade the police. At the scene, he was alert and orientated. On arrival in the A&E Department he has a localised left fronto-parietal boggy swelling. Approximately one hour later whilst waiting for further assessment, he suddenly collapses in the waiting room. At this time his speech is confused, he has eye opening to speech and he localises pain.

3. A 31-year-old woman has fallen from the second floor of her house on to concrete. She has fractures to both wrists and a large frontal haematoma. On examination her speech is confused and she localises and opens her eyes to pain.

4. A 46-year-old publican is attacked whilst leaving his bar one night after closing. He describes being punched and kicked in the face and the head. On examination, he is alert and orientated, has multiple facial injuries and scalp lacerations. He has bilateral black eyes, a left sub-conjunctival haemorrhage and blood is visible in the left external auditory meatus.

5. A 28-year-old professional boxer is brought to hospital immediately after a heavyweight world title fight. The paramedics in attendance at the event inform you that he had collapsed in his corner at the end of the 8th round. At this time he was confused and drowsy. His condition has rapidly deteriorated on the way to the A&E Department. At the time you assess him he has no verbal response or eye opening. Examination reveals a unilateral fixed dilated pupil on the right and flexion to pain only on the left side.

9. THEME: INTRACRANIAL HAEMORRHAGE

A   Acute subdural haemorrhage
B   Chronic subdural haemorrhage
C   Extradural haemorrhage
D   Intracerebral haemorrhage: anterior cerebral artery territory
E   Intracerebral haemorrhage: middle cerebral artery territory
F   Intracerebral haemorrhage: posterior cerebral artery territory
G   Intracerebral haemorrhage: vertebro-basilar artery territory
H   Intracerebellar haemorrhage
I   Intraventricular haemorrhage
J   Subarachnoid haemorrhage

The patients below have all had intracranial bleeding. Please select the most appropriate diagnosis from the above list. Any item may be used more than once.

1. A 60-year-old woman presents 30 minutes after a sudden onset of severe headache. She initially lost consciousness but is now conscious but drowsy and confused (GCS 14). She continues to complain of severe headache and on examination has marked neck stiffness. A lumbar puncture performed in the A&E Department demonstrates xanthochromia.

2. A 27-year-old DJ presents with a twelve hour history of severe headache which started suddenly the night before whilst he was at a party. He has mild photophobia and neck-stiffness and feels nauseous. Neurological examination is otherwise normal but a large ballotable mass is present in the right flank. On further questioning, he admits that the headache started whilst having sexual intercourse after having taken a considerable quantity of cocaine.

3. A 90-year-old woman is a resident in a nursing home. The duty doctor has referred her to the A&E Department because of worsening confusion and fluctuating drowsiness over the last few days. She had a minor head injury sustained whilst falling out of bed two weeks before. On examination she has a mental test score of 2/10 but no focal neurological signs. Her PaO_2 on air is 11.0 kPa , metabolic and septic screens are negative.

4. A 55-year-old hypertensive man with no previous history of neurological events presents with an abrupt onset of right-sided hemiparesis (arm > leg) and hemisensory loss. He is also noted to have an expressive aphasia. He is right-handed.

5. A 36-year-old man is ejected from the passenger seat of a vehicle during an RTA. Following full trauma team assessment, he was found to have an isolated head injury with an initial GCS of 8. He is managed non-operatively and makes a reasonable recovery over the next few weeks. He is referred to you for assessment for neuro-rehabilitation. His main problem is now one of intellectual slowness and behaviour. He finds it difficult to find words, is emotionally labile and has exhibitionist antisocial behaviour. Examination also reveals weakness with hypertonia in the left lower > upper limb > face.

10. THEME: HEADACHE I

A   Benign intracranial hypertension
B   Cervical spondylosis
C   Cluster headache
D   Giant cell arteritis
E   Meningitis
F   Migraine
G   Sinusitis
H   Space-occupying lesion
I   Stress
J   Subarachnoid haemorrhage

The patients below have all presented with a headache. Choose the most appropriate diagnosis from the above list.

1. A 19-year-old obese woman presents to her GP with an eight week history of morning headache, made worse by coughing, and of several episodes of transient blurring of vision. Fundoscopy demonstrates bilateral papilloedema.

2. A 71-year-old man presents to his GP with a six month history of gradually worsening neck pains which radiate to the occiput and to the temples. There is no abnormality on examination but cervical spine X-ray shows osteophyte formation at the levels of C4–C7.

3. A 19-year-old geography student presents to her GP with a twelve hour history of diarrhoea, malaise and severe bifrontal aching headache. She suffers an episode of vomiting whilst on the examination couch, following which the GP notices conjunctival petechiae.

4. A 34-year-old man presents to his GP with a fortnight's history of severe, stabbing right-sided headache centred behind the orbit and radiating to the cheek and jaw. The pain wakes him from sleep at about 1 a.m. every night and he has noticed that his right eye becomes bloodshot and waters profusely. He seeks relief by pacing up and down outside his front door; the headache passes after about an hour.

5. A 68-year-old woman presents to her GP with a constant, throbbing, generalised headache that has been increasing in intensity since it started three weeks ago. She has also noticed pain on chewing for the last five days. On examination she has a low grade pyrexia, a tender scalp and decreased visual acuity in the left eye. ESR is 108 mm/hr. Temporal artery biopsy is normal.

11. THEME: HEADACHE II

A   Benign intracranial hypertension
B   Cervical spondylosis
C   Cluster headache
D   Meningitis
E   Migraine
F   Sagittal sinus thrombosis
G   Sinusitis
H   Space-occupying lesion
I   Subarachnoid haemorrhage
J   Temporal arteritis

The following patients have all presented with a headache. Please choose the most appropriate diagnosis from the above list.

1. An 81-year-old man is referred to Medicine for the Elderly outpatients with a three month history of worsening occipital headaches associated with stiffness and pain in the shoulders. On examination he has old osteoarthritic changes of the hands and a limited range of movement of the shoulders and neck. His ESR is 9 mm/hr.

2. A 36-year-old housewife presents to her GP with a six week history of headaches associated with blurring of her vision and nausea. The headaches are worse on waking in the mornings and are exacerbated by coughing and laughing. On examination she is not acutely unwell but is in obvious distress. A hard 2 cm by 3 cm mass is felt in her left breast with associated lymphadenopathy in the left axilla.

3. A 24-year-old woman presents to her GP with a four month history of severe, episodic headaches associated with visual disturbances and vomiting. The day before each episode she feels unwell, off her food and a little nauseated. Within 24 hours an 'unbearable' left side headache begins, associated with flashing lights across her visual field.

4. A 31-year-old businessman presents to his GP with a three to four month history of daily headaches. The headaches seem to come on at the same time each day, 10:30 am, and last between 20–60 minutes. They are severe and mainly right-sided and seem to be relieved with paracetamol. They are not associated with any pre-warning symptoms, visual changes or vomiting.

continued . . .

5. A 24-year-old student presents in the A&E Department with a six hour
    history of a severe generalised headache associated with vomiting. Of
    note she is on the oral contraceptive pill. On examination she is in
    obvious distress with mild meningism but she is apyrexial and has no
    rash. Fundoscopy reveals bilateral papilloedema and a CT head scan
    with contrast confirms the diagnosis.

12. THEME: STROKE DISEASE

A   Antiphospholipid syndrome
B   Arteriovenous malformation
C   Atrial myxoma
D   Berry aneurysm
E   Carotid dissection
F   Giant cell arteritis
G   Hyperviscosity
H   Left ventricular thrombus
I   Mycotic aneurysm
J   Paradoxical embolism

The following patients have all presented with slightly unusual causes of stroke.
Please choose the most appropriate diagnosis from the above list.

1. A 33-year-old previously fit and well woman is admitted to hospital
    with a low grade fever, vasculitic lesions around her nailbeds, a harsh
    pansystolic murmur and bibasal crepitations. A few days after admission
    she is found slumped to the left with a marked left-sided weakness and
    facial palsy.

2. A 61-year-old woman presents in the A&E Department with a marked
    left-sided weakness and dysarthria. Investigations reveal: full blood
    count: Hb 9.2 g/dl, MCV 98 fl, WCC 2.9 x 10^9/l, Plt 76 x 10^9/l; U&Es:
    Na^+ 134 mmol/l, K^+ 5.7 mmol/l, Urea 22.2 mmol/l, Cr 512 μmol/l;
    CCa^{2+} 3.08 mmol/l; ESR 122 mm/hr.

3. A 29-year-old man with known adult polycystic kidney disease presents
    in the A&E Department with a severe headache and a decreased level of
    consciousness. On examination he has a GCS of 6, BP 200/100 mmHg
    and pulse 60/min. There is no focal neurological deficit but he has
    bilateral extensor plantar responses.

4. A 34-year-old woman with a previous history of several miscarriages and deep vein thromboses of the lower limbs presents in the A&E Department with a right hemiparesis and dysphasia. Routine investigations including FBC, clotting, U&Es, LFTs, RBG, lipids, CXR and echocardiogram are within normal limits but her ESR is 76 mm/hr.

5. A 61-year-old man presents in the A&E Department with a left hemiparesis and a decreased level of consciousness. On examination BP 145/75 mmHg, Pulse 110/min regular; on auscultation he has crepitations to the midzones and mild ankle oedema. Of note he had an acute anterior myocardial infarction eight months previously and an ECG confirms persistent ST segment elevation in leads $V_1 - V_4$.

13. THEME: SITE OF STROKE

A   Cerebellar
B   Frontal cortex
C   Medullary
D   Occipital cortex
E   Parietal cortex
F   Pontine
G   Subcortical
H   Temporo-parietal cortex

The following right-handed patients have presented with a stroke. Please choose the most appropriate anatomical site of their stroke from the above list.

1. A 71-year-old man with long-standing hypertension is admitted to the local stroke unit several days after his initial presentation. He has a right upper limb weakness, expressive dysphasia, urinary incontinence and a change in his normal placid persona to an aggressive, disinhibited manner.

2. A 63-year-old diabetic smoker presents in the A&E Department with a stroke. Examination reveals a right hemiparesis, right inattention and dyspraxia. On further examination several days later he is unable to draw a clock face correctly.

3. A 45-year-old poorly controlled hypertensive woman presents in the A&E Department with a stroke. Further testing after admission shows a marked receptive dysphasia, jargon speech, a right hemiparesis and a right homonymous hemianopia.

4. A 67-year-old man with known diabetes mellitus and ischaemic heart disease presents in the A&E Department with a collapse. After admission it becomes obvious that he is blind but he continues to deny this and has several falls on the ward.

5. A 54-year-old woman presents in the A&E Department after a sudden collapse at home. On examination she has nystagmus to the left, dysdiadochokinesia and past pointing on the left.

14. THEME: SPEECH AND LANGUAGE PROBLEMS

A   Cerebellar speech
B   Dysnomia
C   Expressive dys/aphasia
D   Facial dysarthria
E   Glossal dysarthria
F   Hoarseness
G   Jargon speech
H   Pharyngeal dysarthria
I   Receptive dys/aphasia
J   Speech dyspraxia

The following right-handed patients have all presented with speech and language problems. Please choose the most appropriate diagnosis from the above list. There may be more than one correct answer and options may be used more than once.

1.   A 45-year-old man with known hypertension and diabetes mellitus presents in the A&E Department with a grade 4/5 right hemiparesis and speech problems. He is able to follow three stage commands but can not find the correct words at certain times, and is unable to name a pen and a watch despite being able to show the doctor what to do with them.

2.   A 69-year-old chronic smoker with a previous history of ischaemic heart disease presents in the A&E Department with a six hour history of right-sided weakness and communication problems. On examination he has a dense right hemiparesis and is unable to follow single stage commands or make any verbal responses.

3.   A 58-year-old life-long smoker presents to his GP with a three month history of weight loss, worsening shortness of breath and recent voice change. On examination he has signs of a left pleural effusion. His speech is difficult to hear but is appropriate.

4.   A 57-year-old life-long smoker presents to her GP with a twelve hour history of right-sided weakness, facial droop and speech problems. Her husband says she is making no sense at all but does seem to understand some of his requests.

5.   A 66-year-old man presents to his GP with a four month history of weight loss, speech and swallowing problems. On examination he has marked wasting of his upper limbs associated with weakness and fasciculation. He is able to follow three stage commands (with a little difficulty due to the weakness) and correctly identifies a pen and watch. However, he seems to have particular problems with 'L' and 'K/C' sounds.

15. THEME: PERIPHERAL SENSORY NEUROPATHY

A   Alcohol
B   Amiodarone
C   Carcinoma
D   Demyelination
E   Diabetes mellitus
F   HIV infection
G   Isoniazid
H   Rheumatoid arthritis
I   Uraemia
J   Vitamin B12 deficiency

The following patients have all presented with a peripheral sensory neuropathy. Please choose the most appropriate diagnosis from the above list.

1. A 37-year-old man presents to his GP with increasing parasthesiae and numbness in his hands. On examination he has bilateral Dupuytren's contracture, spider naevi and gynaecomastia. Investigations reveal: FBC: Hb 8.2 g/dl, MCV 109 fl, WCC 7.2 x 10^9/l, Plt 89 x 10^9/l; U&Es: Na$^+$ 127 mmol/l, K$^+$ 4.1 mmol/l, Urea 2.2 mmol/l, Cr 112 μmol/l; B12 and red cell folate – normal.

2. A 79-year-old man presents in outpatients with lethargy, malaise and numbness in his feet. On examination he is clinically anaemic and has signs of a peripheral sensory neuropathy but is otherwise well. Routine investigations reveal: FBC: Hb 6.2 g/dl, MCV 112 fl, WCC 3.5 x 10^9/l, Plt 109 x 10^9/l; U&Es: Na$^+$ 137 mmol/l, K$^+$ 3.9 mmol/l, Urea 4.2 mmol/l, Cr 107 μmol/l; Blood film shows 'hypersegmented neutrophils'.

3. A 21-year-old woman presents to her GP with blurring of her vision associated with numbness in her feet. Examination confirms loss of joint position sense and light touch in her feet but fundoscopy is normal. Routine investigations including: FBC, U&Es, RBG, LFTs, TFTs, B12 and red cell folate are all within normal limits.

4. A 38-year-old man with Kaposi's sarcoma and a previous history of CMV retinitis presents to his GP with a three week history of worsening numbness and pain in his hands. On examination he has multiple Kaposi's lesions and signs of a peripheral sensory neuropathy but is otherwise relatively well.

5. A 66-year-old man presents to his GP with a three month history of weight loss, night sweats and haematuria. More recently he has been dropping objects and has been unable to feel the pedals of his car whilst driving. On examination he is anaemic, has reduced sensation to light touch, pinprick and joint position sense in his hands and feet, and has a ballotable mass in the right loin.

16. THEME: MOTOR–SENSORY NEUROPATHY

A   Beriberi
B   Carcinoma of the lung
C   Charcot-Marie-Tooth syndrome
D   Critical illness polyneuropathy
E   Demyelination
F   Diabetes mellitus
G   Lyme disease
H   Multiple myeloma
I   Refsum's disease
J   Sarcoidosis

The following patients have all presented with a mixed motor-sensory neuropathy. Please choose the most appropriate nerve palsy from the above list.

1. A 24-year-old man returns from a walking holiday in the USA. Whilst away he developed a red rash associated with a headache and a 'flu-like illness'. On his return he has had generalised weakness in all four limbs and 'pins and needles' in his hands. His symptoms improve with a course of penicillin.

2. A 37-year-old man is invited to be a patient in the MRCP clinical examinations. He has a chronic condition causing lower limb weakness, pes cavus deformity of the feet, 'inverted champagne bottle' shaped legs and decreased sensation and areflexia.

3. A 61-year-old woman presents to her GP with a three month history of weight loss, bruising and lethargy. In the last few weeks she has had generalised weakness of the limbs associated with numbness in the feet. Bladder and bowel control is normal. Investigations reveal: FBC: Hb 7.9 g/dl, MCV 89 fl, WCC 2.2 x 10^9/l, Plt 49 x 10^9/l; U&Es: Na$^+$ 129 mmol/l, K$^+$ 6.1 mmol/l, urea 22.9 mmol/l, Cr 612 μmol/l; ESR 125 mm/hr; CCa^{2+} 3.12 mmol/l.

4. A 48-year-old 'down and out' presents in the A&E Department with painful feet and calves, increasing peripheral oedema and shortness of breath on exertion. On examination he has marked peripheral oedema to the groin, pulse 110 bpm regular, BP 100/70 mmHg, JVP raised +5 cm, signs of bilateral effusions and a mixed motor and sensory neuropathy.

5. A 51-year-old obese man with a known peripheral sensory neuropathy and retinopathy presents to his GP with increasing pain and weakness in his thighs, the right being worse than the left.

17. THEME: MOTOR WEAKNESS

A   Alcoholic myopathy
B   Guillain-Barré syndrome
C   Hypocalcaemia
D   Hypokalaemia
E   Middle cerebral artery infarct
F   Motor neurone disease
G   Multiple sclerosis
H   Myasthenia gravis
I   Poliomyelitis
J   Spinal cord compression

The following patients have all presented with weakness. Please choose the most appropriate diagnosis from the above list.

1. A 34-year-old previously well man presents with a ten day history of a 'flu-like illness' and weakness in his lower limbs. Neurological examination of his cranial nerves and upper limbs are normal but his lower limbs have grade 4/5 distal weakness, diminished reflexes and equivocal plantar responses. Vibration, joint position sense and light touch are also reduced distally.

2. A 71-year-old woman on metolazone and frusemide for cardiac failure presents in the outpatient department with insidious worsening of generalised weakness. She has well controlled cardiac failure and respiratory, abdominal and neurological examination are essentially normal.

3. A 63-year-old man with known hypertension presents in the A&E Department with a grade 0/5 weakness in his right upper and lower limbs associated with expressive dysphasia, right homonymous hemianopia and right-sided sensory inattention.

4. An 82-year-old woman with known multiple myeloma presents in the A&E Department with a four week history of increasing weakness in her lower limbs associated with multiple falls. On examination she has a bilateral grade 3/5 weakness in the lower limbs associated with hyper-reflexia and extensor plantars, and a sensory level at T10. Of note she is extremely constipated and has a palpable bladder to above the level of the umbilicus.

continued . . .

5. A 24-year-old woman presents to her GP with a three week history of increasing weakness in her upper and lower limbs associated with 'double vision' and difficulty chewing and swallowing her food particularly at Sunday lunch. Subsequent investigations reveal high titres of acetylcholine receptor antibodies.

18. THEME: PARKINSONISM

A   Arteriosclerotic
B   Chlorpromazine
C   Haloperidol
D   Idiopathic Parkinson's disease
E   Metoclopramide
F   Multisystem atrophy
G   Postencephalitic parkinsonism
H   Prochlorperazine
I   Progressive supranuclear palsy
J   Wilson's disease

The following patients below have all presented with parkinsonism. Please choose the most appropriate cause from the above list.

1. A previously fit and well 73-year-old man presents to his GP with a three month history of insidious worsening of a tremor of the right hand. He is on no medication. On examination his gait is slow and he has poor 'swing through' of the right upper limb. There is a resting tremor of the right hand with associated 'cogwheeling' of the right upper limb. Routine investigations are all within normal limits and he improves dramatically with the addition of *Sinemet*.

2. A 69-year-old man with a long history of dizziness, for which he takes regular medication, is seen by his GP for a 'chesty cough'. The GP notes he is very slow, rigid and his speech is monotoned and tends to fall away. The GP gives him a course of antibiotics and stops his dizziness treatment and all his symptoms and signs improve.

3. A 67-year-old woman is referred to medical outpatients with falls. On examination she appears parkinsonian but is also noted to be unable to follow the movement of objects in a vertical plane, and she is dysarthric. She initially appears quite confused but given time is able to score 8/10 on an AMTS.

4. A 51-year-old woman presents to her GP with a five month history of progressive unsteadiness, and falls associated with dizziness on standing. On examination she is clinically parkinsonian, has marked postural hypotension and is ataxic.

5. A 19-year-old man is referred to neurology outpatients with falls and 'features of Parkinson's disease'. On examination he has marked Kayser-Fleischer rings of the eyes, dysarthria and parkinsonism. Investigations confirm deranged LFTs and reduced serum copper and caeruloplasmin levels.

19. THEME: CEREBELLAR DISEASE

A   Alcohol excess
B   Arnold-Chiari malformation
C   Cerebellar haemorrhage
D   Cerebellar infarction
E   Cerebello-pontine angle tumour
F   Demyelinating disease
G   Friedreich's ataxia
H   Hypothyroidism
I   Metastatic deposits
J   Phenytoin toxicity

The following patients have all presented with cerebellar signs. Please choose the most appropriate cause of their cerebellar disease from the above list.

1. A 49-year-old hypertensive man presents in the A&E Department with acute dizziness and vomiting associated with a posterior headache. On examination he has a regular pulse 88 bpm, BP 220/110 mmHg, his speech is slurred and he has nystagmus to the right. A subsequent CT head scan shows a 'low attenuation area in the right cerebellar peduncle'.

2. A 37-year-old man presents to his GP with falls. On examination he has marked bruising, leukonychia and spider naevi. He has an ataxic gait and bilateral intention tremor.

3. A 12-year-old schoolgirl is referred to the paediatric outpatient clinic with unsteadiness and falls. On examination she is noted to have a wide based, ataxic gait with abnormal, deformed feet, with loss of joint position sense, and nystagmus. Examination is otherwise unremarkable but her routine ECG reveals widespread T wave inversion and the voltage criteria of LVH.

4. A 79-year-old woman is brought in to the A&E Department by ambulance having been found unconscious at home by her home carer. She is treated for a severe right lower lobe pneumonia and recovers. She is slow to mobilise and the SHO notes her to have coarsened facies, a croaky voice and slow relaxing reflexes as well as an ataxic gait and nystagmus in both directions.

5. A 25-year-old man presents to his GP with double vision, increasing unsteadiness and falls, vertigo, speech and swallowing problems. On examination he is unsteady with an ataxic gait, he is dysarthric and has signs of an internuclear ophthalmoplegia.

20. THEME: SEIZURES I

A   Anoxia
B   Cerebral abscess
C   Cerebral metastases
D   Hypocalcaemia
E   Hypomagnesaemia
F   Hyponatraemia
G   Meningitis
H   Phenytoin toxicity
I   Subarachnoid haemorrhage
J   Uraemia

The following patients have all presented with seizures. Please choose the most appropriate diagnosis from the above list.

1. A 24-year-old, known HIV positive man presents in the A&E Department with a decreased level of consciousness associated with two tonic-clonic seizures. On examination he is unwell, pyrexial, T 38.5°C, and is drowsy. A subsequent CT head scan reveals a ring enhancing lesion in the left temporo-parietal region with surrounding cerebral oedema. He improves with a combination of pyrimethamine and sulphadiazine.

2. A 79-year-old man who is on fluoxetine for depression, is started on bendrofluazide for hypertension. Two weeks later he is brought to the A&E Department by ambulance after a tonic-clonic seizure. His wife says he has been extremely confused for several days. Initial investigations reveal: FBC: Hb 13.2 g/dl, MCV 89 fl, WCC 11.2 x 10⁹/l, Plt 419 x 10⁹/l; U&Es: Na⁺ 107 mmol/l, K⁺ 3.1 mmol/l, Urea 7.2 mmol/l, Cr 122 μmol/l; CCa²⁺ 2.31 mmol/l; Mg²⁺ 0.98 mmol/l.

3. A 72-year-old man who underwent excision of a benign meningioma 18 months ago is seen in the A&E Department after a tonic-clonic seizure. Examination reveals him to be drowsy and he has nystagmus. Initial investigations reveal: FBC: Hb 9.2 g/dl, MCV 101 fl, WCC 11.2 x 10⁹/l, Plt 109 x 10⁹/l; U&Es: Na⁺ 137 mmol/l, K⁺ 5.1 mmol/l, Urea 6.2 mmol/l, Cr 108 μmol/l; CCa²⁺ 1.98 mmol/l; Mg²⁺ 0.78 mmol/l. CT head scan is remarkable only for the old neurosurgical procedure with no evidence of a space occupying lesion or collection.

continued . . .

4. A 19-year-old woman presents in the A&E Department with a complex partial seizure. On examination she looks unwell, is distressed and agitated and is pyrexial, T 38.9°C. She has marked meningism and is noted to have a scabbing lesion on the outer third of her upper lip. Investigations reveal: FBC: Hb 12.8 g/dl, MCV 80 fl, WCC 11.2 x 10^9/l (lymphocytosis), Plt 69 x 10^9/l; U&Es: Na$^+$ 127 mmol/l, K$^+$ 4.1 mmol/l, Urea 4.2 mmol/l, Cr 99 μmol/l; CCa^{2+} 2.38 mmol/l; Mg^{2+} 0.74 mmol/l.

5. A 41-year-old woman is recovering in hospital, 24 hours after a thyroidectomy when she has a tonic-clonic seizure on the ward. On examination she is drowsy but rouseable and has a positive Chvostek's sign. Whilst the nurse is trying to take her blood pressure the patient's hand begins to twitch and spasm.

21. THEME: SEIZURES II

A   Absence attack
B   Atonic seizure
C   Atypical absence
D   Clonic seizure
E   Complex partial seizure
F   Partial with secondary generalisation
G   Simple partial seizure
H   Tonic-clonic seizure
I   Tonic seizure
J   Typical absence

The following patients have all presented with varying types of seizures. Please choose the most appropriate type from the above list.

1. A 19-year-old man presents to his GP with a three week history of 'funny turns'. According to his partner he has had three episodes starting with twitching of his right thumb and index finger and then spreading up his right upper limb. He has had no loss of consciousness, tongue biting or urinary incontinence and is otherwise systemically well.

2. A 14-year-old schoolgirl presents to her GP with a five day history of 'strange feelings'. Her mother has witnessed several occasions during this period where her daughter becomes suddenly vague but appears to be able to understand what she is saying. She then starts to screw up her face and smacks her lips several times. The episodes last a few minutes and then she returns to normal. The girl says she experiences a 'warm glow' in her tummy prior to the episodes and feels like she is 'floating in space' during them.

3. A 6-year-old boy is referred to the paediatric neurology clinic with 'funny turns' at school. During the last term his teachers report multiple episodes whereby he becomes momentarily 'vacant' and still, stopping whatever he is doing and then within a few seconds continuing as if nothing has happened. A subsequent EEG shows 'a spikes and waves discharge pattern at a frequency of 3 Hz'.

4. A 19-year-old student with known epilepsy presents in the A&E Department with three seizures in the last two hours. His flatmate who witnessed the episodes says he suddenly became vague and then dropped to the floor. He then went rigid and started shaking violently. He was frothing at the mouth and his face went very purple. During the first two seizures he was incontinent of urine and was very drowsy after each.

5. A 12-year-old schoolgirl presents to her GP with several 'fits' in the last week. Her father describes how she initially becomes vague but seems to hear what he is saying to her. The girl describes a feeling of 'worry and fear' spreading over her and then she 'blacks out'. During this phase her father describes how she becomes unconscious, falls to the floor and starts shaking. On a couple of occasions she has bitten her tongue and has been incontinent of urine.

22. THEME: SEIZURES III

A   Anoxia
B   Cerebral abscess
C   Cerebral metastases
D   Hypocalcaemia
E   Hypomagnesaemia
F   Hyponatraemia
G   Meningitis
H   Phenytoin toxicity
I   Subarachnoid haemorrhage
J   Uraemia

The patients below have all presented with seizures. Choose the most appropriate diagnosis from the above list.

1. You are fast-bleeped to the ward at 3 a.m. to see a 37-year-old woman who has just started fitting. She underwent total thyroidectomy for papillary carcinoma of the thyroid yesterday morning, was maintained on normal saline infusion until the afternoon and then ate a light supper.

2. You are fast-bleeped to the ward to see a 22-year-old man who has just had a brief seizure. He underwent clipping of a Berry aneurysm two days ago following a subarachnoid haemorrhage the previous week. He was given a standard intravenous loading dose of phenytoin in theatre and, since then, has received maintenance doses eight-hourly. On examination he is pyrexial, tachycardic and hypotensive. He has a stiff neck but the chest is clear, heart sounds are normal and the abdomen is soft. Catheter specimen of urine is normal on dipstick and, apart from drowsiness, there is no change in his neurology.

3. An 89-year-old woman is brought into the A&E Department by ambulance having suffered two brief fits at home. She is currently drowsy but denies having a headache. Her husband tells you that she has never been admitted to hospital before but that her GP started her on an antihypertensive three weeks ago, the name of which the husband cannot remember. On examination, the patient's skin turgor is reduced and there is no focal neurology.

4. A 48-year-old man is brought into the A&E Department by ambulance having fitted at home. His wife has accompanied him and tells you that he has felt unwell since squeezing a large boil on his neck eight days ago. On examination you find an ejection systolic murmur and an early diastolic murmur in the aortic area, multiple splinter haemorrhages, a left VIth cranial nerve palsy, and a Roth spot on the right fundus.

5. A 16-year-old girl is brought into the A&E Department by ambulance having collapsed at school. Just before she starts fitting, she tells you she has been vomiting continuously for the last fortnight and has not kept any food down. On examination you find a mass arising from the pelvis.

23. THEME: PSYCHIATRIC PRESENTATIONS

A   Bipolar affective disorder
B   Drug induced psychosis
C   Generalised anxiety disorder
D   Depression (mild)
E   Depression (severe)
F   Mania
G   Obsessive-compulsive disorder
H   Phobic anxiety disorder
I   Psychopathic disorder
J   Schizophrenia

The following patients have all presented with psychiatric disorders. Please choose the most appropriate diagnosis from the above list.

1. A previously fit and well 37-year-old woman is taken to her GP by her husband. Several months ago she lost her job and has been increasingly unwell since. She is sleeping poorly, waking at 4 to 5 a.m. She has little to eat or drink and wanders aimlessly around the house, rarely getting dressed or going out. She has told him on several occasions that she wants to be left alone to die, is a worthless individual who deserves all this misery. He does not think she has had any visual or auditory hallucinations.

2. A previously well 28-year-old man is brought to the A&E Department by the police after being involved in an argument in a car dealership. His wife is called and she tells the doctor that her husband has been acting very strangely for several weeks. He sleeps very little and almost has to be 'tied down' to eat or slow down. She received their credit card bill a few days ago and he has spent £16,000 in one week on luxury items that they can ill afford. On talking to the patient he has pressure of speech, flight of ideas and grandiose ideation. His parting remark is 'what do you expect from the king of France'.

3. A 58-year-old woman, who has always been 'nervous', is referred to psychiatry outpatients. During the last few months she describes feelings of increasing fear about her future. She has had to take time off work and tells the doctor 'Everything worries me' 'I just can't concentrate on anything'. She has generalised aches and pains, sweats, shakes and finds it difficult to sleep.

4. A 49-year-old man suddenly becomes housebound, telling his wife that he is unable to leave the house. His wife has managed to coax him to take a couple of drives but he refuses to go to his bowls club, his local pub and feels 'increasingly cut off from the world'.

5. A 21-year-old student is brought to the A&E Department by ambulance after having been found at the wheel of a crashed motorcar. He is extremely agitated and distressed, and keeps repeating that his life is in danger. On further questioning he tells the doctor that 'those men told me that I was an evil influence on my family and needed to die'. His girlfriend arrives and says he has become increasingly withdrawn and 'strange' over the past few weeks. She excludes any illicit drug use.

24. THEME: PSYCHIATRIC MEDICATIONS

A   Amitriptyline
B   Chlormethiazole
C   Diazepam
D   Fluoxetine
E   Fluphenazine
F   Haloperidol
G   Lithium
H   Lofepramine
I   Risperidone
J   Thioridazine

The following patients have all presented with side-effects of their psychiatric medications. Please choose the most appropriate cause from the above list.

1. A 61-year-old woman with long-standing depression is admitted to hospital with increasing falls, constipation and blurred vision. On examination she has postural hypotension, a resting tachycardia and is heavily bruised. Initial investigations reveal: FBC: Hb 11.2 g/dl, MCV 81 fl, WCC 3.9×10^9/l, Plt 37×10^9/l; U&Es: Na$^+$125 mmol/l, K$^+$ 3.9 mmol/l, Urea 5.0 mmol/l, Cr 78 μmol/l; Glucose 5.4 mmol/l.

2. A 73-year-old woman with bipolar affective disorder is admitted to hospital with increasing confusion, drowsiness and weakness. On examination she has a coarse tremor, peripheral oedema and generalised weakness. She is also noted to be ataxic and dysarthric. Initial investigations reveal: U&Es: Na$^+$ 127 mmol/l, K$^+$ 2.9 mmol/l, Urea 4.7 mmol/l, Cr 98 μmol/l; Glucose 7.4 mmol/l; TFTs: TSH 24.2 mu/l, $_f$T$_4$ 7.9 mu/l.

3. A 29-year-old alcohol abuser with chronic alcoholic liver disease is admitted under the care of the gastroenterologists requesting detoxification. He is given intravenous multivitamins and is placed on appropriate withdrawal medication. The next day he is sleepy but easily rouseable and complains of a cough, dripping nose and 'itchy eyes'. Examination is largely unchanged from his initial review.

4. An 82-year-old woman is placed on an antidepressant by her GP. Two weeks later she is admitted to hospital with increasing confusion and diarrhoea. On examination she is confused with an AMTS 3/10. There are no focal neurological signs and the rest of the examination, including abdominal and per rectal examination, is essentially normal. Initial investigations reveal: FBC: Hb 14.6 g/dl, MCV 92 fl, WCC 6.9 x 10^9/l, Plt 437 x 10^9/l; U&Es: Na^+ 112 mmol/l, K^+ 4.9 mmol/l, Urea 7.0 mmol/l, Cr 128 μmol/l; Glucose 4.8 mmol/l; CXR – nil of note; CT head scan – 'involutional changes only'.

5. A 77-year-old man with known Alzheimer's disease is placed on medication to help with increasing bouts of shouting and behavioural problems at night. Several weeks later he is brought in to hospital by a paramedic team, having suffered a cardiac arrest whilst out shopping with his daughter. On arrival in the A&E Department the monitor shows 'torsade de pointes'.

25. THEME: DELIRIUM

A   Diabetic ketoacidosis
B   Encephalitis
C   Hepatic encephalopathy
D   Hypercalcaemia
E   Hypercapnia
F   Hyperosmolar, non-ketotic precoma
G   Hyponatraemia
H   Opiate analgesia
I   Subdural haemorrhage
J   Urinary tract infection

The following patients have all presented with confusion. Please choose the most appropriate diagnosis from the above list.

1. A previously fit and well 17-year-old schoolgirl presents in the A&E Department with a 24 hour history of increasing confusion. On examination she looks very unwell, is dehydrated, T 39.5°C; BP 100/50 mmHg, pulse 120 bpm regular, poor volume, respiratory, cardiac and abdominal examinations otherwise unremarkable. Initial investigations reveal: FBC: Hb 12.2 g/dl, MCV 81 fl, WCC 19.2 x 10^9/l, Plt 109 x 10^9/l; U&Es: Na^+ 147 mmol/l, K^+ 5.1 mmol/l, urea 26.2 mmol/l, Cr 208 μmol/l; glucose 34.9 mmol/l; ABGs pH 7.13, $PaCO_2$ 3.6 kPa, PaO_2 15.3 kPa, HCO_3^- 12.6 mmol/l, base excess –10.4. Urinalysis: blood ++, protein – nil, ketones 4+, nitrites – negative.

2. A 64-year-old lifelong smoker presents in the A&E Department with a 36 hour history of increasing confusion. On auscultation of his chest there is bronchial breathing and coarse crackles are heard in the right upper and mid zones. The chest radiograph is suggestive of a right hilar mass with upper lobe collapse and consolidation. Investigations reveal: FBC: Hb 10.2 g/dl, MCV 86 fl, WCC 15.2 x 10^9/l, Plt 419 x 10^9/l; U&Es: Na^+ 127 mmol/l, K^+ 4.1 mmol/l, urea 6.7 mmol/l, Cr 128 μmol/l; glucose 5.4 mmol/l; CCa^{2+} 3.37 mmol/l; PO_4^{2-} 1.07 mmol/l.

3. A 63-year-old lifelong smoker presents in the A&E Department with a 36 hour history of increasing dyspnoea associated with a cough productive of yellow sputum, and increasing aggression and confusion. On examination he is centrally cyanosed and his oxygen saturation on air is 71%. Initial investigations reveal: FBC: Hb 17.2 g/dl, MCV 81 fl, WCC 14.2 x 10^9/l, Plt 329 x 10^9/l; U&Es: Na^+ 137 mmol/l, K^+ 4.3 mmol/l, urea 12.9 mmol/l, Cr 119 μmol/l; glucose 4.9 mmol/l; ABGs (on air): pH 7.23, $PaCO_2$ 10.6 kPa, PaO_2 6.3 kPa, HCO_3^- 34.6 mmol/l.

4. A previously fit and well 67-year-old woman presents in the A&E Department with increasing confusion and falls. On examination she is drowsy and confused with an MTS 3/10. Neurological examination reveals a left-sided weakness and an equivocally upgoing plantar. Initial investigations reveal: FBC: Hb 10.7 g/dl, MCV 88 fl, WCC 12.2 x 10^9/l, Plt 488 x 10^9/l; U&Es: Na^+ 129 mmol/l, K^+ 4.0 mmol/l, urea 9.9 mmol/l, Cr 122 μmol/l; glucose 6.9 mmol/l; CXR – nil of note; CT head scan – 'high attenuation rim around the right frontal and temporoparietal lobes with marked mass effect to the left'.

5. A previously fit and well 31-year old woman presents in the A&E Department with a severe headache, increasing confusion and a partial complex seizure. On examination she is obviously distressed, has mild meningism but no rash and is pyrexial, T 39.2 °C. A CT head scan shows changes in the left temporal lobe associated with marked cerebral oedema. She improves with intravenous acyclovir.

26. THEME: DEMENTIA

A   Alcoholic dementia
B   Alzheimer's disease
C   Creutzfeldt-Jakob disease
D   Hypothyroidism
E   Lewy body dementia
F   Neurosyphilis
G   Normal pressure hydrocephalus
H   Pick's disease
I   Pseudodementia
J   Vascular dementia

The following patients have all presented with dementia. Please choose the most appropriate diagnosis from the above list.

1. A 72-year-old man with a long history of hypertension, IHD and several TIAs and strokes presents to his GP with increasing behavioural problems, wandering and forgetfulness. His Folstein score is 17/30. The GP notes that three months ago it was 21/30 and six months ago 24/30.

2. A previously fit and well 67-year-old woman, is taken by her husband to see her GP. He tells the doctor that for the past seven months she has become increasingly forgetful, has word finding problems and can no longer go out alone as she gets lost. He is now having to help her get dressed and washed. Routine examination and investigations are largely unremarkable but her Folstein score is 20/30.

3. A 78-year-old man is referred to the Medicine for the Elderly outpatients with a five month history of increasing confusion, falls and urinary incontinence. On examination he has a dyspraxic gait and a Folstein score of 19/30. CT head scan shows 'marked dilatation of the ventricles with some involutional changes'.

4. An 83-year-old woman presents in the A&E Department with increasing lethargy, confusion and general deterioration. On examination she is obese, pale, confused and speaks with a 'croaky' voice. Her Folstein score is 17/30. Initial investigations reveal: FBC: Hb 11.2 g/dl, MCV 106 fl, WCC 10.2 x 10^9/l, Plt 337 x 10^9/l; U&Es: Na$^+$126 mmol/l, K$^+$ 4.1 mmol/l, urea 4.7 mmol/l, Cr 104 μmol/l; glucose 5.4 mmol/l; CCa^{2+} 2.37 mmol/l; PO$_4$$^{2-}$ 0.88 mmol/l.

5. A previously fit and well 71-year-old man presents to his GP with increasing agitation, a marked change in his personality and disinhibition. His wife says she has become increasingly concerned for his safety. On examination he is relatively unkempt but is otherwise well and cardiovascular, respiratory, abdominal and neurological examinations are unremarkable. His Folstein score is surprisingly 25/30 but he repeats many of the questions and tends to confabulate.

CHAPTER 4

Cardiovascular and Haematology

1. THEME: SURFACE MARKINGS OF THE HEART

A Left costoxiphoid angle
B Left fifth intercostal space in the anterior axillary line
C Left fifth intercostal space in the mid-clavicular line
D Left third costosternal junction
E Medial end of the second left intercostal space
F Medial end of the second right intercostal space
G Medial to the fourth costosternal junction
H Medial to the third left intercostal space
I Midsternal at the level of the fourth intercostal space
J Right sternal border, in line with the fourth intercostal space

For each of the descriptions below, select the most appropriate marking from the above list.

1. Access site for drainage of a pericardial fluid collection. ☐

2. Surface marking of the apex of the heart. ☐

3. Optimal site for auscultation of the aortic valve. ☐

4. Optimal site for auscultation of the tricuspid valve. ☐

5. Surface marking of the pulmonary valve. ☐

2. THEME: BLOOD SUPPLY OF THE HEART

A Anterior interventricular artery
B Circumflex artery
C Coronary sinus
D Diagonal artery
E Great cardiac vein
F Left coronary artery
G Left marginal artery
H Posterior interventricular artery
I Right coronary artery
J Right marginal artery

For each of the descriptions below, indicate the most appropriate vessel from the above list.

1. Opens in the left posterior aortic sinus.

2. Opens into the right atrium.

3. Lies in the anterior atrioventricular groove.

4. Supplies the AV node.

5. Supplies the apex of the heart.

3. THEME: CHEST PAIN

A   Decubitus angina
B   Dissecting thoracic aortic aneurysm
C   Metastatic rib pain
D   Myocardial infarction
E   Oesophagitis
F   Pericarditis
G   Pulmonary embolism
H   Syndrome X
I   Tietze's syndrome
J   Unstable angina

The patients below have presented with chest pain. Choose the most appropriate diagnosis from the above list.

1. A 32-year-old man presents to his GP with a two day history of dyspnoea and retrosternal chest pain which came on gradually. The patient cannot recall any trauma or abnormal exertion and has never been ill before. The pain is stabbing in quality; radiates to the neck and left shoulder; is relieved by sitting upright, and is made worse by lying flat and coughing.

2. A 35-year-old man is brought to the A&E Department by ambulance having collapsed at work. His chest pain began forty minutes ago and has worsened gradually. It is now in a tight band across his chest and radiates to his neck but not his arms. On examination, he is grey, sweaty and short of breath with a pulse of 40 bpm.

3. A 67-year-old hypertensive, obese man is brought to the A&E Department by ambulance having collapsed whilst moving a chest of drawers. His chest pain, which began suddenly as he started lifting, is central, severe, burning and tearing in quality, and radiates through to his back and up to the neck. Measured with a thigh cuff, BP is 190/120 mmHg in the right arm and 160/90 mmHg in the left.

4. A 68-year-old woman presents to the A&E Department with heavy central chest pain radiating to her left arm which began an hour ago and woke her from sleep. The pain is similar to, but more severe than, her usual angina, and her glyceryl trinitrate spray has not relieved it. Serum creatine kinase levels taken in the A&E Department and again the following morning are normal.

continued . . .

5. A 38-year-old woman with systemic lupus erythematosus presents to the A&E Department with a 24 hour history of sharp, right-sided chest pain which is made worse by deep inspiration. She is not short of breath. She suffered a miscarriage five days ago, necessitating overnight admission to hospital for evacuation of retained products of conception. Since leaving hospital her left leg has become erythematous, swollen, warm and tender to palpation.

4. THEME: SHORTNESS OF BREATH

A   Anaemia
B   Angina
C   Aortic stenosis
D   Atrial fibrillation
E   Cardiac tamponade
F   Cardiomyopathy
G   Constrictive pericarditis
H   Left ventricular failure
I   Silent angina
J   Ventricular septal defect

The patients below have all presented with shortness of breath. Choose the most likely diagnosis from the above list.

1. A 62-year-old man presents to his GP with shortness of breath on exertion which has been getting worse for the last six months. On examination the carotid pulse is slow-rising, apex beat is heaving but undisplaced and there is an ejection systolic murmur which is heard over the left sternal edge, the right second intercostal space and radiating to the carotids.

2. A 69-year-old man who has suffered four myocardial infarctions presents to his GP with shortness of breath which has become gradually worse over the last six months. He has to sleep in an armchair and becomes breathless on minimal exertion. On examination, the apex beat is in the sixth intercostal space, mid-axillary line. A gallop rhythm is evident on auscultation of the heart and, in the chest, there are bilateral basal crepitations. Echocardiography shows an ejection fraction of 20%.

3. A 53-year-old woman with rheumatoid arthritis presents to her GP with a three month history of gradually increasing shortness of breath. Examination findings include atrial fibrillation at a rate of 80 bpm; raised jugular venous pressure (JVP); pulmonary basal crepitations and pitting ankle oedema. She improves initially on diuretics and digoxin but, gradually, the symptoms worsen again so the GP arranges referral to a cardiologist, who notices prominent *x* and *y* descents in the jugular venous pulsation and on auscultation hears a third heart sound.

4. You are called to the ward to see a 48-year-old man who underwent coronary artery bypass grafting two days ago. He started to feel breathless ten minutes ago but does not have chest pain. On examination he is grey and sweaty. Pulse is 120 bpm, regular but impalpable during respiration. Blood pressure is 78/40 mmHg. Jugular venous pressure is grossly elevated. There is not time to listen to the heart sounds before he arrests. The monitor shows electromechanical dissociation.

5. A 51-year-old woman presents to her GP with palpitations and shortness of breath. She has lost one-and-a-half stones over the last four months. On examination she appears anxious with greasy skin and a fine tremor. Her pulse is 140 bpm, irregular. Although heart sounds are normal with no murmurs, a bruit is audible in the neck.

5. THEME: MURMURS AND ADDED SOUNDS

A Atrial 'plop'
B Early diastolic murmur
C Ejection systolic murmur
D Late systolic murmur
E Machinery murmur
F Mid-diastolic murmur
G Mid-systolic click
H Opening snap
I Pan-systolic murmur
J Venous hum

The patients below have all presented with abnormal cardiac auscultatory signs. Choose the most likely auscultatory abnormality from the above list.

1. A 67-year-old man presents to his GP with a four-month history of exertional chest pain. The GP notices that the carotid pulse is slow-rising.

2. A 48-year-old publican presents to his GP with a six-month history of gradual onset fatigue, dyspnoea and ankle swelling. In addition to signs of chronic liver disease, the GP finds the apex beat in the mid-axillary line, sixth intercostal space.

3. A 33-year-old woman presents to her GP after an episode of transient left-sided weakness. The GP arranges an urgent echocardiogram which shows an intra-cardiac tumour.

4. A 58-year-old man presents to his GP with malaise, fever, night sweats and exertional dyspnoea. The GP notices several splinter haemorrhages and capillary pulsation beneath the fingernails.

5. A 16-year-old girl is found at a routine medical examination to have a small patent ductus arteriosus.

6. THEME: ST SEGMENT CHANGES ON ECG

A   Anterior myocardial infarction
B   Digoxin effect
C   High take off in the anterior leads
D   Inferior myocardial infarction
E   Lateral myocardial infarction
F   Left ventricular aneurysm
G   Myocarditis
H   Pericarditis
I   Posterior myocardial infarction
J   Prolonged QT interval

For each of the ST segment ECG changes below, choose the most likely diagnosis from the above list.

1. Widespread T wave inversion with sloping depression of the ST segment.

2. Widespread saddle-shaped ST elevation.

3. Tall R wave in V1 and V2 with deep ST depression in V1–V3.

4. Q waves and 4 mm ST elevation in leads II, III and aVF.

5. Deep Q waves and 5 mm elevation of ST segments in leads V1 to V4.

7. THEME: COMPLICATIONS OF MYOCARDIAL INFARCTION

A   Atrial fibrillation
B   Cardiogenic shock
C   Dressler's syndrome
D   Left ventricular failure
E   Mitral valve incompetence
F   Mural thrombus
G   Pericarditis
H   Pulmonary embolus
I   Recurrent infarction
J   Ventricular aneurysm
K   Ventricular fibrillation
L   Ventricular wall rupture

For each of the patients below, select the complication that the patient is most likely to have from the above list.

1. Three days after an anterior myocardial infarct, a 63-year-old man develops a sharp chest pain which is worse on movement and lying down. Auscultation reveals a pericardial rub. ECG shows ST segment elevation.

2. A 70-year-old woman suffers an anterolateral myocardial infarct. Two weeks later she develops sudden right hemiparesis and difficulty in talking.

3. A 60-year-old man is hospitalised for an inferior myocardial infarct. Despite appropriate treatment he dies six days later. Post-mortem examination shows massive distension of the pericardial sac by organising haematoma.

4. A 65-year-old woman suffers a large anteroseptal myocardial infarct. Six months later a left ventricular 'bulge' is seen on X-ray. Echocardiogram shows that the bulge expands during systole.

5. 3 months after a myocardial infarct, a 71-year-old man develops pyrexia and chest pain. Blood tests show a high ESR. A pericardial effusion is seen on echocardiogram.

6. A 59-year-old man suffers a large myocardial infarct. Four days later he develops left ventricular failure. Examination of the chest reveals a systolic thrill and a pansystolic murmur.

8. THEME: ARRHYTHMIA AND CONDUCTION DISTURBANCES

A   Atrial fibrillation
B   Atrial flutter with 2:1 block
C   Complete heart block
D   First degree heart block
E   Left bundle branch block
F   Mobitz type 1 block
G   Mobitz type 2 block
H   Sinus arrhythmia
I   Ventricular fibrillation
J   Ventricular tachycardia

The patients below have all presented with an arrhythmia or conduction disorder. Choose the most likely ECG diagnosis from the above list.

1. A 67-year-old man who suffers from angina presents to the A&E Department with dyspnoea, chest pain and palpitations. His pulse is 120 bpm and regular. ECG shows a regular, broad complex tachycardia with atrioventricular dissociation.

2. A 24-year-old medical student presents to the A&E Department after developing palpitations in a pub. His pulse is 150 bpm and regular. ECG shows a narrow QRS complex tachycardia.

3. An 84-year-old woman presents to the A&E Department with shortness of breath. Her pulse is 168 bpm and irregular.

4. A 71-year-old man presents to the A&E Department with an inferior myocardial infarction. His pulse is 32 bpm and regular.

5. A 65-year-old woman presents to the A&E Department with an anterior myocardial infarction. Her pulse is 88 bpm and regular but with dropped beats. ECG shows wide QRS complexes with a fixed PR interval but with occasional failure of conduction of a P wave.

9. THEME: SIDE-EFFECTS OF ANTIARRHYTHMIC DRUGS

A Adenosine
B Amiodarone
C Atropine
D Bretylium
E Digoxin
F Isoprenaline
G Lignocaine
H Propranolol
I Sotalol
J Verapamil

The following are side-effects of antiarrhythmic medications. Choose the most likely causative drug from the above list.

1. Intravenous injection of this drug to a patient taking beta-blockers may result in asystole.

2. Bolus intravenous injection of this drug may result in transient chest tightness and bronchospasm.

3. Prolonged administration of this drug may cause pulmonary fibrosis.

4. Torsade de pointes may occur, especially in patients with a prolonged QT syndrome.

5. Vivid and often disturbing dreams are common with this drug.

10. THEME: LEFT VENTRICULAR FAILURE

A   Aortic regurgitation
B   Aortic stenosis
C   Atenolol toxicity
D   Complete heart block
E   Hypertrophic obstructive cardiomyopathy
F   Mitral regurgitation
G   Mitral stenosis
H   Myocardial infarction
I   Supraventricular tachycardia
J   Ventricular septal defect

The patients below have all presented with left ventricular failure. Choose the most likely diagnosis from the above list.

1. A 22-year-old man, with a family history of sudden death under the age of 40, presents to his GP with left ventricular failure. The GP notices an ejection systolic murmur on auscultation and therefore requests an echocardiogram, which is reported as showing gross thickening of the ventricular septum.

2. A 76-year-old woman presents to her GP with left ventricular failure. Her pulse is 80 bpm, in atrial fibrillation; there is a tapping apex beat, and a rumbling mid-diastolic murmur radiating up into the axilla.

3. A 58-year-old man, who has been stable for four hours having presented with an inferior myocardial infarction, suddenly develops left ventricular failure. His pulse is 120 bpm, in sinus rhythm. Auscultation reveals a new, loud, pan-systolic murmur heard throughout the praecordium.

4. A 67-year-old woman with severe untreated hypertension presents to her GP with left ventricular failure. On examination she has a collapsing pulse, a laterally-displaced apex beat and a soft early diastolic murmur heard best at the left sternal edge.

5. An 82-year-old man, with a history of angina for which he has recently been started on verapamil, presents with acute left ventricular failure. His ECG shows dissociation between P waves, which are occurring at a rate of 80/min, and QRS complexes, which are broad and occur at a rate of 32/min. ST segments are normal.

11. THEME: SECONDARY CAUSES OF HYPERTENSION

A   Acromegaly
B   Coarctation of the aorta
C   Conn's syndrome
D   Cushing's syndrome
E   Diabetic nephropathy
F   Phaeochromocytoma
G   Polyarteritis nodosa
H   Polycystic kidney disease
I   Pregnancy
J   Renal artery stenosis

The patients below have all presented with secondary hypertension. Choose the most appropriate diagnosis from the above list.

1. A 61-year-old man with diet-controlled type 2 diabetes mellitus and coronary artery disease develops asymptomatic hypertension. 24 hour urine is negative for protein. Urea and electrolytes are normal. He is started on lisinopril and seen again a week later. Repeat blood tests show urea 19.2 mmol/l and creatinine 287 μmol/l.

2. A 30-year-old woman presents to her GP with fatigue and ankle swelling. BP is 200/120 mmHg, Na^+ 141 mmol/l, K^+ 2.8 mmol/l, Cl^- 100 mmol/l, HCO_3^- 35 mmol/l, urea 6.9 mmol/l, Cr 84 μmol/l. Plasma ACTH 22 pg/ml (=4.8 pmol/l). Plasma renin is undetectable. CT abdomen shows a 1.2 cm diameter nodule in the left adrenal gland.

3. An 18-year-old man is found to be hypertensive during a routine medical. Examination reveals radio-femoral delay, an ejection systolic murmur and tortuous retinal arteries.

4. A 31-year-old man presents to his GP with a three-week history of malaise, weight loss, abdominal pains and ankle swelling. Urine dipstick is strongly positive for blood and protein. BP is 190/110 mmHg. Blood tests show WBC 15.2 x 10^9/l, ESR 67 mm/hr, CRP 80 g/l and positive p-ANCA.

5. A 43-year-old woman presents to her GP with frequent, rapid palpitations associated with a pounding headache, sweating and a feeling of impending doom. 24 hour urinary catecholamines are elevated on three separate occasions but CT scan of the adrenals is normal.

12. THEME: SIDE-EFFECTS OF ANTIHYPERTENSIVE DRUGS

A   Atenolol
B   Bendrofluazide
C   Clonidine
D   Doxazosin
E   Enalapril
F   Hydralazine
G   Losartan
H   Minoxidil
I   Moxonidine
J   Nifedipine

The following are side-effects of antihypertensive medication. Choose the most appropriate causative medication from the above list.

1. Bronchospasm

2. Gum hyperplasia

3. Persistent dry cough

4. Hypertrichosis

5. Systemic lupus erythematosus-like syndrome

13. THEME: TYPES OF ANAEMIA

A Anaemia of chronic disease
B Anaemia of chronic renal failure
C Aplastic anaemia
D Autoimmune haemolytic anaemia
E Fanconi anaemia
F Iron deficiency anaemia
G Macrocytic anaemia
H Megaloblastic anaemia
I Microangiopathic haemolytic anaemia
J Pernicious anaemia
K Sickle cell anaemia
L Sideroblastic anaemia

For each of the patients below, select the type of anaemia they are most likely to have from the above list.

1. A 63-year-old man presents with a three month history of right-sided abdominal pain. Haematological investigations show a haemoglobin of 8.0 g/dl, a low MCV and a low MCHC. Colonoscopy shows an ulcerating mass in the ascending colon.

2. A 25-year-old man presents with a one year history of abdominal discomfort and more recently steatorrhoea. He had also felt tired recently and had been taking iron supplements. Blood tests show a haemoglobin of 9.2 g/dl, a high MCV and a normal MCHC. A blood film shows hypersegmented neutrophils. Serum and red cell folate concentrations are low. A duodenal biopsy shows subtotal villous atrophy consistent with coeliac disease.

3. A 35-year-old man presents with a two month history of tiredness, lethargy and easy bruising. Blood tests show a haemoglobin of 4.5 g/dl with low white cell and platelet counts and a virtual absence of reticulocytes. Bone marrow examination shows a hypocellular marrow with increased fat spaces.

4. A 64-year-old chronic alcoholic presents to the A&E Department with a minor head injury. On examination he is found to be pale. Blood tests show a haemoglobin of 9.6 g/dl with a high MCV and a normal MCHC. Subsequent bone marrow examination shows no evidence of megaloblastic change.

5. A 54-year-old woman with long-standing chronic osteomyelitis has a routine blood test taken by her GP. This shows a haemoglobin of 9.8 g/dl with a normal MCV and MCHC.

6. A 48-year-old woman with known SLE presents with recent onset of jaundice. Blood tests show a haemoglobin of 10.1 g/dl with a normal MCV and MCHC and a high reticulocyte count. A blood film shows spherocytes. The direct antiglobulin test is positive. Liver function tests show an unconjugated hyperbilirubinaemia.

14. THEME: MACROCYTOSIS

A   Alcohol excess
B   B12 deficiency
C   Cytotoxic drugs
D   Folate deficiency
E   Hypothyroidism
F   Liver disease
G   Myelodysplasia
H   Myeloma
I   Pregnancy
J   Reticulocytosis

The following patients have all presented with a macrocytosis. Please choose the most appropriate cause from the above list.

1. A 49-year-old woman presents to her GP with malaise, pruritus and early Dupuytren's contracture. Routine investigations show significant titres of anti-mitochondrial and anti-smooth muscle antibodies.

2. A 23-year-old previously fit and well Nigerian man presents to the A&E Department with a one week history of 'flu-like illness and a dry cough. On examination he is clinically anaemic, pyrexial and has coarse crackles on auscultation of the base of his right lung. FBC: Hb 7.9 g/dl, MCV 104 fl, WCC 7.9 x 10^9/l and Plt 234 x 10^9/l.

3. A 78-year-old woman presents to her GP with malaise, pallor and poor concentration. On examination she has dry skin and hair, slow relaxing reflexes and is noted to have a croaky voice.

4. A 47-year-old man presents to his GP with a two month history of back and hip pain associated with malaise. On examination he is pale, has multiple areas of bruising and is very tender over his left upper femur and over L3 and L4. Routine investigation show a macrocytosis, pancytopenia and ESR 122 mm/hr. Urinary Bence-Jones proteins are present.

15. THEME: HAEMOLYTIC ANAEMIA

A   Blood transfusion reaction
B   Beta-thalassaemia
C   CLL induced AIHA
D   Disseminated intravascular coagulopathy
E   G6PD deficiency
F   Hereditary elliptocytosis
G   Hereditary spherocytosis
H   Methyldopa induced AIHA
I   Prosthetic heart valve fragmentation
J   Sickle cell disease

The following patients have presented with a haemolytic anaemia. Please choose the most likely cause from the above list.

1.   A 79-year-old man presents to his GP with exertional dyspnoea and bruising. On examination he is anaemic, bruised and has discrete, non-tender cervical lymph nodes. His blood tests reveal: FBC: Hb 6.7 g/dl, MCV 99 fl, WCC 65 x 10^9/l (60 lymphocytes), Plt 37 x 10^9/l.

2.   A 15-year-old Jamaican girl presents to the A&E Department with bony pain and shortness of breath. Her oxygen saturation is 87% on air. Investigations reveal: FBC: Hb 5.3 g/dl, MCV 101 fl, WCC 13.2 x 10^9/l, Plt 199 x 10^9/l.

3.   A 24-year-old pregnant woman is admitted to hospital with malaise and extreme lethargy. She is being treated for pregnancy-induced hypertension. Investigations reveal: FBC: Hb 6.4 g/dl, MCV 102 fl, WCC 5.6 x 10^9/l, Plt 342 x 10^9/l; Coombs' test positive.

4.   A 29-year-old man is found to have splenomegaly and a macrocytic anaemia on routine investigation for a life assurance policy. The Coombs' test is negative but the osmotic fragility test is strongly positive.

5.   A 7-year-old Greek boy presents to the paediatric outpatients with severe anaemia. On examination he is anaemic and has frontal and parietal bossing of the skull. He is also noted to have hepatosplenomegaly. Skull X-ray reveals a 'hair on end' appearance of the cortex.

16. THEME: APLASTIC ANAEMIA

A   Carbimazole
B   Chlorpromazine
C   Chlorpropamide
D   Cyclophosphamide
E   Gold
F   Indomethacin
G   Methotrexate
H   Phenytoin
I   Propylthiouracil
J   Tolbutamide

The following patients have all presented with aplastic anaemia secondary to their drug therapy. Please choose the most appropriate cause from the above list.

1. A 23-year-old man with recent onset of paranoid delusions and auditory hallucinations becomes acutely unwell with a pyrexial illness and epistaxis after starting antipsychotic medication.

2. A 37-year-old woman with known rheumatoid arthritis, who is receiving regular intramuscular injections in the outpatient clinic, presents to her GP with malaise and severe pharyngitis.

3. A 45-year-old woman who is two weeks post excision of a large frontal meningioma, develops severe bruising and menorrhagia.

4. A 29-year-old woman is started on carbimazole but two weeks later develops a skin rash and has to change to another antithyroid treatment. After a further two weeks she develops a severe sore throat and reports to her GP as instructed.

5. A 86-year-old NIDDM patient who is on a short-acting sulphonylurea presents with a severe systemic infection following a chest infection.

17. THEME: WHITE CELL DISORDERS

A   Acute lymphoblastic leukaemia
B   Acute myeloid leukaemia
C   B-cell chronic lymphocytic leukaemia
D   Burkitt's lymphoma
E   Chronic myeloid leukaemia
F   Hairy cell leukaemia
G   Hodgkin's disease
H   Langerhans' cell histiocytosis
I   Lymphoplasmacytic lymphoma
J   Mantle cell lymphoma
K   Mycosis fungoides
L   Plasma cell myeloma

For each of the patients below, select the white cell disorder that they are most likely to have from the above list

1. A 32-year-old man presents with a two month history of enlarged lymph nodes in the neck which are painful after drinking alcohol. He has also had episodes of swingeing pyrexia and drenching night sweats. Biopsy of one of the nodes shows diffuse replacement of the architecture by a mixed infiltrate of lymphocytes, plasma cells and eosinophils with scattered Reed-Sternberg cells.

2. A 65-year-old man presents with a four month history of worsening back pain. X-rays show many lytic lesions in the lumbar vertebrae and in the iliac crest. Blood tests show hypercalcaemia, mild anaemia and low white cell and platelet counts. An IgG paraprotein is detected on electrophoresis. Examination of a bone marrow aspirate shows that 40% of the cells are cytologically abnormal plasma cells.

3. A 45-year-old woman presents with a two month history of tiredness, intermittent pyrexia and abdominal pain. On examination she is found to have a palpable spleen 7 cm below the costal margin. Blood tests show a moderate anaemia with a substantially raised white cell count. Examination of the bone marrow trephine shows a hypercellular marrow with an increase in myeloid precursors. Cytogenetic analysis detects the Philadelphia chromosome t(9:22).

4. A 7-year-old Ugandan boy presents with a three week history of an enlarging swelling in his jaw. X-rays show a lytic lesion unrelated to his teeth. Biopsy of the lesion shows a high grade B-cell lymphoma that expresses Epstein-Barr virus-related antigens. Cytogenetic analysis shows t(8:14).

continued . . .

5. A 26-year-old woman presents with a one month history of tiredness, dyspnoea on exercise and easy bruising. Blood tests show severe pancytopenia and a blood film shows 50% myeloblasts. Examination of the bone marrow shows increased cellularity with predominance of myeloblasts and profoundly reduced platelet and red cell precursors.

6. A 58-year-old man presents to his GP two weeks after noticing enlarged lymph nodes in the neck, both axillae and the right groin. Blood tests show a mild anaemia and a white cell count of 18. A blood film shows that 60% of the white cells are small mature lymphocytes that express B-cell markers and CD5 antigen on flow cytometry. Examination of the bone marrow shows widespread interstitial infiltrates of small lymphocytes without blasts.

18. THEME: COMPLICATIONS OF BLOOD TRANSFUSION

A   Anaphylactoid reaction
B   Bacterial contamination
C   Delayed haemolytic transfusion reaction
D   Fluid overload
E   Graft *vs.* host disease
F   Immediate haemolytic transfusion reaction
G   Iron overload
H   Non-haemolytic febrile transfusion reaction
I   Transmission of viral disease
J   Urticaria

The patients below all have complications of blood transfusion. Please select the most appropriate cause or description from the above list.

1. You are asked to review a 59-year-old male who has developed fever, rigors and severe chest and lower back pain a few minutes after the start of a blood transfusion. On examination, he is dyspnoeic, tachycardic and hypotensive. Urinalysis reveals haemoglobinuria.

2. An 87-year-old female who lives alone was found collapsed at home. When admitted she was severely anaemic, with a raised urea and creatinine. Over the next 24 hours, 3 litres of fluid were infused followed by transfusion of two units of blood. During the blood transfusion she became dyspnoeic, hypoxic and tachycardic. Examination revealed a raised JVP, basal crepitations and ankle oedema.

3. A 37-year-old multiparous female receiving a blood transfusion developed fever and rigors, facial flushing and tachycardia approximately one hour after the transfusion was started. She had had one previous transfusion seven years ago.

4. A GP noted that a new patient who had just moved to the area, a 16-year-old male with β-thalassaemia, was of short stature and had failed to develop secondary sexual characteristics. Further investigations also revealed poor cardiac function.

5. A pyrexia (> 40°C) and shock develop shortly after the start of a blood transfusion to a previously healthy male with no past history of blood transfusion. Clerical error is suspected, but laboratory testing excludes ABO blood group or rhesus incompatibility.

19. THEME: VASCULAR ANATOMY OF THE HEAD AND NECK

A Abdominal aorta
B Aortic arch
C Coeliac trunk
D Descending thoracic aorta
E Inferior mesenteric artery
F Left external iliac artery
G Right common iliac artery
H Right internal iliac artery
I Right renal artery
J Superior mesenteric artery

Please choose the most appropriate artery from the above list to match the following statements:

1. Posterior relation of the left renal vein

2. Posterior relation of the left pulmonary artery

3. Closely related to the fibres of the greater splanchnic nerves

4. Passes anterior to the uncinate process of the pancreas

5. Anterior relation of the left common iliac vein

20. THEME: VENOUS ANATOMY OF THE LOWER LIMB

A   Anterior to the lateral malleolus
B   Anterior to the medial malleolus
C   Deep to the popliteal artery at the level of the knee joint
D   Lateral to the femoral artery in the femoral triangle
E   Medial to the femoral artery in the femoral triangle
F   Posterior to the lateral malleolus
G   Posterior to the medial malleolus
H   Subcutaneously, anterolateral to the knee joint
I   Subcutaneously, posteromedial to the knee joint
J   Superficial to the popliteal artery at the level of the knee joint

For each of the structures below, select the most appropriate anatomical relationship from the above list.

1.   The great saphenous vein at the ankle   ☐

2.   The great saphenous vein at the knee   ☐

3.   The saphenofemoral junction   ☐

4.   The small saphenous vein   ☐

5.   The popliteal vein   ☐

21. THEME: LIMB ISCHAEMIA

A   Acute on chronic lower limb ischaemia
B   Aortic dissection
C   Embolism
D   Femoral artery transection
E   Intra-arterial heroin injection
F   Popliteal artery entrapment
G   Post-catheter femoral artery false aneurysm
H   Post-traumatic femoral artery occlusion
I   Thrombosis of a femoropopliteal graft
J   Thrombosis of a popliteal aneurysm

The following patients all present with an ischaemic leg. Please choose the most appropriate diagnosis from the above list.

1. A 26-year-old lady presents to the A&E Department with acute onset of severe back pain starting beneath the left scapula, radiating down the back and into the right thigh. Her previous medical history is unremarkable – her mother died at the age of 34 during her second pregnancy. On examination the patient has a pulseless and ischaemic right leg; the left leg is normal.

2. Coronary angiography undertaken in a 45-year-old man is complicated by extensive bruising of the right thigh. Two weeks later he notes a swelling in his right groin and four days after this, he presents to the A&E Department with acute pain of his right leg. On examination the leg is severely ischaemic with the staining of old bruising. The femoral artery is enlarged, firm and pulseless.

3. A 72-year-old known male arteriopath presents to the A&E Department with acute pain in his right leg. Fifteen years previously he developed claudication of the left calf and although this has improved, three years later symptoms started on the right side and progressed over the subsequent years: his claudicating distance is currently 100 metres. On examination there are no pulses palpable in the right leg. It is dusky blue on dependency but becomes white with venous guttering on elevation above 10°.

4. A 57-year-old gentleman presents to the A&E Department with acute pain of his left leg, accompanied by pallor, numbness and weakness. He admits to a mild attack of pain and some discoloration of his other leg seven years before, but this improved overnight and had not been reported to any doctor. On examination the patient is otherwise well. Both femoral pulses are normal but the left leg is acutely ischaemic below the knee.

5. A 63-year-old gentleman with known carcinoma of the bronchus presents to the A&E Department with acute severe pain of his left leg, which is numb and weak. On examination the right leg pulses are normal but none are palpable on the left, and the leg is pale with weakness and sensory loss below the knee.

22. THEME: VENOUS THROMBOSIS

A   Axillary vein thrombosis
B   Deep venous thrombosis
C   Disseminated intravascular coagulation
D   Inferior vena caval obstruction
E   Postphlebitic syndrome
F   Pulmonary embolism
G   Superior vena caval obstruction
H   Superficial venous thrombosis
I   Thrombophlebitis
J   Varicose veins

The following patients all have thrombotic problems. Please choose the most appropriate diagnosis from the above list.

1. A fit 48-year-old quantity surveyor presents to the A&E Department with a painful right arm that was present when he woke up that morning. He is otherwise well and there is no history of trauma or abnormalities of any system. On examination there is marked tenderness and mild erythema along the anterolateral aspect of the forearm and cubital fossa, with no abnormality of the upper arm or axilla.

2. A 45-year-old lady, a known heavy smoker with chronic respiratory problems, presents to her GP with increasing dyspnoea and swelling of her right arm and face. On examination of her chest there is no asymmetry or tracheal deviation, but there are added sounds over the right upper lobe and on bending forward her face becomes congested.

3. A 56-year-old lady returns to the Vascular Clinic with recurrence of her left leg ulcer after the area has been knocked by a shopping trolley. On examination the ulcer is situated above the medial malleolus, its dimensions being 6 cm x 5 cm. The base is filled with yellowish slough and the surrounding area is erythematous, with prominent oedema.

4. A 48-year-old gentleman develops right-sided pleuritic chest pain and coughs up a trace of bloodstained sputum eight days after a right hemicolectomy. He has mild dyspnoea but chest examination and chest radiography are normal.

5. A 32-year-old lady develops acute swelling of her left leg two days postpartum. She had bilateral leg swelling during the pregnancy but the delivery was normal. On examination there is tense swelling of the leg and thigh and some deep tenderness over the calf and medial aspect of the thigh.

23. THEME: LEG PAIN

A Bone tumour
B Fracture of the patella
C Fracture of the tibial condyle
D Haemarthrosis
E Osteochondritis
F Ruptured Baker's cyst
G Torn cartilage
H Torn fibres of the soleus muscle
I Torn medial ligament
J Venous thrombosis

The following patients all present with leg pain. Please choose the most appropriate diagnosis from the above list.

1. A 45-year-old male physician is persuaded to make up the numbers in the staff-student tennis match. Although involved in competitive sport as a student, he has not undertaken any regular exercise for fifteen years. When running for a ball at 5–2 up in the first set, he experiences severe pain of the right calf and is unable to take any further part in the proceedings.

2. A 54-year-old gentleman, admitted to hospital for the management of an acute myocardial infarction, develops an acute painful leg ten days later. On examination the leg is white and tensely swollen, with altered sensation over the dorsum of the foot and lower leg.

3. A 16-year-old boy presents to his GP with a two month history of an aching pain in his right lower thigh. This is particularly noticeable at night, keeping him awake. He plays regular first team football but does not remember a specific injury. On examination there are no obvious abnormalities. He is apyrexic with no local tenderness or problems with joint movement.

4. A 27-year-old insurance agent who plays minor league football is brought to the A&E Department with an acutely swollen right knee. He had been involved in a heavy tackle and had to be carried off. Walking was subsequently very painful and tended to 'catch' in certain positions: he is still unable to fully straighten the knee. On examination there is an effusion with tenderness over the anterolateral aspect of the knee joint. Movements are still very painful and the knee is held in 10° of flexion. Radiographs are normal.

continued . . .

5. A 27-year-old man who plays regular Saturday football was on his way home after the match and subsequent celebrations when his right knee locked. He was able to get up from the fall and continue home and attends the A&E Department the next morning. The knee is swollen but there is no local tenderness around the knee and the movements are full. Radiographs show some irregularity of the medial femoral condyle.

24. THEME: PAIN AND SWELLING IN THE LOWER LIMB

A   Atherosclerosis
B   Buerger's disease
C   Congestive cardiac failure
D   Deep vein thrombosis
E   Osteoarthritis of the hip
F   Primary lymphoedema
G   Raynaud's disease
H   Secondary lymphoedema
I   Spinal stenosis
J   Osteoarthritis of the knee

The patients below have all presented with pain and/or swelling in the lower limb. Please select the most appropriate diagnosis from the above list.

1. A 72-year-old woman presents with a ten week history of progressive non-painful swelling of her right lower limb. On questioning she has noted some vaginal bleeding for the past year. Pelvic examination reveals an ulcerating mass of the uterine cervix.

2. A 58-year-old Australian woman complains of a sudden onset of pain and swelling in the left ankle and calf causing her difficulty in walking shortly after arriving on holiday in the UK. On examination, the calf is swollen in comparison to the opposite side, and the muscles are firm and tender to palpation. There is unilateral ankle oedema.

3. A 40-year-old woman presents with a six month history of slowly progressive non-painful swelling of her left lower limb. She has no significant past medical history, but notes that her mother also suffered with swollen legs. Cardiovascular, abdominal and pelvic examination and examination of the inguinal lymph nodes are unremarkable.

4. A 76-year-old man presents with a three month history of a continuous severe aching pain in the toes and left forefoot. The pain is worse at night and he can only sleep if in a chair, and with the aid of 10 mg of morphine sulphate. On general examination he appears haggard and thin. Buerger's angle is 20° on the left and the foot becomes reddish-purple colour on dependency. Foot pulses are absent bilaterally, and the ankle-brachial pressure index (ABPI) is 0.3.

5. A 70-year-old man complains of a six month history of aching pain and weakness in both calves when walking. The pain starts with ambulation and resolves only after resting for some time following exercise. Foot pulses are present. ABPI is 1.0 on exercise testing.

25. THEME: LEG SWELLING

A   Cardiac
B   Chronic infection
C   Filariasis
D   Hepatic failure
E   Malignancy
F   Malnutrition
G   Nephrotic syndrome
H   Post-radiotherapy
I   Primary lymphoedema
J   Venous thrombosis

The following patients all present with leg swelling. Please choose the most appropriate diagnosis from the above list.

1. A 25-year-old West African lady who has recently arrived in the UK presents to her GP with an eight month history of painless swelling of her left leg. She is otherwise well. On examination, the maximum circumference of the left calf is 5 cm greater than the right and the left thigh 8 cm greater than the right. The skin over the leg is normal. FBC shows: Hb 10.1 g/dl, WBC 11.6 x 10^9/l, neutrophils 6 x 10^9/l, lymphocytes 2.6 x 10^9/l, eosinophils 2.9 x 10^9/l.

2. A 15-year-old West Indian schoolgirl presents to her GP with a five month history of painless swelling of her right leg. She is otherwise well. She is on no medication. On examination, the maximum circumference of the right lower leg and thigh are 2 cm greater than the left, and there is pitting oedema of the anterior shin. The skin is normal. Investigations, including FBC, U&Es, LFT, are normal.

3. A 35-year-old Caucasian lady who has been brought up in West Africa presents to her GP with painless swelling of her left leg. She is otherwise well. She had an operation on the sole of her foot eight years previously, but is not sure of the diagnosis. On examination she is well. The left leg is mildly swollen, with pitting oedema over the shin. There are prominent inguinal lymph nodes and palpable external iliac nodes. There is a healed skin graft over the medial aspect of the sole.

4. A 45-year-old native West African lady who is known to be Hep B positive, develops left leg swelling eight days post-hysterectomy for fibroids. On examination she has marked swelling of the leg and thigh. Investigations show: FBC: Hb 10.3 g/dl, WBC 12.6 x 10⁹/l; LFT: bilirubin 23 μmol/l, ALT 121 iu/l, AST 86 iu/l.

5. A 35-year-old West African lady presents to her GP with a two week history of bilateral leg oedema and mild breathlessness for one week. She has been hypertensive since the birth of her fourth child four years previously. Examination confirms pitting oedema and left basal crepitations. Investigations show: Hb 10.0 g/dl; U&Es: urea 7 mmol/l, Cr 95 μmol/l; LFT: bilirubin 8 μmol/l, ALT 25 iu/l, total protein 51g/l, albumin 19 g/l.

26. THEME: LEG ULCERS I

A   Arterial
B   Basal cell carcinoma
C   Intravenous drug abuse
D   Neuropathic
E   Nutritional
F   Pyoderma gangrenosum
G   Sickle cell disease
H   Traumatic
I   Vasculitic
J   Venous

The patients below have all presented with leg ulcers. Please choose the most appropriate diagnosis from the above list.
(The Doppler ratio is the ratio of the ankle:brachial systolic pressure e.g. ankle =120 mmHg; brachial = 120 mmHg; ratio = 1.0)

1. A 47-year-old obese woman with lipodermatosclerosis and 'eczema' over both calves presents to her GP with a large ulcer over the medial malleolus of the right ankle. Doppler ratios (L) = 0.95, (R) = 1.05.

2. A 61-year-old man with known IHD and diabetes mellitus presents with a large, penetrating ulcer over the lateral malleolus of the left leg. Sensory examination of the lower limbs is unremarkable. Doppler ratios (L) = 0.44, (R) = 0.65.

3. A 29-year-old known alcohol abuser presents to his GP with paraesthesiae in his feet associated with ulceration over the distal tips of three toes on the left foot and the dorsal aspect of the right ankle. Doppler ratios (L) = 0.96, (R) = 0.98.

4. A 30-year-old man with known inflammatory bowel disease presents to his GP with a large ulcerating lesion over the anterior shin of the left leg. He is otherwise systemically well and his bowel disease is quiescent. Doppler ratios (L) = 1.04, (R) = 1.01.

5. A 24-year-old Jamaican woman presents to her GP with a three month history of a painful ulcer over the anterior shin of the right leg. Doppler ratios (L) = 1.0, (R) = 1.03.

27. THEME: LEG ULCERS II

A   Artefactual
B   Ischaemic
C   Malnutrition
D   Neuropathic
E   Osteomyelitis
F   Scleroderma
G   Squamous cell carcinoma
H   Tropical
I   Tubercular
J   Venous

The following patients all present with leg ulcers. Please choose the most appropriate diagnosis from the above list.

1. A 32-year-old lady is referred to the vascular clinic for a second opinion of a chronic ulcer of her right leg. This has been present for six years and has not responded to any of a wide range of treatments. On examination she is fit and cheerful: there is a 12 cm wide and 15 cm long ulcer over the upper anterolateral aspect of the shin. This has a prolific overlying green slough with two longitudinal grooves, the edges are straight and the surrounding skin and foot are normal. There are no associated varicose veins and peripheral pulses are normal.

2. A 43-year-old gentleman is found to have a perforating ulcer of the sole of his right foot on routine follow-up in the Diabetic Clinic. This is giving him no discomfort and his diabetes is well-controlled. On examination the ulcer is circular, 4 mm in diameter, situated over the head of the second metatarsal. It is surrounded by a rim of keratinisation but there are no adjacent inflammatory changes. Pedal pulses are just palpable and the pressure is normal within them.

3. A 35-year-old gentleman presents to his GP with a circular ulcer over his left shin. This has been gradually getting larger for a year. Although it initially has shown some signs of healing, it is now well-established and there is contact bleeding along one edge. On examination the ulcer is 4 cm in diameter over the mid–tibia, its edge is raised medially and the base covered with green slough, except laterally, where there is evidence of some pink granulation. There is no palpable inguinal lymphadenopathy.

continued . . .

4. A 35-year-old lady has noticed a cold sensitivity of her hands for a decade, the fingers going white with the cold: on rewarming, they are painful, with blue and then red discoloration. For two years there has been a superficial ulcer above the right lateral malleolus which is occasionally very painful. She has also noticed that her fingers are becoming spindle-shaped and occasionally she has small, painful ulcers over their tips.

5. A 53-year-old accountant presents to the Outpatient Department with recurrent ulceration of the medial and lateral supramaleolar regions of his right lower leg. He had a motorcycle accident at the age of 23, with a complicated fracture of the mid-shaft of the tibia and fibula. The fracture and skin healing had taken eighteen months, but this was complete, with no local discharge or subsequent infection.

Respiratory

1. THEME: SURFACE MARKINGS OF THE LUNG AND PLEURA

A   1st rib
B   2nd rib
C   3rd rib
D   4th rib
E   6th rib
F   8th rib
G   9th rib
H   10th rib
I   11th rib
J   12th rib

For each of the descriptions below, choose the most appropriate surface markings from the above list.

1. The lower posterior limit of the parietal pleura.

2. The lower limit of the parietal pleura in the mid-axillary line.

3. The lower limit of the parietal pleura in the mid-clavicular line.

4. The upper marking of the cardiac notch.

5. The upper anterior level at which the two lungs meet.

2. THEME: RELATIONSHIPS OF THE LUNG

A Aortic arch
B Azygos vein
C Body of the 5th thoracic vertebra
D Body of the 7th thoracic vertebra
E Descending thoracic aorta
F Inferior vena cava
G Left vagus nerve
H Left ventricle
I Right ventricle
J Superior vena cava

For each of the descriptions below, select the most appropriate structure from the above list.

1. Lies posterior to the tracheal bifurcation.

2. Lies anterior to the hilum of the right lung.

3. Lies superior to the hilum of the left lung.

4. Produces the cardiac impression of the left lung.

5. Lies superior to the hilum of the right lung.

3. THEME: CHEST PAIN

A   Bony metastases
B   Dissecting thoracic aortic aneurysm
C   Pancoast's tumour
D   Pneumothorax
E   Pulmonary embolism
F   Rib fracture
G   Sarcoidosis
H   T6 herpes zoster rash
I   Tietze's syndrome
J   Viral pneumonia

The patients below have all presented with chest pain. Choose the most appropriate diagnosis from the above list.

1. A 19-year-old woman presents to her GP with a small, firm, tender lump 2 cm lateral to the manubrio-sternal joint on the right side. She first noticed it a month ago and it has become gradually more tender. In addition she is experiencing moderate pleuritic-type pains. There is no history of trauma. Routine blood tests, including ESR, are normal.

2. A 57-year-old woman presents to her GP with a continuous ache on the right side of her chest. She also admits to weight loss and haemoptysis, and volunteers that her right eyelid has recently begun to droop.

3. A 26-year-old woman who was recently started on an oral contraceptive presents to the A&E Department with sudden onset left-sided chest pain which came on whilst smoking a cigarette. The pain is sharp, pleuritic and severe and is associated with shortness of breath. Clinical examination is normal except for swelling of the right leg.

4. A 29-year-old basketball player presents to the A&E Department with sudden onset left-sided chest pain which came on during training without a history of trauma. The pain is sharp, pleuritic and severe and is associated with shortness of breath. Clinical examination reveals reduced breath sounds on the left.

5. A 38-year-old man presents to his GP with a year's history of vague central chest pains which are not related to exertion or food intake. Nevertheless he is troubled by increasingly frequent palpitations and by a bruising-like rash on his shins. Apart from this rash, clinical examination is normal.

4. THEME: SHORTNESS OF BREATH

A   Asbestosis
B   Asthma
C   Cryptogenic fibrosing alveolitis
D   Emphysema
E   Farmer's lung
F   Mycoplasma pneumonia
G   Pleural effusion
H   Pneumothorax
I   Pulmonary embolism
J   Sarcoidosis

The patients below have all presented with shortness of breath. Choose the most appropriate diagnosis from the above list.

1. A 19-year-old man presents to his GP with a two day history of shortness of breath on exertion and a non-productive cough. He has felt non-specifically unwell with a headache for several days. Clinical examination is normal but a chest X-ray shows patchy shadowing of both lower lobes.

2. A 64-year-old man with a six month history of weight loss, constipation and rectal bleeding presents to his GP with shortness of breath and pleuritic chest pain which came on suddenly during a meal. Chest examination is normal.

3. A 22-year-old woman known to have asthma presents to the A&E Department acutely short of breath. On examination there are polyphonic wheezes throughout the chest; these gradually disappear as her condition worsens.

4. A 28-year-old woman presents to the chest clinic with a six month history of dyspnoea on exertion. She also admits to weight loss, malaise and polyuria. Apart from a nodular rash on her nose and forehead, clinical examination is normal.

5. A 58-year-old policeman presents to the chest clinic with an 18-month history of increasing shortness of breath. On examination he is tachypnoeic and has gross clubbing of the fingers. Auscultation reveals bibasal fine end-inspiratory crackles.

5. THEME: HAEMOPTYSIS

A   Goodpasture's disease
B   Mesothelioma
C   Microscopic polyarteritis
D   Pulmonary abscess
E   Pulmonary embolism
F   Pulmonary metastases
G   Small cell carcinoma
H   Squamous cell carcinoma
I   Streptococcal pneumonia
J   Tuberculosis

The patients below have all presented with haemoptysis. Choose the most appropriate diagnosis from the above list.

1. A 63-year-old tramp presents to the A&E Department with a four day history of haemoptysis. He has felt unwell for about two months with a cough, loss of weight and generalised weakness. He attributes his diplopia, which started a fortnight ago, to excessive alcohol consumption. On examination he has bilateral ptosis and proximal weakness in the limbs which improves on repeated testing.

2. A 20-year-old man with cystic fibrosis presents to the chest clinic with haemoptysis. He has felt unwell for a fortnight with increased sputum production, fever and rigors. Gram stain of the sputum shows Gram-positive cocci in clusters.

3. A 48-year-old woman with ovarian carcinoma presents to the A&E Department with a 12 hour history of haemoptysis associated with dyspnoea and pleuritic pains. On examination she is apyrexial and has a right-sided pleural rub. The chest X-ray shows a wedge-shaped infarct peripherally on the right but is otherwise normal.

4. A 51-year-old social worker presents to her GP with haemoptysis. On further questioning she admits to having had a productive cough for six months and to losing two stones in weight over the same time. Chest X-ray shows patchy consolidation and scarring in both apices.

5. A 34-year-old man presents to the A&E Department with a short history of haemoptysis. He has had a cough for a fortnight and noticed his ankles beginning to swell five days ago. Initial blood tests show a creatinine of 400 µmol/l. An autoantibody screen is positive for p-ANCA and anti-glomerular basement membrane antibodies.

6. THEME: AUSCULTATORY FINDINGS

A   Absent breath sounds left base
B   Absent breath sounds right hemithorax
C   Bronchial breathing right base
D   Coarse crackles right apex
E   Coarse crackles right axilla
F   Fine inspiratory bibasal crackles
G   Monophonic wheeze
H   Pleural rub
I   Polyphonic wheeze
J   Whispering pectoriloquy

The patients below have all presented with thoracic disease. Choose the sign you expect to elicit on clinical examination from the above list.

1. A 74-year-old woman who has recently suffered a major stroke and is therefore fed via a nasogastric tube becomes confused, pyrexial and dyspnoeic five hours after some visitors helped her to drink a cup of tea.

2. A 22-year-old man is brought to the A&E Department complaining of new dyspnoea and chest pain which came on suddenly during a coughing fit. Chest X-ray shows absent lung markings on the right side.

3. A 63-year-old smoker is required to have a chest X-ray performed during a routine insurance medical. A 2 cm diameter, round, spiculated mass of soft tissue density is seen close to the left hilum.

4. A 65-year-old woman is referred to the chest clinic with dyspnoea at rest. She is cyanosed and has clubbing of the fingers. Respiratory function tests show a restrictive defect and a CT scan of the thorax demonstrates a honeycomb pattern in the lower zones of both lungs.

5. A 19-year-old man is brought to the A&E Department after sustaining a single stab wound. The knife entered the left side of the chest anteriorly, just above the nipple and has lacerated the left internal mammary artery.

7. THEME: ABNORMAL RESPIRATORY CLINICAL FINDINGS

A Absent or reduced breath sounds
B Bronchial breathing
C Coarse inspiratory crackles
D Fine inspiratory crepitations
E Decreased or absent tactile vocal fremitus
F Dullness to percussion
G Stony dullness to percussion
H Tracheal deviation to the left
I Tracheal deviation to the right
J Reduced expansion

Listed below are five clinical diagnoses. Please choose the most appropriate COMBINATION of options from the above list which would lead one to make the diagnosis in each case. The options may be used more than once.

1. A large left-sided pneumothorax.

2. A large right-sided pleural effusion to the lung apex.

3. A right middle lobe pneumonia.

4. Left upper lobe collapse.

5. Right-sided apical fibrosis.

8. THEME: FINGER CLUBBING

A Alcoholic cirrhosis
B Congenital cyanotic heart disease
C Cryptogenic fibrosing alveolitis
D Empyema
E Infective endocarditis
F Inflammatory bowel disease
G Mesothelioma
H Pulmonary abscess
I Squamous cell carcinoma
J Tuberculosis

The patients below all have clubbing of the fingers. Choose the most appropriate diagnosis from the above list.

1. A 44-year-old investment banker who has recently spent several months working in Thailand presents to her GP with weight loss, malaise and a productive cough. Sputum culture is negative after five days.

2. A 71-year-old retired electrician presents to his GP with pleuritic chest pain and dyspnoea. After initial investigations, a CT scan of the chest demonstrates a right pleural effusion with lobular pleural thickening in the right mid-zone.

3. A 28-year-old male intravenous drug abuser presents to the A&E Department feeling unwell with intermittent fevers and weight loss. He is found to have a raised jugular venous pressure, a pansystolic murmur at the left sternal edge which is accentuated by inspiration, and a pulsatile liver.

4. An 84-year-old woman who worked in a munitions factory during the second world war presents to her GP with abdominal pain, constipation, polyuria, cough, haemoptysis and weight loss. A chest X-ray taken three years ago showed multiple pleural plaques only.

5. A 52-year-old man presents to his GP with dyspnoea. On examination he is cyanosed and mildly dyspnoeic at rest with fine late inspiratory crackles heard bilaterally in the chest.

9. THEME: RESPIRATORY INVESTIGATIONS

A   Arterial blood gases
B   Bronchoscopy and bronchial aspirate
C   Chest X-ray
D   CT scan of the chest
E   Flow-volume loop
F   Peak expiratory flow rate diary
G   Pleural biopsy and aspiration
H   Spirometry
I   Sputum culture
J   Ventilation-perfusion scan

The patients below have presented with respiratory diseases. Choose the most appropriate investigation to perform next from the above list.

1. A 32-year-old man is being treated empirically for pneumonia but is not improving. Chest X-ray shows patchy consolidation bilaterally. Three successive sputum cultures have yielded nothing. Further careful questioning elicits a history of unprotected sex with prostitutes.

2. A 58-year-old woman is referred to the chest clinic with a four month history of weight loss, malaise, night sweats and back pain, and a three week history of shortness of breath with a dry cough. Radiography demonstrates loss of intervertebral disc space between T12 and L1, with partial wedge collapse of L1 and a large right pleural effusion.

3. A 27-year-old woman presents to her GP with weight loss, a tender bruising-like rash on her shins and vague chest discomfort. On examination the chest is clear but there is bilateral mild anterior uveitis.

4. A 15-year-old boy presents to his GP with nocturnal and post-exercise cough. On examination the chest is clear and his peak expiratory flow rate is just below the median for his age and height.

5. A 74-year-old man with chronic obstructive pulmonary disease is seen in outpatients and started on a new inhaler. A convenient measure of response to treatment is required.

10. THEME: ARTERIAL BLOOD GASES

Patient	A	B	C	D	E	F	G
pH	7.03	7.5	7.51	7.29	7.32	7.41	7.12
P_aCO_2	2.8	3.9	3.4	2.7	7.8	5.1	8.5
P_aO_2	13.0	7.0	13.2	12.9	7.1	12.6	24.0
HCO_3-	11	28	24	10	33	26	30
Base excess	-18	+1	0	-1	+2	+1	−1

The patients below have all had their arterial blood gases measured whilst breathing room air. Choose the most likely set of results from the above table.

1. A 25-year-old woman who uses the oral contraceptive pill but does not smoke becomes acutely short of breath with pleuritic chest pain after a long-haul flight. VQ scan shows multiple large ventilation-perfusion mismatches.

2. A 68-year-old woman with severe chronic obstructive pulmonary disease is brought to the A&E Department having become more short of breath. She is coughing up purulent sputum and the chest X-ray shows hyper-expanded lungs with shadowing at the right base.

3. A 16-year-old girl who suffers from anxiety notices tingling in her fingertips and around her mouth and becomes dyspnoeic in a crowded supermarket. After measuring her blood gases, the Casualty Officer treats the girl successfully by asking her to rebreathe from a brown paper bag.

4. A 36-year-old man with ulcerative colitis, who underwent total colectomy with formation of an ileal pouch, has suffered profuse diarrhoea continuously since the operation six weeks previously. Over the past 48 hours he has become increasingly dyspnoeic but a chest X-ray and VQ scan are both normal.

5. A 17-year-old boy is found at home, semiconscious and hyperventilating, by his mother. He has been unwell for a fortnight with polyuria and increasing lethargy. A BMstix reading of 29.8 mmol/l is recorded and urinalysis is strongly positive for ketones.

11. THEME: CHEST INJURY

A   Aortic arch injury
B   Cardiac tamponade
C   Diaphragmatic rupture
D   Flail segment with pulmonary contusion
E   Massive haemothorax
F   Myocardial contusion
G   Open pneumothorax
H   Simple pneumothorax
I   Tension pneumothorax
J   Tracheobronchial disruption

The patients below have all had thoracic injuries. Please select the most appropriate diagnosis from the above list.

1. A 26-year-old man is the driver in a high speed RTA. He has a serious head injury and is intubated and ventilated at the scene. On arrival some 15 minutes later he becomes tachycardic and hypotensive. Examination of the chest demonstrates decreased air entry and increased resonance to percussion on the left side. The neck veins are distended.

2. An 18-year-old man is brought to hospital following a stab wound to the left side of the chest. A left-sided chest drain was inserted at the scene. This has drained approximately 200 ml of blood in 30 minutes. In the A&E Department he rapidly becomes severely hypotensive (BP 70/30 mmHg). Re-examination of the chest shows bilateral equal air entry/expansion and the chest drain is still only slowly draining blood (further 50 ml). His neck veins are distended.

3. A 19-year-old man is brought to A&E following a gunshot wound to the left side of the chest. He is shocked (pulse 130 bpm; BP 90/50 mmHg) and dyspnoeic (RR 38; pulse oximetry: SaO_2 82%). Examination of the chest reveals decreased breath sounds and dullness to percussion of the left side.

4. A 32-year-old female pedestrian is brought to A&E after being hit by a car travelling at approximately 30 mph. She has abrasions and bruising down the left side (chest, flank and pelvis) and a fractured right wrist. In A&E she develops left-sided chest pain and mild dyspnoea (RR 30; SaO_2 93%). On examination of the chest, she has decreased air entry and hyper-resonance on the left side. The pulse and blood pressure are normal.

continued . . .

5. A 60-year-old builder is crushed by a fork-lift truck at work. His signs are initially stable but a chest X-ray shows fractures of ribs 4–9 on the left side and a small amount of pleural fluid. Several hours later he becomes increasingly dyspnoeic (RR 36; SaO$_2$ 78%). Re-examination of the chest demonstrates equal air entry bilaterally and a normal percussion note. ABG: P$_a$O$_2$ 8.1 mmol/l.

12. THEME: LUNG DISEASES ASSOCIATED WITH COUGH

A   Bronchial asthma
B   Bronchiectasis
C   Croup
D   Cystic fibrosis
E   Emphysema
F   Fibrosing alveolitis
G   Legionnaire's disease
H   Mycoplasma pneumonia
I   Pertussis (whooping cough)
J   Pneumococcal pneumonia
K   Sarcoidosis
L   Tuberculosis

For each of the results below, select the disease most likely to account for them from the above list.

1. White cell count 32 x 10 ^{9}/l, 90% lymphocytes.

2. Transbronchial biopsy showing non-caseating granulomas.

3. Sputum showing neutrophils and Gram-positive cocci in pairs.

4. Mucoid *Pseudomonas aeruginosa* isolated from sputum.

5. Open lung biopsy showing widening of the interstitium by broad bands of fibrous tissue.

13. THEME: CAUSATIVE ORGANISMS IN PNEUMONIA

A   *Chlamydia psittaci*
B   *Coxiella burneti*
C   *Haemophilus influenzae*
D   *Klebsiella pneumoniae*
E   Legionella pneumonia
F   *Mycobacterium tuberculosis*
G   *Mycoplasma pneumoniae*
H   *Pseudomonas aeruginosa*
I   *Staphylococcus aureus*
J   *Streptococcus pneumoniae*

The following descriptions give details of several pneumonia-causing organisms. Choose the most appropriate organism from the above list.

1. Rough, dry, yellow colonies growing after two to three weeks' incubation on Löwenstein-Jensen medium.

2. Gram-negative motile bacilli growing in yellowish, non-lactose-fermenting colonies on MacConkey agar.

3. Gram-positive diplococci growing in alpha-haemolytic 'draughtsman' colonies on blood agar.

4. Slender Gram-negative rods growing in milky-white colonies on charcoal yeast extract agar.

5. Pleomorphic bacteria growing in 'fried egg' colonies on semi-solid enriched medium which are nominally Gram-negative but which stain poorly owing to the lack of a cell wall.

14. THEME: PLEURAL EFFUSION

A   Cannonball metastases
B   Cardiac failure
C   Cirrhosis
D   Hypothyroidism
E   Mesothelioma
F   Renal failure
G   Rheumatoid arthritis
H   Squamous cell carcinoma
I   Streptococcal pneumonia
J   Tuberculosis

The following patients have all presented with a pleural effusion. Please choose the most appropriate diagnosis from the above list.

1. A 17-year-old student presents in the A&E Department with increasing shortness of breath on exertion. On examination he is very thin and has signs consistent with a large right pleural effusion. Abdominal examination reveals 5 cm hepatomegaly and a hard irregular mass in the left side of the scrotum.

2. A 58-year-old retired pipe lagger presents to his GP with exertional dyspnoea and weight loss. On examination he has signs of a large left pleural effusion and his chest radiograph confirms pleural thickening on the left, a left pleural effusion and pleural and diaphragmatic calcification.

3. A 51-year-old life-long smoker is referred to the respiratory outpatient clinic with a three month history of weight loss, shortness of breath and haemoptysis. Routine investigations organised by his GP reveal: FBC: Hb 10.7 g/dl, MCV 81 fl, WCC 12.2 x 10^9/l, Plt 256 x 10^9/l; ESR 87 mm/hr; U&Es: Na$^+$ 125 mmol/l, K$^+$ 4.1 mmol/l, urea 5.3 mmol/l, Cr 96 μmol/l; CCa^{2+} 3.05 mmol/l. CXR – 'Right pleural effusion with large mass in the right midzone and hilar enlargement'.

4. A 38-year-old woman presents to her GP with weight loss, night sweats, haemoptysis and increasing shortness of breath. On examination she is thin, has supraclavicular and axillary lymphadenopathy and signs of bilateral pleural effusions with consolidation in the right apex and midzones. Sputum and pleural aspirate cultures confirm the presence of acid and alcohol fast bacilli.

5. An 81-year-old woman presents to the A&E Department with fever, anorexia and increasing confusion. On examination she is unwell, very confused and has signs of a right middle lobe pneumonia with a basal pleural effusion. Sputum cultures confirm the presence of Gram-positive diplococci.

15. THEME: RESPIRATORY FAILURE

A   Acute asthma
B   Chronic bronchitis
C   Fibrosing alveolitis
D   Guillain-Barré syndrome
E   Motor neurone disease
F   Myasthenia gravis
G   Mycoplasma pneumonia
H   *Pneumocystis carinii* pneumonia
I   Pulmonary embolism
J   Pulmonary oedema

The following patients have all presented with respiratory failure. Please choose the most appropriate diagnosis from the above list.

1. A 26-year-old man with a two week history of an upper respiratory tract infection presents in the A&E Department with increasing weakness and numbness in his lower limbs. On examination he looks unwell, has a low grade fever and has grade 3+/5 distal weakness of the lower limbs associated with loss of joint position sense and light touch below the knee. The plantars are down going. Two days after admission he becomes increasingly dyspnoeic at rest. His ABGs on air show: pH 7.31, pCO_2 6.7 kPa, pO_2 8.1 kPa, Sats 88%, HCO_3^- 26 mmol/l, BXS – 4.2 mmol/l.

2. A 63-year-old life-long smoker presents in the A&E Department with a ten day history of worsening shortness of breath, wheeze and a cough productive of greenish sputum. On examination he is unwell, tachypnoeic and deeply cyanosed. Auscultation of his chest reveals a harsh polyphonic wheeze and signs of a right lower lobe pneumonia. His initial ABGs on air show: pH 7.23, P_aCO_2 8.1 kPa, P_aO_2 6.4 kPa/l, Sats 77%, HCO_3^- 36 mmol/l, BXS – 7.6 mmol/l.

3. A 21-year-old woman presents in the A&E Department with a two day history of increasing shortness of breath associated with left-sided pleuritic chest pain. On examination she is tachypnoeic at rest, unwell and in obvious distress. Respiratory examination is remarkable only for a left mid zone pleural rub. Initial ABGs on air show: pH 7.48, P_aCO_2 2.7 kPa, P_aO_2 7.1 kPa, Sats 85%, HCO_3^- 23 mmol/l, BXS 2.9 mmol/l.

4. A 79-year-old man presents in the A&E Department with a three day history of increasing confusion, dry cough and fever. On examination he is unwell, pyrexial and dyspnoeic at rest. Respiratory examination reveals a mild expiratory wheeze. Investigations reveal: FBC: Hb 10.7 g/dl, MCV 96 fl, WCC 12.9 x 10^9/l, Plt 256 x 10^9/l; ESR 67 mm/hr; U&Es: Na$^+$ 127 mmol/l, K$^+$ 4.7 mmol/l, urea 7.9 mmol/l, Cr 126 μmol/l; his chest radiograph is unremarkable. Initial ABGs on air show: pH 7.40, P$_a$CO$_2$ 4.1 kPa, P$_a$O$_2$ 8.3 kPa, Sats 83%, HCO$_3^-$ 26 mmol/l, BXS 0.9 mmol/l.

5. A 61-year-old woman is referred to medical outpatients with a three month history of worsening shortness of breath on exertion. On examination she has clubbing of her fingernails and fine inspiratory crepitations at the bases of her lungs. ABGs on air show: pH 7.43, P$_a$CO$_2$ 3.9 kPa, P$_a$O$_2$ 8.0 kPa, Sats 87%, HCO$_3^-$ 25 mmol/l, BXS – 0.8 mmol/l.

16. THEME: COMPLICATIONS OF RESPIRATORY THERAPIES

A   Beclomethasone inhaler
B   Gentamicin
C   High flow oxygen
D   Ipratropium bromide inhaler
E   Leukotriene antagonist
F   Penicillin
G   Prednisolone
H   Salbutamol inhaler
I   Sodium cromoglycate
J   Theophylline

The patients below have all presented with complications of their respiratory treatments. Choose the most appropriate cause from the above list.

1. A few weeks after starting this medicine, the patient notices that her mouth is sore and red with soft, white patches on the tongue and pharynx which are easily dislodged.

2. 24 hours after being admitted as an emergency, this patient finds that she is unable to write owing to severe hand tremor.

3. This patient, who is on the waiting list for a transurethral resection of the prostate, is brought to the A&E Department in acute urinary retention one week after starting this medicine.

4. This patient has been taking her medicine for several years before she falls and sustains a Colles' fracture. No sooner has she been discharged from hospital than she is readmitted with excruciating back pain. X-ray shows crush fractures of T10 and T11.

5. This patient, who has smoked all his life and suffers from angina as well as the respiratory problem for which he is currently being treated, collapses on the ward. His blood pressure is 60/40 mmHg and the ECG monitor shows broad complex tachycardia.

17. THEME: COMPLICATIONS OF TUBERCULOSIS

A   Cerebral abscess
B   Glomerulonephritis
C   Lobar collapse
D   Lupus vulgaris
E   Meningitis
F   Osteomyelitis
G   Pericardial effusion
H   Pericarditis
I   Renal abscess
J   Terminal ileitis

The following patients have all presented with complications of tuberculosis. Please choose the most appropriate complication from the above list.

1. A 23-year-old man presents in the A&E Department with a five week history of night sweats, anorexia and cough productive of yellowish sputum. In the last three days he has become increasingly short of breath at rest and his ankles have begun to swell. On examination he is tachypnoeic, tachycardic and BP 105/70 mmHg. The medical registrar thinks he has a positive Kussmaul's sign and comments that the apex beat is impalpable and the heart sounds are difficult to hear. His ECG confirms small QRS complexes.

2. A 19-year-old Asian man presents in the A&E Department with a six week history of weight loss, a cough with several episodes of haemoptysis and fever. On examination he is noted to have dullness to percussion with reduced breath sounds at the left base. His chest radiograph reveals apical shadowing associated with a 'double left heart border'.

3. A 24-year-old man is referred to the chest clinic with suspected pulmonary tuberculosis. On examination he is noted to have a plaque-like lesion over the radial aspect of his left forearm. A subsequent Mantoux test confirms the diagnosis.

4. A 29-year-old HIV positive man presents in the A&E Department with a severe left sided headache and two generalised tonic-clonic seizures. A CT head scan confirms the presence of a contrast enhancing ring lesion in the left temporoparietal area and subsequent neurosurgical aspiration and culture confirms the presence of acid and alcohol fast bacilli (AAFBs).

continued . . .

5. A 3-year-old Asian girl presents in the A&E Department with a two day history of fever, increasing drowsiness and a seizure. A CT head scan confirms the presence of raised intracranial pressure but no mass lesion is seen. She improves with empirical treatment for tuberculosis and subsequent blood cultures confirm the presence of acid and alcohol fast bacilli.

18. THEME: ANTI-TUBERCULOUS THERAPY

A   Ciprofloxacin
B   Cycloserine
C   Dapsone
D   Ethambutol
E   Isoniazid
F   Pyrazinamide
G   Pyridoxine
H   Rifampicin
I   Streptomycin
J   Trimethoprim

The following adverse effects are characteristically associated with various drugs used in the treatment of pulmonary tuberculosis. Choose the most appropriate drug from the above list.

1. Tendon damage

2. Peripheral neuropathy

3. Failure of oral contraceptive medication

4. Red-green colour blindness

5. Ototoxicity

19. THEME: SARCOIDOSIS

A   Anterior uveitis
B   Cardiomyopathy
C   Choroidoretinitis
D   Conduction system disease
E   Diabetes insipidus
F   Erythema nodosum
G   Facial nerve palsy
H   Lupus pernio
I   Parotitis
J   Peripheral neuropathy

The following patients have all presented with complications of sarcoidosis. Please choose the most appropriate complication from the above list.

1. A 26-year-old woman is referred to Ophthalmology outpatients with a three day history of 'acute, painful red eyes'. Her symptoms improve with topical corticosteroids but she is referred to the chest clinic where a diagnosis of sarcoid is confirmed.

2. A 31-year-old man presents to his GP with increasing exertional dyspnoea associated with a macular papular violaceous rash over his nose. His chest radiograph confirms bilateral hilar lymphadenopathy and formal respiratory function tests show a restrictive defect.

3. A 29-year-old woman with known sarcoidosis is admitted for investigation of polyuria and polydypsia. Routine investigations confirm hypernatraemia, normal blood glucose and large volumes of urine with low osmolality. As a result of further investigations she is placed on nasal DDAVP and her symptoms improve.

4. A 24-year-old woman presents to her GP with worsening exertional dyspnoea and a large lesion over the anterior surface of her right shin. Her chest radiograph confirms bilateral hilar lymphadenopathy.

5. A 37-year-old woman with known sarcoidosis presents to her GP with increasing exertional dyspnoea and peripheral oedema. On examination she is normotensive, BP 120/70 mmHg, pulse 40 bpm regular, JVP raised with cannon waves. Auscultation of the heart is unremarkable. An ECG shows A-V dissociation with a narrow escape rhythm.

20. THEME: INTRATHORACIC TUMOURS

A   Adenocarcinoma of the bronchus
B   Atrial myxoma
C   Carcinoid tumour of lung
D   Germ cell tumour
E   Hodgkin's disease
F   Leiomyosarcoma of lung
G   Malignant mesothelioma
H   Neurofibroma
I   Rhabdomyoma of heart
J   Small cell carcinoma of the bronchus
K   Squamous cell carcinoma of the bronchus
L   Thymoma

For each of the patients below, select the tumour they are most likely to have from the above list.

1. A 65-year-old man, a life-long heavy smoker, presents with recent onset of haemoptysis and dyspnoea. On examination he has a moon face and truncal obesity. Biochemical investigations show hypokalaemia.

2. A 35-year-old woman presents with respiratory distress, night sweats and weight loss. Chest X-ray shows an anterior mediastinal mass. Biopsy of the mass shows Reed-Sternberg cells.

3. A 51-year-old woman who has never smoked presents with liver metastases. Chest X-ray shows a 2 cm subpleural mass in the right lower lobe. Bronchoscopy is normal.

4. A 70-year-old man who worked as a docker for many years presents with a three month history of worsening dyspnoea and weight loss. Chest X-ray shows diffuse pleural thickening over the left lower lobe.

5. A 62-year-old male smoker presents with haemoptysis for two weeks. On examination he has Horner's syndrome. Sputum cytology reveals malignant keratinised cells.

6. A 42-year-old woman with myasthenia gravis is found to have an anterior mediastinal mass on chest X-ray. Excision of the mass shows a mixture of lymphocytes and epithelial cells.

21. THEME: LUNG CANCER

A   Bony metastasis
B   Eaton-Lambert syndrome
C   Ectopic ACTH secretion
D   Ectopic PTH secretion
E   Inappropriate ADH secretion
F   Horner's syndrome
G   Hypertrophic pulmonary osteoarthropathy
H   Pancoast's tumour
I   Peripheral neuropathy
J   Superior vena caval obstruction

The patients below all have lung cancer. Please select the most appropriate cause for the clinical findings in each case from the above list.

1.   A 60-year-old gentleman attends clinic complaining of a three week history of intermittent blackouts, a tightness around the collar and headache usually worse in the morning.

2.   A 49-year-old gentleman is brought in by his wife to the A&E Department. The history is of increased confusion over the last couple of days and now he is drowsy and confused, she mentions that recently he has complained of progressively increasing severe lower back pain. On examination he has poor skin turgor, a dry mouth and his BP is 95/60 mmHg with a mild tachycardia. Initial investigations show: U&Es: Na^+ 129 mmol/l, K^+ 4.2 mmol/l, urea 9.1 mmol/l, Cr 115 μmol/l; corrected Ca^{2+} 3.65 mmol/l; plasma osmolality: 300 mosmol/kg.

3.   A 70-year-old lady is brought in by ambulance after being found collapsed by neighbours. When she is examined she is found to be extremely drowsy and agitated when attempts are made to rouse her. Routine observations show that her BP is 160/100 mmHg and pulse 80 bpm. Her biochemistry results come back as U&Es: Na^+ 119 mmol/l, K^+ 3.0 mmol/l, urea 6.5 mmol/l, Cr 92 μmol/l; corrected Ca^{2+} 2.45 mmol/l; plasma osmolality: 255 mosmol/kg.

4.   A 55-year-old gentleman goes to his GP complaining of progressive weakness in his left hand. On examination, as well as discovering weakness and wasting of the intrinsic muscles of the hand, his GP notes a mild ptosis and meiosis on the left hand side.

continued . . .

5. A 67-year-old man is seen by the palliative care team after complaining of severe fatigue and weakness. He is now unable to stand from sitting, has problems chewing and gets occasional double vision. Examination shows normal power in the hands and feet, but weakness of the girdle muscles and an oculomotor nerve palsy on the right with ptosis. The doctor is surprised that the weakness improves after repeated demonstrations to colleagues.

ANSWERS

ANSWERS TO CHAPTER – GENERAL PATHOLOGY

1. PATHOLOGICAL PROCESSES

1. **I – Metaplasia**
    Metaplasia is a change in cell type from one fully differentiated form to another fully differentiated form. It is usually a protective response to chronic irritation or cell damage, the new cell type being more able to withstand the irritating agent than the original. A common cause of 'acid heartburn' is gastro-oesophageal reflux, during which gastric acid refluxes from the stomach into the lower oesophagus. The oesophagus is normally lined by stratified squamous epithelium. This type of epithelium cannot easily withstand the damage caused by gastric acid so metaplasia occurs to gastric-type glandular epithelium, which is better able to bear the damage. Endoscopically the metaplastic mucosa has a red, velvety appearance in contrast to the smooth white appearance of normal oesophageal epithelium. This condition is known as Barrett's oesophagus. Like many other metaplastic conditions, Barrett's oesophagus is associated with an increased risk of malignancy.

2. **F – Hyperplasia**
    Hyperplasia is an increase in the number of cells in a given cell population. In contrast, hypertrophy is an increase in size of cells without an increase in number. Hyperplasia is usually hormonally driven while hypertrophy occurs in response to an increased workload. Prostatic enlargement in men is common with increasing age. The growth is hormonally driven and involves an increase in cell number rather than cell size. The process is therefore hyperplasia rather than hypertrophy.

3. **B – Atrophy**
    Atrophy is a decrease in the size of cells, tissues or organs, often leading to a loss of function. Lack of use of striated muscles, as often occurs in patients who are bed-bound, leads to shrinkage in the size of myocytes and to loss of muscle bulk. This is known as disuse atrophy.

4. **L – Thrombosis**
    Thrombosis is the formation of an intravascular mass from the constituents of blood in a flowing circulation. Factors that predispose to the development of thrombosis include prolonged immobility, as occurs during long-distance flying and the oral contraceptive pill. In susceptible patients, transatlantic flights may well cause thrombosis in deep calf veins, which manifests as a swollen painful calf.

5. **C – Dysplasia**

The term dysplasia literally means abnormal growth, but it is most often used to describe failure of normal maturation of an epithelium with partial expression of a neoplastic phenotype. In a cervical biopsy this is recognised as large pleomorphic nuclei above the basal layer. This condition is known as Cervical Intraepithelial Neoplasia (CIN) and is graded 1–3 according to the severity of the abnormality. Dysplasia is a pre-malignant condition.

6. **G – Hypertrophy**

As described above, hypertrophy is an increase in size of cells without an increase in number and usually occurs in response to an increased workload. In patients with hypertension, the heart has to pump against increased vascular resistance and its workload is therefore increased. The consequent increase in size of the cardiac myocytes leads to left ventricular hypertrophy and enlargement of the heart.

2. CELLS OF THE IMMUNE SYSTEM

1. **I – Plasma cell**

Memory B cells and plasma cells are both fully differentiated B-lymphocytes. Memory B cells maintain memory of the encounter with antigen and become activated if the antigen is encountered again, while plasma cells produce and secrete antibody to a specific antigen. Plasma cells have a single eccentrically placed nucleus in which the chromatin is peripherally aggregated at the nuclear membrane, giving a 'clock-face' appearance. They also have a perinuclear halo, the site of the Golgi apparatus, and basophilic cytoplasm indicating abundant RNA secretion.

2. **B – Dendritic cell**

Dendritic cells and macrophages are both antigen presenting cells. Dendritic cells are named after their irregular shape with numerous dendritic processes. Dendritic cells play an important role in establishing the first time response to an antigen by 'virgin' T-lymphocytes and, like other antigen presenting cells, express high surface levels of class II MHC molecules which augment antigen presentation.

3. **C – Helper T-lymphocyte**

The CD4 molecule is a transmembrane glycoprotein found on the surface of both macrophages and helper T-lymphocytes, although the concentration is considerably lower in macrophages. This molecule interacts with class II MHC molecules on antigen presenting cells and increases the affinity of binding. The CD3 complex, on the other hand, is expressed only in T-cells and is an absolute requirement for T-cell function. It acts as a signal transducer for the T-cell receptor to initiate T-cell activation.

4. **E – Macrophage**

Macrophages act not only as antigen presenting cells but also as phagocytes and are therefore important in bacterial killing. Lysozyme is an enzyme that attacks the bacterial cell wall (see question 1.6, *Theme: Mediators of acute inflammation* page 10) and is found within lysosomes in macrophage cytoplasm.

5. **A – Cytotoxic T-lymphocyte**

T-lymphocytes that express the CD8 molecule are called cytotoxic T-cells. Like CD4, the CD8 molecule is also a transmembrane protein. Its function is to bind with class I MHC molecules on cells, thereby stabilising T-cell interactions with cells presenting antigen through the class I MHC molecule.

6. **H – Natural killer cell**

Natural killer (NK) cells are a population of cells that resemble lymphocytes morphologically but form a separate lineage from B- and T-lymphocytes. NK cells carry two distinct surface molecules, one is CD16 and the other is CD56, the function of which is unknown. NK cells can kill target cells, such as tumour cells and virally infected cells, without previous known sensitisation to that target. This contrasts with cytotoxic T-cells which can also kill target cells, but require prior exposure.

3. COMPONENTS OF ANTIGENS AND ANTIBODIES

1. **A – Epitope**

An antigen is the structure that generates a response by the immune system. An antibody is a glycoprotein that recognises an intact antigen. The precise part of the antigen bound by antibody is called the epitope. This region of the antigen determines which antibody will bind and so is also referred to as an antigenic determinant.

2. **B – Fab fragment**

Treatment of an immunoglobulin molecule with the proteolytic enzyme papain cleaves it into three fragments. Two of the fragments are identical and each contains an intact light chain and part of one heavy chain. These fragments can bind to antigen and are thus known as the Fab fragments (fragment antigen binding). The third fragment is composed of part of both heavy chains. It cannot bind to antigen but is easily crystallised and so is termed the Fc fragment (fragment crystallisable). It is the site of important functions such as complement activation and adherence to specific receptors on the surface of neutrophils and macrophages.

3. **H – IgE**

IgE is present at extremely low levels in the serum of normal individuals but is increased in individuals who are atopic or in patients with allergies and type 1 (immediate) hypersensitivity. IgE is also raised in response to parasitic infections. The main effector function of IgE is to bind to mast cells through Fc receptors on the mast cell surface and to activate them. Activation causes mast cell degranulation resulting in potent localised, and occasionally generalised, vascular effects.

4. **D – Hapten**

Some molecules are too small to act as antigens themselves. Such molecules, known as haptens, can only elicit an immune response when bound to carrier proteins. In the resulting hapten-carrier complex, the hapten acts as an epitope. The antibodies formed against this complex can react specifically in solution with the free hapten (e.g. in sensitivity reactions to certain drugs).

5. **F – HLA**

The major histocompatibility complex (MHC) describes a collection of genes that code for proteins involved in immune functions such as recognition of antigen by T-lymphocytes. The human MHC system is also called the HLA (human leucocyte antigen) system and is coded for on chromosome 6 where there are six loci, three for class I antigens (A, B and C) and three for class II antigens (DP, DQ and DR). Class I molecules are expressed on virtually all nucleated cells whereas class II molecules are found only on antigen presenting cells and B-lymphocytes. HLA molecules are the dominant group of antigens governing transplant rejection reactions.

6. **K – Superantigen**

A few antigens can bind to MHC class II proteins without first being processed by antigen-presenting cells. These are known as superantigens. They are implicated in several disorders such as rabies, acquired immune deficiency syndrome and acute T-lymphocyte responses to certain bacterial exotoxins such as those of *Staphylococcus aureus*, responsible for toxic shock syndrome.

4. TECHNIQUES IN MOLECULAR MEDICINE

1. **H – Transfection**

Transfection is a method of putting genes into mammalian cells. The term arises because the transfer of genes is similar to viral infection. In contrast, bacterial cells are said to be transformed because in a classic (historical) experiment non-pathogenic bacteria were made pathogenic by addition of the 'transforming principle'. Both cell types spontaneously pick up DNA, but efficiency is very low. Selection and screening techniques allow 'stable' trans-fectants to be detected.

2. C – Hybridisation

Hybridisation is the formation of base pairs between nucleic acids. The term was originally restricted to the formation of hybrid double-stranded molecules as in a Northern blot where DNA/RNA hybrids are formed. Typically, a mixture of nucleic acids is resolved on a gel, blotted on to nitrocellulose, and the blot is hybridised with a labelled (easily detectable) piece of DNA or RNA – the probe. The probe sticks to its complementary strand, the blot is then washed to remove unbound and non-specifically bound probe and the remaining probe is then detected (usually by using radioactive labelling and autoradiography). A modification of the technique can be used *in situ* to detect the presence of mRNA in tissues.

3. J – Western blotting

Blotting is a descriptive term for the transfer of molecules out of a gel and onto a filter membrane by wicking action, although the term is now used for electro- or vacuum transfers. In the original description of blotting, Dr Edwin Southern developed the technique to make the gel-resolved nucleic acid DNA more accessible to subsequent manipulation, such as identification by hybridisation – Southern blotting. Northern and Western blotting followed the original nomenclature (perhaps not very helpfully). In Western blotting proteins are separated on a gel, and blotted then probed with antibodies to detect the specific protein of interest. Northern blotting is the similar separa-tion and blotting of RNA.

4. F – Polymerase chain reaction (PCR)

The polymerase chain reaction (PCR) is still a relatively new technique which has revolutionised many aspects of molecular biology. It amplifies DNA to produce adequate amounts for subsequent use. In principle, two synthetic oligonucleotide primers are designed, which are typically 20–25 nucleotides long, and flank the DNA segment to be amplified. These primers, orientated 5' to 3', are hybridised to opposite strands of the target sequence and extended using DNA polymerase until the region between the two primers is completely replicated. Initial hybridisation of the two oligonucleotides requires heat denaturation of the double-stranded DNA template. The temper-ature is then lowered to an optimum at which primers anneal to their comple-mentary sequences. Finally, polymerase elongation, again requiring an optimal temperature, completes the synthesis which effectively results in doubling the concentration of the target DNA segment. This cycle is repeated for 25–35 rounds using commercially available thermal cyclers.

5. **D – Linkage analysis**
    If the only information about a gene is the phenotype that it produces (e.g. a disease or characteristic), the gene may be demonstrated to lie near to a chromosomal region containing an established marker (usually a restriction length polymorphism or another gene whose genomic position is known), that therefore tends to be inherited with it. The region of interest can then be examined for the presence of a candidate gene causing the disorder or characteristic in question and the exact mutation identified by other techniques such as direct DNA sequencing.

5. TYPES OF INFLAMMATION

1. **C – Caseating granulomatous**
    Tuberculosis is the archetypal granulomatous disease. The granulomas are composed of histiocytes, a Langhans' type multinucleate giant cell and a peripheral rim of lymphocytes. Typically there is central caseating necrosis. The term caseating or caseous is used when the necrosis appears soft and 'cheesy' macroscopically and structureless histologically.

2. **D – Chronic**
    Helicobacter pylori causes a chronic gastritis with numerous lymphocytes and plasma cells in the lamina propria. Often there are also numerous lymphoid follicles. Neutrophils are commonly seen within surface and gland epithelium, in which case the term *active* chronic gastritis is used, but they are never the predominant T cell as they would be in acute gastritis.

3. **F – Fibrinous**
    Fibrinous pericarditis is the most common pathological type of pericarditis. Common causes include acute myocardial infarction, uraemia, rheumatic fever and SLE. In fibrinous pericarditis, the surface is dry with a fine granular roughening. At autopsy, the strands of fibrin on the surfaces of the parietal and visceral pericardium pull apart like two pieces of buttered bread, giving rise to the term 'bread and butter' pericarditis. A pericardial friction rub is the most striking clinical feature. The development of a pericardial effusion may obliterate the friction rub by separating the two layers of pericardium.

4. **H – Non-caseating granulomatous**
    Like tuberculosis, sarcoidosis is a granulomatous multisystem disease, but in contrast to tuberculosis, the granulomas are not caseating. This feature can be helpful in distinguishing pulmonary tuberculosis from pulmonary sarcoid in lung biopsies, but cannot be completely relied upon as tuberculosis occasionally causes non-caseating granulomas.

5. **A – Acute suppurative**

In bacterial meningitis, the subarachnoid space contains a creamy, purulent acute inflammatory exudate that is rich in neutrophils. The cerebrospinal fluid (CSF), which circulates in the subarachnoid space, is therefore turbid and shows many neutrophils on microscopic examination. This contrasts with viral meningitis in which the CSF contains scattered lymphocytes but no neutrophils.

6. **E – Eosinophil-rich**

Eosinophils play an important role in defence against parasitic infestation. Tissue and blood eosinophilia is often seen in such infections. Hookworm larvae penetrate human skin and pass in the bloodstream to the lungs, where they can cause an eosinophilic pneumonia. From the lungs the larvae ascend through the bronchi into the pharynx and are then swallowed, ending up in the small intestine where they mature into adult worms. The adults 'suck' blood from the small intestinal mucosa causing an iron deficiency anaemia.

6. MEDIATORS OF ACUTE INFLAMMATION

1. **B – C3b**

Opsonisation is one of the steps involved in the phagocytosis of bacteria by macrophages and neutrophils. Bacteria coated with certain substances are ingested more readily. The factors that coat bacteria are called opsonins (from the Greek word *opson* meaning 'ready for eating') and the process is termed opsonisation. There are two main opsonins: immunoglobulin (IgG) and the C3b component of complement. There are receptors for both these opsonins on the cell surface of phagocytic cells. Opsonised fragments attach to the phagocytic cell and are internalised to become phagosomes. Lysosomes fuse with the phagosome and release proteolytic enzymes that result in killing bacteria.

2. **E – Histamine**

Histamine is a vasoactive amine that is stored in and released from mast cells, basophils and platelets. It causes vasodilatation and increases the permeability of venules. The action of histamine on vessels is mediated via H_1 receptors while some of its other actions, such as bronchoconstriction, are effected by H_2 receptors. Factors that stimulate histamine release include physical injury from heat, mechanical trauma or radiation, and chemical agents, such as immunoglobulins, bee sting venom, C3a and C5a, and IL1. Anti-H_1 antihistamines only inhibit the immediate phase of the vascular response to injury, implying that histamine is only important during this early phase.

3. **L – Superoxide anion**
    After an invading bacterium has been phagocytosed, its killing involves oxygen-dependent and oxygen-independent mechanisms. The oxygen-dependent mechanism is associated with a burst of oxidative activity known as the respiratory burst. This essentially results in the stepwise reduction of molecular oxygen into an oxygen free radical, the superoxide anion, and then to hydrogen peroxide. Phagocytes cannot kill ingested organisms in the absence of the respiratory burst and without production of the superoxide anion. Indeed, lack of one of the enzymes involved in this process, NADPH oxidase, leads to chronic granulomatous disease of childhood, an inherited disease in which neutrophils are able to ingest bacteria but cannot kill them.

4. **F – Intercellular cell adhesion molecule 1 (ICAM-1)**
    The immunoglobulin gene superfamily is a group of intercellular adhesion molecules so named because each contains several domains resembling the structure of immunoglobulins. Three such molecules have been identified: intercellular cell adhesion molecules 1 and 2 (ICAM-1 and ICAM-2) and vascular cell adhesion molecule (VCAM-1). ICAM-1 is expressed at low levels normally but its expression is increased in acute inflammation by stimulants such as IL-1. Leucocytes bind to ICAM-1 through ligands on their surface known as integrins.

5. **H – Interleukin 1 (IL-1)**
    Interleukin 1 (IL-1) is a potent regulator both of local inflammatory events and of several systemic ones. Many of its activities are similar to those of tumour necrosis factor-alpha. The synthesis of IL-1 is stimulated by other cytokines and by various microbial products such as bacterial endotoxin. Locally it upregulates expression of ICAM-1, thus increasing leucocyte adhesion, it stimulates release of histamine and stimulates macrophages to produce chemokines. Systemically, IL-1 acts as an endogenous pyrogen (i.e. it produces fever), induces glucocorticoid synthesis and stimulates the release of prostaglandins and acute phase proteins.

6. **I – Lysozyme**
    Lysozyme is a low molecular weight cationic enzyme that attacks the mucopeptide cell walls of some bacterial species, particularly Gram-positive cocci. It is found in lysosomes and is one of the oxygen-independent mechanisms of bacterial killing.

7. INFECTIOUS DISEASES

1. **B – Amoebiasis**
    Infection with *Entamoeba histolytica* causes amoebiasis. Both this and schistosomiasis can lead to colonic ulceration, but in schistosomiasis the ulcers are not typically flask-shaped. The finding of PAS-positive trophozoites with ingested red cells is diagnostic of amoebiasis.

2. **L – Toxoplasmosis**

Congenital toxoplasmosis is caused by maternal infection with *Toxoplasma gondii* in the first trimester. In normal adults, this parasite causes subclinical infection or mild lymphadenopathy, but in infants without developed cell-mediated immunity, infection leads to severe abnormalities. There is widespread necrosis of the brain, liver, heart, lungs and retina. Calcification can occur in foci of long-standing necrosis in the brain.

3. **I – Pneumocystis pneumonia**

Pneumocystis carinii is an ubiquitous organism that does not cause disease in normal individuals but causes a severe pneumonia in immunosuppressed patients, including those on chemotherapy. The organism cannot be grown in culture, so diagnosis requires cytological or histological identification. Useful cytological preparations include bronchial washings or lavage. Transbronchial biopsy shows foamy eosinophilic material in the alveolar spaces. On both cytology and histology, the organism is seen as a boat-shaped or cup-shaped structure on silver stain.

4. **J – Schistosomiasis**

Infection with *Schistosoma haematobium* is endemic in parts of the Middle East and Africa. Biopsy of the infected bladder shows parasite ova surrounded by granulomatous inflammation and numerous eosinophils. Healing by fibrosis leads to ureteric obstruction with consequent hydronephrosis and chronic pyelonephritis. There is also an association between urinary schistosomiasis and squamous cell carcinoma of the bladder.

5. **F – Falciparum malaria**

Malaria is caused by four species of *Plasmodium* and is transmitted by the female *Anopheles* mosquito. Falciparum malaria is caused by *Plasmodium falciparum* and is the most common type. The signs, symptoms and pathological features of malaria are related to the sequelae of various aspects of the parasite's life cycle in man. Diagnosis is by finding ring trophozoites inside red cells on a blood smear.

6. **D – Candidiasis**

The finding of fungal hyphae in this patient's biopsy are diagnostic of fungal oesophagitis. The differential diagnosis lies between aspergillosis, caused by Aspergillus species, and candidiasis caused by Candida species, usually Candida albicans. The fact that yeast forms were also present rules out Aspergillus as this is not a yeast-forming fungus. In addition, the endoscopic appearance of white plaques on the mucosal surface is typical of candidiasis. This disease is common in immunosuppressed patients such as those with AIDS.

8. BACTERIAL INFECTIONS

1. **H – *Neisseria meningitidis***
   This patient has bacterial meningitis. The two most likely causes from the list are *Neisseria meningitidis* (meningococcus) and *Streptococcus pneumoniae* (pneumococcus). The petechial rash is characteristic of meningococcal septicaemia. This is confirmed by finding Gram-negative cocci on CSF examination.

2. **E – *Escherichia coli***
   The patient's symptoms and findings on urinalysis are typical of urinary tract infection. *Escherichia coli* is the cause of 60–90% of urinary tract infections. This organism is a normal commensal of the large intestine and in women enters the urinary tract by direct spread up the urethra from the perineum. *Escherichia coli* is a Gram-negative, lactose-fermenting bacillus

3. **C – *Clostridium difficile***
   This patient has a complication of antibiotic therapy, namely pseudomembranous colitis. The finding of white plaques on the large bowel mucosa is characteristic of this disease. The causative organism is a toxigenic strain of *Clostridium difficile*, an anaerobic Gram-positive bacillus. *Clostridium difficile* produces two toxins: Toxin A is an enterotoxin responsible for the gut symptoms, Toxin B is a cytotoxin which has a cytopathic effect in cell cultures.

4. **K – *Streptococcus pneumoniae***
   This patient is suffering from lobar pneumonia. Vagrants and alcoholics who have poor social and medical care are particularly prone to this type of pneumonia. The causative organism in approximately 90% of cases is *Streptococcus pneumoniae*. These occur as Gram-positive diplococci which show alpha-haemolysis on blood agar. The colonies are typically described as draughtsman-shaped on account of their sunken centre.

5. **J – *Staphylococcus aureus***
   Wound infection is an important cause of post-operative sepsis. The most common cause is *Staphylococcus aureus*, but other possible organisms include *Streptococcus pyogenes*, particularly when there is associated cellulitis, and *Escherichia coli* when the wound follows abdominal surgery. In this patient, Gram stain of the pus from the wound shows Gram-positive cocci, thus ruling out *Escherichia coli*. *Staphylococcus aureus* and *Streptococcus pneumoniae* are both Gram-positive cocci, but the finding of coagulase-positive organisms is diagnostic of *Staphylococcus aureus*.

6. **A – *Campylobacter jejuni***
   Campylobacter species, particularly *Campylobacter jejuni*, are now recognised as a major cause of diarrhoeal disease in the UK. Common sources of

infection are poultry, meat and milk. *Campylobacter jejuni* is a Gram-negative curved or spiral-shaped rod. It is a flagellate organism and therefore highly motile. This feature distinguishes it from enteropathogenic strains of *Escherichia coli* which are also Gram-negative rods but are non-flagellate.

9. PATHOGENIC VIRUSES

1.   G – Human papilloma virus
Warts are benign tumours of squamous epithelium known as squamous cell papillomas. They arise not only in keratinised squamous epithelium, such as the skin, but also in non-keratinised squamous epithelium such as that lining the ectocervix. All warts are caused by human papilloma virus (HPV), a DNA virus belonging to the papovavirus family. There are many serotypes of HPV. Genital warts are sexually transmitted and are caused by HPV types 6 and 11. Other serotypes, notably 16, 18 and 31 have been implicated in the development of high grade cervical intraepithelial neoplasia (CIN) and invasive cervical carcinoma.

2.   C – Epstein-Barr virus
Infectious mononucleosis is a multisystem disorder caused by Epstein-Barr virus (EBV). This is a DNA virus belonging to the herpes virus family. Diagnosis of infectious mononucleosis is made by finding heterophil antibodies to sheep erythrocytes in the patient's serum. As well as causing infectious mononucleosis, EBV has a strong association with certain human malignancies, particularly Burkitt's lymphoma and nasopharyngeal carcinoma.

3.   I – Parainfluenza virus
Croup or acute laryngotracheobronchitis, is most commonly associated with parainfluenza virus type 1. This is an RNA virus belonging to the paramyxovirus family. Croup is seen mainly in infants and young children; the symptoms include hoarseness, cough and inspiratory stridor. As well as croup, parainfluenza viruses are associated with bronchiolitis and pneumonia in young children and the 'common cold' in adults.

4.   A – Coxsackie virus
In 'aseptic' meningitis, the CSF contains lymphocytes rather than neutrophils and CSF culture is negative. Aseptic meningitis is usually due to viruses of the enterovirus group, of which Coxsackie virus is a member. Enteroviruses are RNA viruses that belong to the picornavirus family. Other enteroviruses that cause aseptic meningitis include echovirus and poliovirus.

5.   L – Rotavirus
Viruses are an important cause of acute diarrhoea, particularly in children. In

the developing world, viral gastroenteritis is a major cause of infant mortality but is less severe in the UK. A common cause of viral gastroenteritis is rotavirus; this is an RNA virus that belongs to the reovirus family. Other causes include adenovirus and astrovirus.

6. **H – Measles virus**
   Subacute sclerosing panencephalitis is a rare, severe, progressive neurological disease occurring in children and young adults. It presents with personality change and intellectual impairment followed by convulsions and myoclonic movements, and eventually coma and death. It is caused by persistent infection with defective measles virus following primary measles infection several years previously. Measles is an RNA virus that belongs to the paramyxovirus family.

10. TYPES OF AMYLOID PROTEIN

1. **B – AL amyloid**
   Amyloid deposited in this disease is often systemic in distribution and is of the AL type. The malignant plasma cells produce abnormal amounts of monoclonal immunoglobulin, either the whole molecule or just the light chains, usually of λ type. These light chains are referred to as Bence-Jones protein and are found in the serum and urine of patients with plasma cell myeloma and other monoclonal B-cell proliferations. 5–15% of patients with plasma cell myeloma who have free light chains develop clinical amyloidosis.

2. **D – Beta amyloid protein**
   Beta amyloid protein (Aβ is a 4000 dalton peptide that constitutes the core of cerebral plaques found in Alzheimer's disease as well as the amyloid deposited in the walls of cerebral blood vessels in patients with this disease. The Aβ protein is derived from a much larger transmembrane glycoprotein called amyloid precursor protein (APP), the function of which is unknown.

3. **A – AA amyloid**
   The amyloid deposits in this condition are systemic in distribution and are composed of AA protein. This is derived from serum amyloid-A associated (SAA) protein, an acute phase protein synthesised by the liver in a number of chronic inflammatory conditions such as rheumatoid arthritis, tuberculosis, chronic osteomyelitis, bronchiectasis and inflammatory bowel disease. Nowadays rheumatoid arthritis is the most commonly associated condition. Amyloidosis occurs in about 3% of patients with rheumatoid arthritis and is clinically significant in about half of those affected.

4. **G – Islet amyloid polypeptide**
    Islet amyloid polypeptide (IAPP), also known as amylin, is a 37 amino acid peptide that is normally produced by the β cells of the islets of Langerhans and is co-secreted with insulin. In patients with type II diabetes mellitus, this protein accumulates in the sinusoidal space outside the β cells in close contact with their cell membranes. It is not known whether deposition of IAPP actually contributes to the pathogenesis of the disease or is a consequence of the disordered β cell function.

5. **F – Calcitonin**
    Medullary carcinoma of the thyroid is one of the endocrine tumours in which localised deposits of amyloid can be found in the stroma, other examples being phaeochromocytoma and islet cell tumours of the pancreas. The amyloid in medullary carcinoma is derived from the peptide hormone calcitonin, which is secreted by the tumour cells.

11. TYPES OF EPITHELIUM

1. **H – Transitional cell**
    Transitional cell epithelium is a special form of stratified epithelium only found in the urinary tract and so is also called urothelium. It is specialised to withstand the toxicity of urine and to accommodate a high degree of stretching. It has an appearance intermediate between that of stratified cuboidal epithelium and stratified squamous epithelium, hence 'transitional'.

2. **G – Stratified squamous, non-keratinising**
    Stratified squamous epithelium is usually several layers thick and matures progressively from the basal layer which has cuboidal-shaped cells through to the surface layer where the cells are flattened. When the maturing cells reach the surface, they degenerate and eventually slough off. Ectocervical epithelium can withstand moderate abrasion due to its thickness but is not keratinised as it does not normally need to withstand desiccation.

3. **A – Pseudostratified ciliated columnar**
    The trachea is lined by pseudostratified ciliated columnar epithelium, also known as respiratory epithelium. This is actually a true simple epithelium because all the cells rest on the basement membrane, but the nuclei of the cells are at different levels, giving the false impression of stratification. The luminal surface of the cells bears cilia, the function of which is to propel surface films of mucus or fluid in a consistent direction over the epithelial surface.

4.   **D – Simple squamous**
Simple squamous epithelium consists of a single layer of flattened cells and is found lining surfaces involved in the transport of gases, namely the alveoli, and fluids (i.e. lymphatics and blood vessels). It also lines the serous body cavities such as the pericardium, pleura and peritoneum where it is termed mesothelium. Mesothelium permits the passage of a small amount of fluid into and out of the cavities as required.

5.   **F – Stratified squamous, keratinising**
Like the cervix, the skin is lined by stratified squamous epithelium. Unlike the cervix, however, the skin is keratinised as it must be able to withstand desiccation.

12. ENVIRONMENTAL CARCINOGENS

1.   **K – Ultraviolet light**
The ultraviolet portion of the solar spectrum can be divided into three wavelength ranges: UVA (320 to 400 nm), UVB (280 to 320 nm) and UVC (200 to 280 nm). Of these, UVB is believed to be responsible for the induction of cutaneous neoplasms, including malignant melanoma, squamous cell carcinoma and basal cell carcinoma. The carcinogenicity of UVB is attributed to its formation of pyrimidine dimers in DNA. This type of damage is repaired by the nucleotide excision repair (NER) pathway. With excessive sun exposure, the NER pathway is overwhelmed, and hence some damaged DNA remains unrepaired. This leads to transcriptional errors and subsequent development of malignancy.

2.   **F – Cigarette smoke**
Cigarette smoke contains a number of carcinogens, among them polycyclic aromatic hydrocarbons which are among the most potent carcinogens known. They are activated by mixed function oxidases to form epoxides which are more water soluble and more reactive than the parent compound. Epoxides bind to DNA, causing mutations, and also to macromolecules in the cytoplasm of target cells.

3.   **D – Beta-naphthylamine**
Beta-naphthylamine has been responsible in the past for an increased incidence of bladder cancer in workers in the aniline dye and rubber industries. By itself, beta-naphthylamine is not carcinogenic, but after absorption it is hydroxylated in the liver to an active form then detoxified by conjugation with glucuronic acid. This non-toxic compound is excreted by the kidney and concentrated in the bladder. The human bladder mucosa contains the enzyme beta-glucuronidase which cleaves the non-toxic substance and in so doing releases the carcinogenic molecule.

4. **A – Aflatoxin B1**
    Aflatoxin B1 is a naturally occurring carcinogen that is produced by some strains of *Aspergillus flavus* that thrive on improperly stored grains and peanuts. A strong correlation has been found between the dietary level of this toxin and the incidence of hepatocellular carcinoma in certain parts of Africa and the Far East. It appears that synergy exists between aflatoxin and chronic hepatitis B virus infection. Aflatoxins produce a point mutation at codon 249 of the p53 gene, leading to production of an abnormal gene product.

5. **I – Nitrosamines**
    Like beta-naphthylamine, nitrosamines require metabolic activation to form a carcinogenic agent. In the course of this activation, alkylating agents are produced that bind to guanine in DNA, thereby enhancing malignant transformation. Nitrosamines are formed in the gastrointestinal tract from the reaction of nitrostable amines and nitrites. Nitrites are present in large amounts in pickled, salted and smoked foods, and the incidence of gastric carcinoma is high in countries such as Japan where the dietary intake of such foods is great. In addition, nitrites can be formed in the stomach from nitrates (found in food preservatives) by the action of bacteria.

6. **H – Ionising radiation**
    There is an increased risk of carcinoma of the thyroid in people who have had ionising radiation to the neck, particularly in childhood. This ionising radiation can be therapeutic, such as treatment for head and neck tumours, or environmental, such as the nuclear explosions at Hiroshima and Nagasaki or the nuclear accident at Chernobyl. The mechanisms by which ionising radiation induces malignancy are unclear. Irradiation causes free radical generation and these active chemical species may react with elements of the target cell genome.

13. VIRAL AND MICROBIAL CARCINOGENS

1. **G – Human papilloma virus**
    Human papilloma viruses (HPV) have been implicated in the genesis of several malignancies, particularly squamous cell carcinoma of the cervix and anogenital region. Approximately 85% of squamous cell carcinomas of the cervix contain DNA sequences of HPV, most commonly types 16 and 18. Studies have shown that the E6 and E7 proteins of HPV disable two important tumour suppressor proteins that regulate the cell cycle, thereby initiating the carcinogenic process. Additional somatic mutations, caused by co-factors such as smoking, co-existing microbial infections or hormonal changes, then complete the malignant transformation.

2. **D – *Helicobacter pylori***
   Primary gastric lymphoma is a low grade B-cell lymphoma that is strongly associated with *Helicobacter pylori* infection. It arises in mucosa-associated lymphoid tissue (MALT), and hence is also known as MALToma. Unlike small intestinal mucosa, the normal gastric mucosa lacks MALT and acquires it only as a result of chronic infection, such as with *H. pylori*. Initially, this MALT is a polyclonal B-cell proliferation, but with continued infection, a monoclonal population emerges that is recognisable as a low grade B-cell lymphoma. Even at this stage, eradication of *H. pylori* with antibiotics can result in regression of the tumour as the stimulus for MALT production is removed. Eventually, however, the tumour becomes *H. pylori* independent and behaves like a typical lymphoma.

3. **F – Human herpesvirus type 8**
   Kaposi's sarcoma is a vascular tumour that is common in patients with AIDS but is rare in the rest of the population. The association with human herpesvirus type 8 (HHV-8) is now firmly established though the precise role the virus plays in the pathogenesis of the tumour is unclear. DNA of HHV-8 is found both in tumour cells and in circulating B-lymphocytes of affected patients. It is thought that these, together with HIV-infected T-lymphocytes, produce a variety of cytokines and growth factors that stimulate proliferation of mesenchymal cells, followed eventually by neoplastic transformation.

4. **E – Hepatitis B virus**
   The evidence linking hepatitis B virus (HBV) with the development of hepatocellular carcinoma is compelling, yet the mechanism of action remains unclear. HBV DNA is integrated into the hepatocyte genome but does not encode any oncoprotein and is not associated with a known proto-oncogene. It is likely therefore that the effect of HBV is indirect and may be multifactorial. Possible factors include liver cell damage and accompanying regenerative hyperplasia, secretion of a protein that disrupts normal growth control of infected liver cells, and disabling of a tumour suppressor gene that controls the cell cycle.

5. **C – Epstein-Barr virus**
   Burkitt's lymphoma is a high grade B-cell lymphoma that is endemic in parts of sub-Saharan Africa where falciparum malaria has a high prevalence. There is a strong association between the endemic form of Burkitt's lymphoma and infection with Epstein-Barr virus (EBV). It is thought that cofactors such as chronic malaria favour sustained proliferation of B-cells immortalised by EBV. The actively dividing B-cell population is at increased risk of developing translocations, particularly involving the c-myc gene on chromosome 8, usually with chromosome 14. These translocations cause c-myc overexpression and ultimately release the cells from normal growth regulation, resulting in malignant transformation.

14. GENE ABNORMALITIES IN NEOPLASIA

1. **H – Overexpression of bcl-2**
    bcl-2 is one of the cellular genes that regulates apoptosis. About 85% of patients with follicular lymphoma have a characteristic t(14:18) translocation which brings the bcl-2 locus on chromosome 18 in close proximity to the immunoglobulin heavy chain promoter region on chromosome 14. Brisk transcriptional activity in this region leads to overexpression of the bcl-2 protein. By mechanisms that are not yet clear, this overexpression protects B-cells from apoptosis and allows them to survive for long periods. Follicular lymphoma arises from this pool of 'immortalised' B-cells.

2. **D – Mutation in BRCA1**
    BRCA1, and the functionally similar BRCA2, are tumour suppressor genes of the 'caretaker' type. They are found on chromosomes 17 and 13, respectively. Germline mutations in BRCA1 and BRCA2 account for about 80% of familial breast cancer but are rare in sporadic breast cancer. The functions of BRCA1 and BRCA2 have not yet been fully elucidated but they are thought to be involved in DNA repair; mutations in these genes therefore lead to replication errors.

3. **J – Translocation t(9:22)**
    This translocation is characteristic of chronic myeloid leukaemia and provides an example of an oncogene formed by the fusion of two separate genes. A reciprocal translocation between chromosomes 9 and 22 relocates a truncated portion of the proto-oncogene c-abl from chromosome 9 to the bcr gene on chromosome 22. The hybrid c-abl-bcr gene (also known as the Philadelphia chromosome) encodes a chimeric protein that has tyrosine kinase activity.

4. **C – Deletion of Rb**
    The Rb (retinoblastoma) gene was the first tumour suppressor gene discovered and is associated with both familial and sporadic retinoblastoma. It is located on chromosome 13 and is a tumour suppressor gene of the 'gatekeeper' type. The Rb gene product is a nuclear phosphoprotein that plays a key role in regulating the cell cycle, acting as a brake on progression from the G1 to the S phase of the growth cycle. Inactivation of the Rb gene, through mutation or deletion, allows cells to progress unchecked through the cell cycle and eventually to undergo mitosis.

5. **B – Deletion of APC**
    APC is also a tumour supressor gene of the 'gatekeeper' type, located on chromosome 5. Individuals with germline mutations in the APC gene develop familial adenomatous polyposis in which hundreds of adenomas develop in the colorectum. Unless the colon is removed, one or more of these adenomas eventually progresses to become invasive adenocarcinoma. An important function of the APC gene product is to cause the degradation of the signal transducer β-catenin. Mutation in the APC gene increases the cellular levels of β-catenin which in turn causes upregulation of cell proliferation.

15. NEOPLASMS

1. **J – Squamous cell carcinoma**
    The most likely diagnosis in a heavy smoker with a lung mass is bronchial carcinoma. The four main types of bronchial carcinoma are: squamous cell carcinoma, small cell carcinoma, large cell undifferentiated carcinoma and adenocarcinoma. Adenocarcinoma is unlikely as it is most often located in the peripheral part of the lung. Well-differentiated squamous cell carcinoma produces keratin and this can be seen on sputum cytology as atypical keratinised cells.

2. **E – Lipoma**
    The fact that this patient's lump is located in the subcutaneous tissue points toward a mesenchymal tumour and the fact that it is mobile implies it is benign. The differential diagnosis therefore lies between a lipoma and a neurofibroma. The soft consistency and yellow colour indicate a lipoma rather than a neurofibroma.

3. **I – Osteosarcoma**
    This is the typical presentation of an osteosarcoma. This is a malignant tumour of osteoblasts (bone-forming cells) which originates in the metaphysis of long bones, most commonly the femur. It spreads extensively within the medullary cavity, eventually eroding through the cortical plate and lifting the periosteum as it does so. This latter feature is visible on X-ray. The malignant osteoblasts produce varying amounts of osteoid, some of which become mineralized, and this too can be seen radiologically.

4. **L – Transitional cell carcinoma**
    The urinary tract is lined with a specialised multilayered epithelium called transitional cell epithelium. The most common neoplasms arising from this epithelium are termed transitional cell neoplasms. Virtually all transitional cell neoplasms of the bladder are carcinomas; benign tumours (papillomas) are extremely rare.

5. **B – Adenoma**
    Adenomas are benign neoplasms of glandular epithelium. Adenomas of the large intestine can be classified as tubular, villous or tubulovillous. Tubular adenomas are pedunculated and have a lobulated red surface. Villous adenomas are sessile and have seaweed-like fronds. Adenomas have distinct malignant potential and are thought to be the precursor of adenocarcinomas of the colorectum. This patient's polyp is unlikely to have developed into an adenocarcinoma because it is pedunculated and small.

6. **A – Adenocarcinoma**
    The endoscopic appearance of this mass, large and ulcerated, strongly suggests a malignant tumour. This is confirmed by finding signet ring cells on biopsy, which indicate a poorly differentiated adenocarcinoma. This is the commonest malignant tumour of the stomach and often presents with vague symptoms of dyspepsia and weight loss.

16. EPONYMOUS CELLS

1. **D – Langhans' cell**
    A Langhans' multinucleate giant cell is formed by the fusion of activated macrophages and is typically found in the granulomas of tuberculosis, sarcoidosis and other granulomatous diseases. It has many peripherally arranged nuclei and a large central cytoplasmic mass. A Langerhans' cell, by contrast, is an antigen-presenting cell found in the skin.

2. **I – Schwann cell**
    In the peripheral nervous system, structural and metabolic support for axons is provided by Schwann cells. Small unmyelinated axons are simply surrounded by the cytoplasm of Schwann cells while large myelinated axons are wrapped in a myelin sheath formed by concentric layers of Schwann cell plasma membrane.

3. **J – Sertoli cell**
    Sertoli cells are found within testicular tubules intimately associated with spermatogenic cells. Sertoli cells have ramifying cytoplasm with extensive intercellular junctions and they support and nourish the developing spermatozoa. Leydig cells, on the other hand, are located in the interstitial spaces between the testicular tubules and they secrete testosterone and other male sex hormones.

4. **H – Reed-Sternberg cell**

    Hodgkin's disease is characterised by the neoplastic proliferation of an atypical form of lymphoid cell termed the Reed-Sternberg (RS) cell. Several forms of RS cell have been described in the different subtypes of Hodgkin's disease, each with a different morphology and immunophenotype. Classical RS cells are binucleate, resembling owls' eyes and show CD15 and CD30 positivity.

5. **B – Kupffer cell**

    Kupffer cells are one of the three types of cell that line the sinusoids of the liver. They are large plump phagocytic cells with oval-shaped nuclei. They form part of the monocyte-macrophage system and, together with the spleen, participate in the removal of effete erythrocytes and other particulate debris from the circulation.

17. VITAMIN DEFICIENCY

1. **D – Vitamin B1 (thiamine)**

    This patient has vitamin B1 (thiamine) deficiency. In developed countries, thiamine deficiency is relatively uncommon in the general population, but affects up to 25% of chronic alcoholics and is a recognised complication of hyperemesis gravidarum. The major targets of thiamine deficiency are the peripheral nerves, the heart and the brain, giving rise to polyneuropathy (dry beri-beri), a cardiovascular syndrome (wet beri-beri) and Wernicke-Korsakoff syndrome, usually in that order. The pedal oedema in this patient is due to cardiac failure, the ataxia and nystagmus are features of Wernicke's encephalopathy while the amnesia and confabulation are due to Korsakoff psychosis.

2. **F – Vitamin B12 (cobalamin)**

    Vitamin B12 is essential for normal DNA synthesis; thus deficiency of this vitamin impairs cell synthesis and regeneration. The effects of deficiency are seen most severely in haemopoietic tissues, with megaloblastic anaemia being the usual outcome. Another feature is subacute combined degeneration of the cord since vitamin B12 is also necessary for maintenance of myelination of spinal cord tracts. In this patient, the deficiency of vitamin B12 is not due to lack of dietary intake but due to failure of absorption. The presence of anti-parietal cell antibodies and atrophic gastritis indicates autoimmune gastritis; the consequent destruction of parietal cells leads to lack of intrinsic factor, which is essential for vitamin B12 absorption. This condition is known as pernicious anaemia.

3. **J – Vitamin K**
    This patient has vitamin K deficiency. Vitamin K is a fat-soluble vitamin that acts as a co-factor in hepatic carboxylation of procoagulants. Deficiency in vitamin K thus leads to a bleeding diathesis, characterised by haematomas, bleeding from mucosal surfaces and ecchymoses. The fact that this patient has steatorrhoea indicates fat malabsorption, a common consequence of chronic pancreatitis due to lack of pancreatic lipase. As vitamin K is fat soluble, its absorption is impaired in patients with steatorrhoea, along with absorption of the other fat-soluble vitamins A, D and E.

4. **G – Vitamin C**
    Deficiency of vitamin C leads to the clinical syndrome of scurvy, characterised by gingival swelling, haemorrhages, a hyperfollicular hyperkeratotic papular skin rash and impaired wound healing. Unlike some other vitamins, vitamin C cannot be synthesised endogenously so humans are dependent on dietary intake. Vitamin C is abundant in many foodstuffs, particularly fresh fruit and vegetables, so scurvy is relatively rare nowadays. It is seen most commonly in elderly patients who live alone and who have erratic and inadequate eating patterns, such as this patient.

5. **H – Vitamin D**
    This child has the classical signs of rickets, the syndrome caused by vitamin D deficiency in children. The major function of vitamin D is the maintenance of normal calcium homeostasis and it therefore plays an important role in bone metabolism. Humans have two possible sources of vitamin D: diet (milk, fish and vegetables) and endogenous synthesis in the skin on exposure to ultraviolet light. Deficiency of vitamin D can therefore result from inadequate diet, failure of absorption or lack of exposure to sunlight. Whatever the cause, the deficiency leads to impaired mineralisation of bone leading to rickets in children and osteomalacia in adults.

ANSWERS TO CHAPTER – HEAD AND NECK

1. PHARMACOLOGY OF THE EYE

1. **F – Hypromellose**
   Schirmer's test measures the rate at which a strip of filter paper suspended from the lower eyelid is wetted by tears. Reduced tear production (keratoconjunctivitis sicca – one of the features of Sjögren's syndrome) causes ocular discomfort and erosion. Artificial tears are the mainstay of treatment.

2. **I – Timolol**
   Chronic simple (open angle) glaucoma is one of the major causes of blindness. In contrast to acute (closed angle) glaucoma, its onset is insidious and painless. Initial treatment is with a topical beta-blocker, such as timolol, with the proviso that significant systemic absorption may occur; the usual cautions and contraindications to beta-blockers should be observed. If initial treatment does not reduce intraocular pressure sufficiently, additional treatments may include parasympathomimetics (e.g. pilocarpine); selective alpha-2-adrenoceptor agonists (e.g. brimonidine); carbonic anhydrase inhibitors (e.g. dorzolamide) and prostaglandin analogues (e.g. latanoprost). If medical treatment fails, surgical trabeculectomy or laser trabeculoplasty may be necessary.

3. **A – Antazoline**
   This woman has seasonal allergic conjunctivitis (hayfever) and her symptoms should respond to a topical antihistamine such as antazoline.

4. **J – Tropicamide**
   Tropicamide is commonly used in many settings as an aid to fundoscopy. Maximal pupillary dilation is achieved about fifteen minutes after instillation of drops and the effect wears off within two hours. Very rarely it may precipitate acute (closed angle) glaucoma in elderly, long-sighted patients; this adverse effect is less likely to occur with tropicamide than with atropine owing to the latter's longer duration of action.

5. **E – Fluorescein**
   This boy may well have sustained an ocular injury and it is important to remove any retained fragments of glass. Fluorescein and rose bengal are both used as aids to ocular examination. Rose bengal is more effective at highlighting conjunctival epithelial defects but it is very irritant if used without local anaesthetic.

2. RED EYE

1. **D – Herpes simplex keratitis**
Keratitis, meaning inflammation of the cornea, may be caused by a wide range of infections. Oedema and inflammatory cell infiltration of the cornea result in pain, photophobia and impaired visual acuity with localised corneal opacity. Permanent blindness may occur if treatment is delayed. Herpes simplex keratitis causes a characteristic dendritic ulcer that may be visualised with fluorescein or rose bengal staining. Treatment is with topical acyclovir. If the diagnosis is missed, injudicious use of steroid drops leads to massive ulceration and blindness.

2. **C – Bacterial conjunctivitis**
Bacterial conjunctivitis is contagious and scrupulous hygiene is necessary to prevent spread within families. Typical causative organisms include staphylococcus, streptococcus and *Haemophilus influenzae*. Topical chloramphenicol is usually effective but swabs should always be taken for culture before treatment is started in case of resistance.

3. **A – Acute (closed angle) glaucoma**
Acute glaucoma is a medical emergency. It is usually unilateral but, because it tends to occur in people with shallow anterior chambers, the other eye is often affected within a few weeks of initial presentation. The condition progresses over a few hours; if treatment is delayed permanent blindness may result. Initial management is with intravenous acetazolamide (to reduce aqueous production), pilocarpine drops (to constrict the pupil and thereby open the angle of the anterior chamber) and, if necessary, intravenous mannitol. Definitive treatment is with surgical iridectomy or laser iridotomy.

4. **G – Pterygium**
A pterygium is a harmless ingrowth and thickening of the conjunctiva which often occurs with exposure to hot, dry, dusty environments. Surgical removal is only indicated if it encroaches on vision or for cosmetic reasons.

5. **B – Acute iritis**
Acute iritis presents similarly to acute glaucoma with rapid onset of unilateral eye pain and blurring of vision. On examination there is reduced visual acuity and ciliary vessel hyperaemia. However, the inflammatory nature of the condition causes pupillary constriction, keratitic precipitates (inflammatory cells deposited on the back of the cornea) and hypopyon (a collection of pus in the anterior chamber of the eye). Treatment includes topical steroids to suppress inflammation, and mydriatics to dilate the pupil, thereby preventing formation of adhesions between iris and lens. Iritis is associated with systemic illnesses, including Still's disease, ulcerative colitis, sarcoidosis and the seronegative arthritides, especially ankylosing spondylitis and Behçet's syndrome.

3. AUDITORY PAIN AND DEAFNESS

1. **J – Wax**
   This patient has wax. This is probably by far the most common cause of unilateral deafness and discomfort. The onset of deafness is often sudden following washing or bathing, when the entrance of water to the meatus closes a previously narrow passage for the transmission of sound by causing the wax to swell.

2. **H – Otitis externa**
   This patient has otitis externa as evidenced by the history and findings on examination. Inflammation of the skin of the external auditory meatus is common. Causes may be primarily otological or dermatological. In addition, the condition may be classified as infective: bacterial, fungal, viral, or reactive (i.e. largely due to allergy). Trauma is the commonest aetiological factor and is usually caused by scratching or inappropriate attempts to clean the canal.

3. **F – Chronic serous middle ear effusion**
   This patient has a chronic middle ear effusion. Middle ear effusions are caused by blockage of the eustachian tube at its opening in the nasopharynx. Acute middle ear effusions usually follow 'flu and upper respiratory tract infections when mucosal oedema causes the obstruction. In children, acute suppurative otitis media may occur. In such cases the tympanic membrane may bulge outwards. However, in all other middle ear effusions (acute and chronic) the drum appears retracted. Whilst chronic effusions may be a sequel to chronic sinusitis/rhinitis: any mass in this region can also cause obstruction. In a 60-year-old (as in this case) a nasopharyngeal carcinoma must always be excluded by examination.

4. **E – Cholesteatoma**
   This patient has cholesteatoma as evidenced by the history and otoscopic findings. This is a form of chronic suppurative otitis media. As a result of a marginal or attic perforation, there is chronic infection of the bone of the attic, antrum and mastoid process, as well as the mucosa of the middle ear. Whilst the disease is less common than in pre-antibiotic times, it is an important disorder not to miss. Cholesteatoma requires chronic treatment, often including surgery (commonly mastoidectomy), and has numerous potentially serious extra- and intracranial complications.

5. **I – Otosclerosis**
   This patient has otosclerosis, a common disorder which affects up to 1:200 people to some degree. The disorder is more common in females, and has a marked hereditary tendency in certain families. It commonly presents between the ages of 18–30. The pathology is one of excessive bone formation in the middle ear which leads to conductive deafness (hence the findings on Rinne's and Weber's tests) and often also tinnitus. The hearing is often

improved in noisy places: so-called Willis' paracousis. The tympanum appears normal in the majority of cases.

6.   **A – Acoustic neuroma**
This patient may have an acoustic neuroma. These represent 80% of cerebel-lopontine angle tumours and 8% of all intracranial tumours. They arise from the neurilemmal cells of a cranial nerve virtually always in the internal audi-tory meatus. Essentially, the tumour is benign histologically, but causes local pressure effects on other cranial nerves (V > VII > others) and the cerebellum. The possibility of an acoustic neuroma should always be considered in cases of unilateral deafness or tinnitus or both, and very strongly suspected if evidence of cranial nerve/cerebellar dysfunction is present (as in this case).

4.   ANATOMY OF THE NOSE AND PARANASAL AIR SINUSES

1.   **D – Frontal sinus**
The frontal sinuses lie on either side of the midline related posteriorly to the frontal lobe of the brain and drain inferiorly into the anterior end of the hiatus semilunaris.

2.   **F – Maxillary sinus**
The maxillary sinus projects into the zygomatic process of the temporal bone, is related posteriorly to the infratemporal and pterygopalatine fossae, and superiorly to the orbit. It is grooved superiorly by the infraorbital nerve and drains into the hiatus semilunaris.

3.   **B – Ethmoid sinus**
The ethmoidal air cells are grouped into anterior, opening into the hiatus semilunaris, middle, within the bulla ethmoidalis, and posterior, draining into the superior meatus.

4.   **H – Sphenoid sinus**
The sphenoidal sinus, in the body of the sphenoid bone, forms the sella turcica housing the pituitary fossa. It forms the posterosuperior boundary of the nasal cavity and drains into the sphenoethmoidal recess.

5.   **E – Inferior concha**
The nasolacrimal duct lies between the maxilla laterally and the lacrimal and inferior concha bones medially. The nasal opening is overlain by a fold of mucosa.

5. EPISTAXIS

1. **C – Foreign body**
    A foreign body may present with bleeding from the nose in the presence of long-standing inflammation. The history of a foul-smelling nasal discharge and the age of the child (foreign bodies in the nose are commonest in children aged 2–3) should alert one to the diagnosis. Treatment is by removal under GA.

2. **D – Leukaemia**
    Leukaemia and other blood dyscrasias may present with epistaxis as a result of clotting abnormalities caused by thrombocytopenia. This diagnosis should always be suspected in patients when the anaemia appears to be out of proportion to the loss of blood (or that the patient may be bleeding from elsewhere e.g. upper or lower gastrointestinal tract).

3. **B – Drug induced**
    Patients who take warfarin quite frequently have nose bleeds that are difficult to stop while the INR remains raised.

4. **G – Pyogenic granuloma**
    Pyogenic granulomas are raised smooth swellings that arise most frequently on Little's area. They may cause severe bleeding and may mimic a neoplasm. They can generally be easily removed under GA. Histology confirms the diagnosis.

5. **F – Osler-Weber-Rendu disease**
    Osler-Weber-Rendu disease (hereditary familial telangiectasia) can give rise to severe and occasionally fatal haemorrhage. Many treatments have been tried, including sclerosants, split skin grafting, ligation or embolisation of the feeding vessels and oestrogens (the condition improves in pregnancy).

6. ANATOMY OF THE LARYNX

1. **B – Cricoid cartilage**
    The signet-ring shaped cricoid cartilage is the foundation of the larynx, giving articulation to the thyroid and arytenoid cartilages. The tracheal and bronchial cartilaginous rings are all incomplete.

2. **I – Thyroid cartilage**
    Each vocal cord is the upper free margin of the cricothyroid membrane and extends from the back of the laryngeal prominence of the thyroid cartilage to the vocal process of the arytenoid cartilage.

3. **D – Epiglottis**
    The epiglottis lies medial to the piriform fossa: it is bounded anteriorly by the valleculae, between it and the back of the tongue, and posteriorly by the inlet (aditus) of the larynx.

4. **E – External laryngeal nerve**
    The cricothyroid muscle is the only laryngeal muscle not supplied by the recurrent laryngeal nerve. The latter also supplies the mucous membrane of the vocal fold and the larynx below this level.

5. **A – Arytenoid cartilage**
    The shorter posterior border of the quadrangular membrane is attached to the anterolateral surface of the arytenoid cartilage and the anterior border to the epiglottis. The upper border forms the aryepiglottic fold and the lower the vestibular fold (false vocal cord).

7. HOARSENESS

1. **I – Singer's nodules**
    This patient has singer's nodules. Although they are said to be caused by vocal abuse, the name is a misnomer, anyone who misuses their voice can get them. The treatment is voice rest for small lesions. Larger lesions require micro-surgical removal. Without the swellings but with redness and swelling of the cords, the diagnosis would be chronic laryngitis.

2. **F – Laryngeal papilloma**
    This boy has laryngeal papillomas. These are viral lesions and must be removed with care, as they can easily be spread to the whole of the larynx and trachea. Laser removal, which vaporises the lesions is the treatment of choice. They normally disappear at puberty.

3. **C – Carcinoma of the bronchus**
    This man has carcinoma of the bronchus, which has locally spread to involve the left recurrent laryngeal nerve as it loops around the remnant of the ductus arteriosus (the subclavian artery on the right side). This diagnosis should be considered in all patients presenting with hoarseness and a chest X-ray ordered accordingly. The vocal cord lies in the mid-abducted (cadaveric) position after complete nerve section. Other causes of recurrent laryngeal nerve palsy include: other local malignancies (e.g oesophagus and thyroid), trauma (thyroidectomy), CNS causes and aortic aneurysm.

4. **E – Laryngeal carcinoma**
   This man has carcinoma of the larynx. Squamous cell carcinoma accounts for 95% of all malignant tumours of the larynx. 50% of these originate on the vocal cords, often at the junction between the anterior third and the posterior two-thirds (the same site as singer's nodules). Diagnosis is by histology. Hoarseness is the only early sign of carcinoma of the larynx. Anyone who has been hoarse for more than three weeks requires laryngoscopy.

5. **B – Candidiasis of the larynx**
   This man has candidiasis affecting both the larynx and pharynx. This is common with the widespread use of steroid inhalers and becoming more common with the increased prevalence of acquired immunodeficiency. Diagnosis is made by fungal culture.

8. UPPER AIRWAYS OBSTRUCTION

1. **J – Papilloma of the larynx**
   Papillomas of the larynx occur in children and are probably viral in origin. Care must be taken when removing them, as it is very easy to spread them in the larynx and trachea. They will often need more than one treatment. They may become numerous and large enough to obstruct the airway. When a tracheostomy has been performed they may also grow around the stoma. Modern treatment is by laser ablation. Papillomas usually regress spontaneously at or after puberty.

2. **F – Fracture of the mandible**
   Certain midfacial injuries may compromise the naso- and oropharynx. Fractures of the mandible, especially bilateral body fractures, may cause a loss of normal support to the muscles of the tongue. Airway obstruction results if the patient is in a supine position.

3. **A – Acute epiglottitis**
   The rapid onset of the stridor and the high temperature give the clue to the diagnosis. The infecting organism is *Haemophilus influenzae B*, which responds to broad-spectrum antibiotics. If there is any but the mildest degree of stridor, the child must be taken to the operating theatre and anaesthetised on the operating table with a surgeon scrubbed up and the instruments opened so that tracheostomy can be performed in the event of the anaesthetist being unable to intubate. In this condition the epiglottis is red and swollen and protrudes above the tongue (the rising sun sign). Patients must never be examined to see this, as to do so may precipitate complete respiratory obstruction. With immunisation, such infections are becoming rarer. The differential diagnosis is acute laryngo-tracheo-bronchitis, and in the third world with an unimmunised population, diphtheria.

4. **C – Carcinoma of the larynx**
    Carcinoma of the larynx may present with upper respiratory obstruction, when the tumour has grown large enough to block the airway. The hoarseness has been accepted by the patient as a consequence of smoking. Stridor is sometimes confused with wheezing (which is also a consequence of smoking). It will nearly always be necessary to perform a tracheostomy prior to biopsy and treatment as the airway is so blocked that an endotracheal tube may not pass.

5. **B – Bilateral recurrent laryngeal nerve paralysis**
    Bilateral recurrent laryngeal palsy is fortunately a rare complication of thyroidectomy. The cords fall into the adducted position blocking the airway. Tracheostomy may be necessary to relieve the obstruction, before trying to abduct one vocal cord surgically.

6. **G – Inhaled foreign body**
    A history of choking on food followed by stridor or wheezing suggests that something has been inhaled. The symptoms may be intermittent when the foreign body lies in the lumen of the trachea and only return when it comes into contact with the larynx. If there is any suspicion that a foreign body has been inhaled, the patient must be laryngoscoped and bronchoscoped.

9. ANATOMY OF THE PHARYNGEAL MUSCLES

1. **C – Middle constrictor**
    The middle constrictor also gains attachment from the greater horn of the hyoid bone, deep to the hyoglossus muscle. Its fibres diverge around the pharynx to the midline posterior raphé.

2. **E – Palatopharyngeus**
    The anterior pillar overlies the palatoglossus muscle, the mucosa being inner-vated by the ninth cranial nerve, producing the afferent fibres for the gag reflex.

3. **A – Inferior constrictor**
    The horizontal cricopharyngeal part of the inferior constrictor produces the lower pharyngeal sphincter. A potentially weak area between the crico- and thyro-pharyngeal components of the inferior constrictor (the dehiscence of Killian) is the site of protrusion of a pharyngeal pouch (a cause of the dysphagia).

4. **H – Stylopharyngeus**
    The stylopharyngeus muscle is supplied by the ninth cranial nerve and the tensor palati muscle by the medial pterygoid branch of the trigeminal nerve. Other pharyngeal wall muscles are supplied from the pharyngeal plexus, derived from branches of the vagus.

5. **I – Superior constrictor**
    The superior constrictor diverges to pass posteriorly around the pharynx, meeting its fellow on the opposite side in the midline raphé. It lies within the middle constrictor, which itself lies within the inferior constrictor muscle. The pharyngeal wall is completed superolaterally by the pharyngobasilar fascia.

10. VESSELS OF THE NECK

1. **G – Subclavian artery**
    The subclavian artery arches over the lung, pleura and suprapleural membrane. The thyrocervical trunk is given off posterior to the internal jugular vein but the vertebral artery lies more medially.

2. **D – Internal carotid artery**
    The last four cranial nerves are related to the internal jugular vein and internal carotid artery at the base of the skull. The 11th nerve passes laterally anterior to the internal jugular vein, the 10th descends between the two vessels in the carotid sheath, and the 9th descends medially between the internal and external carotid arteries.

3. **A – Common carotid artery**
    The common carotid artery ascends through the neck from behind the sternoclavicular joint and is palpable, or can be compressed, on the 4th to 6th cervical transverse processes.

4. **C – Facial artery**
    The facial artery arches over the submandibular gland and then around the inferior margin of the mandible. It is palpable just anterior to the masseter muscle. The superficial temporal artery can be palpated just in front of the tragus as it passes up to the scalp.

5. **B – External jugular vein**
    The external jugular vein descends from behind the angle of the mandible, crosses the sternomastoid muscle, lying on the deep investing layer of fascia, and pierces the fascia just above the clavicle to enter the subclavian vein.

11. NECK LUMPS

1. **I – Thyroglossal cyst**
This patient has a thyroglossal cyst. This is caused by a remnant of the thyroglossal duct left patent after the migratory development of the thyroid gland. The diagnosis is strongly suggested by the position in or very near to the midline, the cystic nature of the swelling (fluctuance), and confirmed by its movement upwards on tongue protrusion. Theoretically, thyroglossal cysts can occur anywhere between the base of the tongue and the thyroid gland, but they are commonly found in two sites – between the isthmus of the thyroid gland and the hyoid bone (pre-tracheal/subhyoid) or just above the hyoid bone as in this case (suprahyoid).

2. **G – Pharyngeal pouch**
This patient has a pharyngeal pouch as evidenced by the characteristic history and findings on examination. In this case regurgitation at night has caused chronic respiratory symptoms and the patient has started to suffer from dysphagia as a result of compression of the oesophagus by the filling pouch. A pharyngeal pouch is a pulsion diverticulum of the pharynx which occurs through a weakness between fibres of the pharyngeal constrictor muscles (Killian's dehiscence). It commonly occurs in the elderly.

3. **D – Lymphoma**
This patient has a lymphoma as evidenced by the finding of supraclavicular lymphadenopathy and the history of constitutive symptoms. The differential diagnosis in such a case should include tuberculous lymphadenopathy and metastatic carcinoma.

4. **A – Branchial cyst**
This patient has a branchial cyst as evidenced by the characteristic position and features of the lump. A branchial cyst is a remnant of the second branchial cleft. They are occasionally complicated by infection and inflammation of the wall when they may cause attacks of pain associated with an increase in size, however, they most commonly present in the 15–25 year age group as painless swellings as in this case.

5. **E – Metastatic carcinoma**
This patient has metastatic carcinoma. This is one of the commonest causes of swelling of the deep cervical nodes, which lie behind the sternomastoid muscles. Primary lesions may occur in the skin of the head and neck, the lips, tongue and buccal cavity and the larynx. The history of dysphonia in a man of this age should point to the diagnosis of a primary laryngeal carcinoma.

12. TUMOURS OF THE HEAD AND NECK

1. **G – Pleomorphic adenoma**
    Pleomorphic adenoma accounts for two-thirds of all salivary gland tumours and is more common in the parotid than in other salivary glands. As the name implies, the tumour has a varied histological appearance and is composed of a mixture of stromal and epithelial elements. The stroma is often myxoid and/or cartilaginous, which explains the gelatinous appearance macroscopically. Pleomorphic adenoma is a benign tumour but it does have a tendency to recur if surgical excision is incomplete.

2. **H – Squamous cell carcinoma**
    About 95% of malignant tumours of the oral cavity are squamous cell carcinomas. In this patient, the focal keratinisation of the malignant cell indicates that the tumour is well differentiated. Squamous cell carcinomas often arise within areas of leukoplakia, as shown in this patient by the thickened white mucosa around the ulcer edge. The aetiology of this tumour is strongly linked to the use of tobacco and alcohol, though in some parts of the world, chewing betel nut is also an important aetiological factor. Despite their easy accessibility, oral squamous cell carcinomas often present late and their prognosis is consequently poor.

3. **A – Acoustic neuroma**
    Acoustic neuromas originate in the nerve sheath of the 8th (vestibulo-cochlear) cranial nerve, most commonly at the cerebello-pontine angle. The symptoms are referable to compression of the nerve, particularly the vestibular branch. Acoustic neuromas arise from Schwann cells and are therefore also known as acoustic schwannomas. Histologically they are composed of elongated cells with 'wavy' nuclei that resemble normal peripheral nerve sheath cells. The tumours are benign but are prone to recur if excision is incomplete.

4. **E – Nasopharyngeal carcinoma**
    The main differential diagnosis of an intranasal undifferentiated malignant tumour lies between nasopharyngeal carcinoma and olfactory neuroblastoma. The fact that this patient is Chinese and that the tumour is associated with a prominent lymphocytic infiltrate and Epstein-Barr virus infection indicate a nasopharygeal carcinoma. Antibodies to Epstein-Barr virus (EBV) are raised in 100% of patients with nasopharyngeal carcinoma and parts of the EBV genome can be detected in the tumour cells. In addition, there is a distinctive geographical distribution; the tumour is rare in Caucasians but in parts of China it accounts for over 50% of all malignant disease. Nasopharyngeal carcinomas tend to grow silently and have often spread to cervical nodes by the time of presentation.

5. C – Ameloblastoma

Ameloblastoma is the most common of the epithelial odontogenic tumours, and the mandible is the most frequent site of origin. Macroscopically they are rounded lytic lesions with solid and cystic areas. Histologically, the tumour cells resemble the epithelium of the developing tooth. The behaviour of ameloblastomas is unpredictable; they have a tendency for local invasion and recurrence after excision but distant metastases are rare.

ANSWERS TO CHAPTER – NEUROLOGY & PSYCHIATRY

1. CRANIAL NERVE ANATOMY

1. **D – Glossopharyngeal nerve**
   The reflex is elicited by stimulating the anterior pillar of the fauces. The efferent pathway is through the vagus, the glossopharyngeal only provides motor innervation to the stylopharyngeus muscle.

2. **C – Facial nerve**
   The muscles of facial expression are innervated by the facial nerve. Those of the forehead receive bilateral innervation and are therefore not paralysed in a unilateral upper motor neurone lesion. Sensation over the face is provided by the trigeminal nerve.

3. **I – Vagus nerve**
   The recurrent laryngeal nerve innervation of the vocal cord muscles is at risk in thyroid surgery, and also in manipulation of the vagus in other procedures, as these fibres are superficially placed in the parent nerve.

4. **H – Trochlear nerve**
   The superior oblique muscle subserves this movement: it passes from the back of the orbit around the trochlear to be attached to the superoposteromedial aspect of the globe.

5. **B – Accessory nerve**
   The accessory nerve innervates the sternomastoid and trapezius muscles. These rotate the head, draw the head backwards, protrude the chin and shrug the shoulders.

2. SPINAL CORD AND PATHWAYS

1. **D – Fasciculus gracilis**
   The dorsal funiculus carries proprioceptive, vibration, pressure and some tactile information. Fibres synapse in the gracile (medial) and cuneate (lateral) nuclei. The secondary neurones pass in the medial lemniscus to the ventral thalamic nuclei and are relayed to the post-central gyrus.

2. **F – Lateral corticospinal tract**
Descending fibres from the motor cortex, including those from the large pyramidal Betz cells, pass through the internal capsule and cerebral peduncle, and in the medullary pyramid, many descend to form the lateral corticospinal tract. The tract contains approximately 1 million fibres of varying calibre. It is probable that the pyramidal pathway is made up of a series rather than single neurons.

3. **J – Ventral spinothalamic tract**
The primary neurone synapses in the dorsal grey matter and the secondary neurone decussates in the anterior white commissure. Fibres ascend in the ventral and lateral spinothalamic tracts, and the spinal lemniscus to the ventralis posterior lateralis nucleus of the thalamus.

4. **B – Dorsal spinocerebellar tract**
The fibres pass to the cerebellar cortex. The ventral spinocerebellar tract is largely a decussating pathway and passes to the cerebellum in the superior cerebellar peduncle.

5. **C – Dorsolateral tract**
The dorsolateral tract carries predominantly proprioceptive neurones from the dorsal root that ascend for one or two segments. The axon, and a number of branches, terminate around neurones of the dorsal grey column.

3. VISUAL DEFECTS I

1. **A – Amaurosis fugax**
This patient describes the classical features of amaurosis fugax (i.e. a screen or curtain of darkness descending over the vision in one eye, which then slowly resolves). Amaurosis is due to retinal artery emboli leading to an ophthalmic transient ischaemic attack). It may precede a full blown anterior circulation stroke and requires further investigation and possible treatment.

2. **D – Cortical blindness**
This patient has cortical blindness due to bilateral posterior cerebral artery strokes. The patient is suddenly blind and has little or no insight into their disability. This condition is known as Anton's syndrome.

3. **B – Bitemporal hemianopia**

    Enlarging pituitary tumours compress the optic chiasma which lies directly above the pituitary sella. Compression classically produces bitemporal hemianopia, which is marked by the inability to see objects in the lateral aspects of the visual fields. However compression may be asymmetrical and produce almost any visual field defect. Bitemporal hemianopia is NOT the same as tunnel vision, which is described as looking at the world through two tubes or tunnels (i.e. complete peripheral field loss). Tunnel vision may be caused by retinal lesions (e.g. retinitis pigmentosa), and bilateral occipital cortical lesions.

4. **E – Diplopia to left gaze**

    This patient has a left sixth nerve palsy which means he will not be able to abduct his left eye. This causes diplopia on looking to the left. In this case the abrupt onset of the symptoms suggest stroke as a likely cause. The nucleus of the sixth nerve lies in the pons and tumours and demyelination may also produce a similar lesion. Raised intracranial pressure can lead to compression of the sixth nerve against the petrous temporal bone and may be a false localising sign.

5. **C – Central scotoma**

    This patient has developed multiple sclerosis. Commonly demyelination occurs in the cervical spine, brain stem, cerebellum and periventricular, most patients present with visual symptoms caused by optic or retrobulbar neuritis. This young woman has a right-sided central scotoma. Bilateral causes include hypertension, alcohol excess and vitamin B12 deficiency.

4. VISUAL DEFECTS II

1. **D – Diabetic proliferative retinopathy**

    This man has features of proliferative diabetic retinopathy. He has exudates and haemorrhages which are background and pre-proliferative changes and neovascularisation (new vessel formation, the retina's response to ischaemic damage) proliferative change. Other diabetic eye changes include 'snowflake' cataracts, maculopathy, optic atrophy and vitreous haemorrhages.

2. **F – Oculomotor nerve palsy**

    This woman has features of a painful third nerve palsy (i.e. a full ptosis, fixed dilated pupil and the eye turned 'down and out' due to the unopposed action of the IVth and VIth nerves). This is a classical presentation due to a posterior communicating artery aneurysm rupture.

3. **B – Cataract**
    This elderly lady has cataracts, seen as opacities in the anterior chamber. These can be operatively excised under a local nerve block and surgery has changed the outlook for millions of people who were previously severely visually impaired.

4. **I – Retrobulbar neuritis**
    This man has developed retrobulbar neuritis which is often a presenting feature of demyelinating disease. The patient complains of loss of vision but due to the fact the inflammation is behind the eye (retrobulbar), fundoscopy is normal (i.e. the patient and the doctor can't see anything). Visual evoked potentials are a method to confirm demyelination. A light is shone into the eye and the time taken for it to register in the occipital cortex is measured using scalp electrodes. A similar presentation may occur with optic neuritis but this can be identified on fundoscopy.

5. **G – Optic atrophy**
    This man has optic atrophy (pale discs) secondary to his chronic alcohol abuse. Other causes include compression of the optic nerve by tumours or aneurysms, vitamin B12 deficiency, diabetes mellitus, lead and mercury toxicity, Paget's bone disease, syphilis and retinal artery occlusion.

5. PUPILLARY ABNORMALITIES

1. **A – Argyll Robertson pupil**
    This patient has Argyll Robertson pupils. Classically this condition was seen in tertiary syphilis. The pupil accommodates but does not react. The condition is rarely seen now and, as in this case, may be caused by diabetes mellitus.

2. **F – Horner's syndrome**
    This patient has a left-sided apical lung tumour, known as a Pancoast's tumour. Invasion of the brachial plexus leads to pain and paraesthesiae along the ulnar border of the forearm and the muscle wasting indicates a T1 root lesion. The interruption of the sympathetic nerve supply to the pupil as it exits from the cord at T1 leads to a Horner's syndrome. The pupil is constricted, the eye is sunken (enophthalmos) and there is a partial ptosis.

3. **E – Holmes-Adie pupil**
    This young woman has a Holmes-Adie pupil. The pupil is larger than the non-affected one and its pupillary reflexes are absent or diminished and slow. This is an idiopathic, benign condition and patients should be reassured. It may be associated with diminished or absent tendon reflexes.

4. **I – Opiate overdose**
    This patient has pinpoint pupils which may be a sign of pontine strokes or more commonly opiate overdose. The unconscious patient with pinpoint pupils may warrant empirical treatment with intravenous naloxone (an opiate antagonist) to see if there is any response.

5. **D – Gunn's pupil**
    This patient has an afferent defect of the right eye. The direct pupillary response will be diminished or absent, and the slight dilation of the pupil as the light is swung back towards the abnormal eye indicates that its consensual light reflex is more active than its direct reaction. This is known as a Gunn's pupil and is characteristic of an optic nerve lesion. It may occur in optic neuritis, retrobulbar neuritis and compression of the nerve by tumours or aneurysm. (Compare these features to the patient in vignette (3), where the abnormal pupil is slightly dilated and has diminished or absent direct and consensual responses.)

6. CRANIAL NERVE LESIONS

1. **B – Facial nerve**
    This woman has a left-sided lower motor neurone facial palsy. The loss of wrinkles on the left side of forehead is typical of a lower motor neurone palsy. An upper motor neurone palsy is characterised by 'forehead sparing' due to the bilateral innervation of the nuclei. In this case the likeliest cause is an idiopathic Bell's palsy. At such an early stage steroids should be given.

2. **G – Trigeminal nerve**
    This man has developed trigeminal neuralgia. This is an idiopathic disorder of later life characterised by shooting pains which may be reproduced at given 'trigger zones'. In the idiopathic condition there are no signs of trigeminal nerve dysfunction. Carbamazepine may be useful in some cases but resistant cases may require surgical intervention.

3. **C, D, I – Glossopharyngeal, hypoglossal and vagus nerves**
    This woman has developed signs and symptoms suggestive of motor neurone disease. The condition classically affects the cranial nerves in the medulla or 'bulb'. Hence patients present with bulbar or pseudobulbar palsy characterised by the speech and swallowing problems.

4. **A – Abducens nerve**
    This woman has signs and symptoms of a breast carcinoma with cerebral metastases. The sixth nerve palsy is a 'false localising sign' and indicates the presence of raised intracranial pressure. The nerve palsy is caused by the compression of the nerve on the tip of the petrous temporal bone.

5. **B, G, J – Facial, trigeminal and vestibulocochlear nerve**

This patient has signs and symptoms of a cerebello-pontine angle lesion. As evidenced by the combination of cerebellar signs associated with Vth, VIIth and VIIIth nerve palsies. The VIth nerve may be affected and the patient may also develop contralateral pyramidal signs. Causes include acoustic neuromas, meningiomas and metastases.

7. FACIAL NERVE PALSY

1. **B – Cerebello-pontine angle tumour**

Neurofibromatosis is an autosomal dominant disorder, divided into two separate conditions. Type I was eponymously known as von Recklinghausen's disease and is considered the peripheral form of the condition. It is characterised by neurofibromas of the skin, café-au-lait spots (six or more is considered pathological), Lisch nodules of the iris, and axillary and inguinal freckling. Neurofibromas may occur in the pelvis, mediastinum and abdomen, as well as paraspinally. Astrocytomas of the central nervous system, including the optic nerve, may also occur. Type II is a more central disorder associated with bilateral acoustic neuromas and other cranial nerve and central nervous system tumours. This patient has signs of a left-sided cerebello-pontine angle tumour which is consistent with an acoustic neuroma

2. **J – Sarcoidosis**

This patient has features of transient, bilateral facial palsies associated with fever, uveitis and parotitis. This combination is known as Heerfordt's syndrome, an acute syndrome seen in sarcoidosis: the features usually resolve spontaneously within a few weeks. Myasthenia gravis and Lyme disease may also cause bilateral facial palsies.

3. **I – Ramsay Hunt syndrome**

This gentleman has a left, lower motor neurone facial palsy associated with a herpes zoster infection of the external auditory meatus. This is known as the Ramsay Hunt syndrome. The palsy is usually rapid in onset and is associated with pain and vesicles in and around the external auditory meatus. Rarely there is also involvement of the VIIIth nerve leading to vertigo, tinnitus and deafness.

4. **G – Pontine demyelination**

This young woman has features suggestive of optic neuritis and pontine demyelination, due to multiple sclerosis. The facial palsy, similar in onset and character to a Bell's palsy, may be associated with facial spasm and myokymic twitching (a diffuse rippling of the muscles).

5.   **D – Mononeuritis multiplex**
This patient has facial, ulnar and lateral popliteal nerve palsies due to mononeuritis multiplex. The diagnosis may be inferred when a patient presents with several non-anatomically related nerve palsies. It has numerous causes including diabetes mellitus, rheumatoid arthritis, SLE, polyarteritis nodosa, Wegener's granulomatosis, sarcoidosis, carcinoma and amyloidosis.

8. HEAD INJURY

1.   **F – GCS 8**
This patient has a GCS of 8 [EO to pain = 2, BMR = normal flexion (withdrawal) = 4, BVR = incomprehensible sounds = 2]. He has by definition a severe head injury (GCS ≤8).

2.   **D – Extradural haematoma**
This patient probably has an extradural haematoma. These are located outside the dura but within the skull. They are most commonly located in and associated with injuries of the temporal or temporoparietal region and often result from tearing of the middle meningeal artery by a fracture. Because they are commonly not associated with primary brain injury, there is classically a 'lucid interval' before a rapid decline in neurological status due to cerebral compression from arterial bleeding. This is commonly referred to as the 'talk and die' scenario. The GCS is 12.

3.   **G – GCS 11**
This patient has a GCS of 11 [EO to pain = 2, BMR = localises pain = 5, BVR = confused speech = 4]. She has a moderate head injury (GCS 9–13).

4.   **A – Basal skull fracture**
This patient has evidence of a basal skull fracture as evidenced by some of the characteristic clinical signs listed. These may include 'panda or racoon eyes', subconjunctival haemorrhage, otorrhoea or blood in the external auditory meatus, and CSF rhinorrhoea. Whilst the fracture itself does not denote the need for emergency intervention, all such patients should be admitted for neurological observation and CT scanning strongly considered because of the likelihood of associated brain injury. Some fractures around the orbit may affect eye movements and require maxillofacial surgical intervention.

5.   **J – Subdural haematoma**
This patient has a subdural haematoma as evidenced by the history and clinical findings. These occur because of rupture of bridging veins between the cerebral cortex and a draining venous sinuous. The brain damage underlying a subdural haematoma is invariably much more severe than with extradural

haematomas and the mortality rate high. In this case the GCS of 5 and fixed dilated pupil with contralateral hemiplegia are indicative of severe brain displacement with uncal herniation through the tentorium cerebelli. Death is imminent without intervention and long-term prognosis very poor.

9. INTRACRANIAL HAEMORRHAGE

1. **J – Subarachnoid haemorrhage**
Subarachnoid haemorrhage is characterised by sudden onset of severe headache; this is classically described as 'like a blow to the head'. The subsequent clinical findings of meningism are caused by irritation of the meninges by blood in the subarachnoid space. This is a common neurosurgical problem. Most (90%) are caused by rupture of Berry aneurysms. Other causes include arteriovenous malformations and trauma, but in some no cause is found. CT and lumbar puncture (LP) are diagnostic. The CSF at LP may be blood-stained or yellow (xanthochromia). Aneurysms (demonstrated by arteriography) may need to be clipped subsequently to prevent rebleeding.

2. **J – Subarachnoid haemorrhage**
This patient has also had a subarachnoid haemorrhage. In this case, the patient is very likely to have congenital Berry aneurysms associated with polycystic kidney disease (hence the flank mass). Bleeding is commonly precipitated by acute rises in arterial pressure (coitus, straining at stool, lifting weights). In addition to coitus, this patient's bleeding has been precipitated by the use of stimulant narcotics which also markedly raise arterial pressure (an increasingly recognised cause).

3. **B – Chronic subdural haemorrhage**
This patient has a chronic subdural haemorrhage. These present weeks or months after an often relatively trivial head injury (some may also be secondary to clotting defects including anticoagulant therapy). Like acute subdurals, they are caused by venous bleeding. About 80% of patients have a headache if questioned, but there are two major presentations. Firstly, there may be local symptoms caused by cerebral compression and therefore focal neurological signs. Secondly, as in this case, there may be a diffuse mental change caused by slight rises in intracranial pressure. Diagnosis is by CT scan, and treatment by burr-hole evacuation.

4. **E – Intracerebral haemorrhage: middle cerebral artery territory**
This patient has an intracerebral haemorrhage: (left) middle cerebral artery territory. Intracerebral haemorrhage is the most common type of intracranial bleeding, accounting for approximately 25% of strokes. Hypertension is a risk factor in all strokes, but especially in haemorrhagic (80%). Other rarer causes include arteriovenous malformations, Berry aneurysms and trauma (see

below). There is no history of transient cerebral episodes (unlike ischaemic strokes). There is usually abrupt or rapidly progressive neurological impairment which is dependent on the focal area affected. Vomiting and headache, suggestive of rising intracranial pressure, may occur and consciousness may be impaired.

5. D – Intracerebral haemorrhage: anterior cerebral artery territory
This patient has an intracerebral haemorrhage: anterior cerebral artery territory. In trauma, the haemorrhage is described as a cerebral contusion. The post-head injury syndrome in this patient is fairly characteristic of frontal brain damage causing behavioural and speech, as well as motor abnormalities. The outcome could also be due to an acute subdural haematoma, but these are almost always managed operatively.

10. HEADACHE I

1. A – Benign intracranial hypertension
Headache is the commonest symptom of benign intracranial hypertension and is characteristically worsened by temporary changes in CSF pressure, such as are caused by coughing, straining or bending over. Papilloedema is invariable and frequently results in transient visual disturbance. Visual field defects often occur, ranging in severity from enlargement of the blind spot to permanent, total loss of vision as a result of optic nerve infarction. In common with other causes of raised intracranial pressure, false localising signs, such as VIth cranial nerve palsy, may occur but, in contrast, cognitive defects and deterioration of conscious level are rare. Most sufferers are female and obesity is characteristic.

2. B – Cervical spondylosis
The headache of cervical spondylosis is usually dull in nature and worse on neck movement. As in raised intracranial pressure, the pain is often worse on waking but, in cervical spondylosis, this is thought to relate to neck positioning during sleep rather than to CSF pressure changes.

3. E – Meningitis
The risk of spontaneous, community-acquired, acute bacterial meningitis in adults is greatest when large numbers of people are brought into close proximity with each other, such as in university halls of residence. Presentation is frequently non-specific, especially in infancy, but, unless the diagnosis is made and treatment started, coma and death may swiftly follow. Typical early signs include irritability, malaise and fever. Diarrhoea is particularly associated with meningococcal infection. Adults complain of severe headache which is usually gradual in onset and associated with vomiting. Photophobia and marked meningism are later signs but some degree of neck stiffness may

be elicited in the early stages by gentle manipulation of the head with the patient supine. The vasculitic rash of meningococcal septicaemia may be subtle at first, as in this patient, and is often noticed initially on the forearms and shins. Progression may be rapid, however, and can result in necrosis of the extremities.

4. **C – Cluster headaches**
Cluster headaches affect men much more commonly than women. The headaches occur at the same time every day during clusters, often shortly after the onset of sleep. Clusters last between one and four months and recur annually. The headaches may be differentiated from migraine by their characteristic pattern of timing; lack of aura; relative brevity and by the fact that sufferers seek relief through movement rather than by remaining still. Transient Horner's syndrome occurs in 25% of cases.

5. **D – Giant cell arteritis**
Being a chronic inflammatory condition, giant cell arteritis is frequently associated with non-specific signs such as fever, malaise and weight loss. The specific clinical features occur as a result of ischaemia caused by inflammatory infiltration, and hence obliteration of the lumen of the large arteries supplying the scalp, face and eyes. Visual involvement presenting as diplopia, transient blurring of vision or permanent total blindness, may be the first sign but it is more usual for headache to be prominent. The temporal arteries are often thickened, tender and non-pulsatile and there is tenderness of the overlying scalp. Jaw and tongue claudication may occur during mastication. The ESR may occasionally be normal but is usually grossly elevated. Temporal artery biopsy is the definitive investigation but it must not be allowed to prevent immediate initiation of corticosteroid treatment, which is vital to prevent blindness. Inflammatory involvement of the temporal arteries may be focal so biopsy is only positive in 70%.

11. HEADACHE II

1. **B – Cervical spondylosis**
This gentleman has cervical spondylosis, degenerative arthritis of the cervical spine, which commonly presents with occipital headaches. The headaches may radiate anteriorly and across the shoulders, and are exacerbated by movements of the cervical spine. If there are associated neurological symptoms in the upper and/ or lower limbs the patient will require an MRI scan of the cervical spine to exclude cord compression.

2. H – Space occupying lesion

This woman has the classical headache of raised intracranial pressure. The headache is often generalised, dull and constant, and exacerbated by straining, coughing or laughing. The headache is worse after prolonged periods of being supine, as after a night in bed and is associated with vomiting and blurring of vision. Examination may be unremarkable other than the presence of papilloedema but such a history warrants urgent investigation, including CT head scan.

3. E – Migraine

This young woman has developed migraine. Patients often get pre-warning symptoms in the 24 hours prior to an acute episode. The headaches are often unilateral but may be generalised and are associated with nausea, vomiting and visual disturbances including flashing lights and zig-zag lines across the visual fields. The headaches may be extremely disabling and require the patient to lie quietly in a darkened room. Patients should be advised to take early treatment (at the start of any symptoms) with aspirin, paracetamol and antiemetics. If this is not sufficient, sumatriptan, a $5HT_1$ antagonist may be required, and in severe cases, prophylaxis with beta blockers or 5HT antagonists may also be of benefit. Other treatments include acupuncture, hypnosis and stress management.

4. C – Cluster headache

This gentleman has developed cluster headaches, so called because they tend to occur in clusters ranging from days to weeks. The headaches are often severe, unilateral and come on at the same time both day and night (e.g. 10:00 am and 22:00 pm). They may be differentiated from migrainous headaches in that they occur daily for as long as the cluster continues, and are associated with ipsilateral watering and reddening of an eye and a nasal drip. They are NOT associated with pre-warning symptoms, visual disturbances or nausea and vomiting. Ergotamine is the mainstay of treatment given just prior to the predicted start of an attack.

5. F – Sagittal sinus thrombosis

This young woman has developed sagittal sinus thrombosis secondary to the use of the oral contraceptive pill. This presents in a similar manner to benign intracranial hypertension, now known as idiopathic intracranial hypertension. Patients have signs of raised intracranial pressure (i.e. headache, blurring of vision and nausea and vomiting which, unlike in the idiopathic condition, is abrupt in onset). CT head scan with contrast will confirm the diagnosis with thrombosis seen in the sagittal vein, classically forming a delta (triangular) shape. Treatment includes stopping the contraceptive pill with alternative advice given and anticoagulation. Other causes include hyperviscosity and pregnancy.

12. STROKE DISEASE

1. **I – Mycotic aneurysm**
This woman presents with signs and symptoms suggestive of infective endocarditis. The subsequent cause of her stroke is a mycotic aneurysm in the right
side of the cerebral circulation. Such aneurysms are the result of bacterial
seeding within the vessel wall causing inflammation, weakening and thus
aneurysm formation. The aneurysm may subsequently rupture causing a
haemorrhagic stroke.

2. **G – Hyperviscosity**
This patient has a pancytopenia, raised ESR, renal impairment and hypercalcaemia which are associated with multiple myeloma and in turn hyperviscosity. Other causes include polycythaemia, Waldenström's macroglobulinaemia
and leukaemias associated with very high white cell counts.

3. **D – Berry aneurysm**
Adult polycystic kidney disease is associated with Berry aneurysms of the
circle of Willis. These in turn may rupture causing a subarachnoid haemorrhage.

4. **A – Antiphospholipid syndrome**
This patient has a history suggestive of the antiphospholipid syndrome. The
syndrome may occur as an idiopathic, isolated disorder or in association with
systemic lupus erythematosus and is characterised by recurrent venous and
arterial thrombosis and miscarriage. It is a recognised cause of stroke in young
adults. The syndrome is confirmed by the presence of autoantibodies to a
number of phospholipids, including cardiolipin. However, these antibodies
are seen transiently in a number of infections including EBV, measles, HBV,
HCV and in chronic conditions such as leprosy and in such conditions require
no treatment. In the appropriate circumstances patients should be placed on
life-long warfarin.

5. **H – Left ventricular thrombus**
This man had an acute anterior myocardial infarction eight months prior to his
presentation with a stroke. The persistent ST segment elevation indicates the
likely presence of a left ventricular aneurysm and possible intraventricular
thrombus. Paradoxical emboli originate in the right side of the heart, usually
from lower limb venous thromboses, and pass through a septal defect into the
left, systemic side of the circulation, leading to arterial thromboses.

13. SITE OF STROKE

1. **B – Frontal cortex**
   This man has frontal signs including monoparesis, personality changes, expressive dysphasia (Broca's dysphasia) and urinary incontinence. The right monoparesis and associated dysphasia localises the lesion to the left frontal lobe.

2. **E – Parietal cortex**
   Parietal strokes produce quite complex disabilities including contralateral sensory inattention and neglect, dyspraxia and homonymous field defects. The construction of a clock face may be seen in such lesions but is also a feature of chronic cognitive impairment.

3. **H – Temporo-parietal cortex**
   Temporo-parietal lesions cause receptive dysphasia associated with jargon speech, contralateral sensory inattention, homonymous field defects and hemiparesis (i.e. a left-sided temporo-parietal stroke will produce a right hemiparesis, right homonymous visual field defect and right-sided inattention).

4. **D – Occipital cortex**
   This gentleman has had bilateral occipital strokes causing 'cortical blindness' or Anton's syndrome. Classically the patient has little or no insight into their blindness and this may lead to rehabilitation problems.

5. **A – Cerebellar**
   This woman has had a left-sided cerebellar stroke. Cerebellar signs are always ipsilateral to the site of the lesion and include past pointing due to an intention tremor, dysdiadochokinesia, nystagmus towards the side of the lesion and may include ipsilateral hypotonia and hyporeflexia. Bilateral or global cerebellar problems will also produce ataxia and slurred or scanning speech. Posterior fossa lesions may also cause vertigo and vomiting.

Note – Recently the use of 'cerebrovascular accident' (CVA) to describe a stroke has become less acceptable. One should say the patient has had a stroke, explaining which side of the brain it has affected and the resulting disability. For example: 'This right handed patient has had a left-sided stroke causing expressive and receptive aphasia, a grade 1/5 right hemiparesis and right-sided inattention'.

14. SPEECH AND LANGUAGE PROBLEMS

1. **B and C – Dysnomia and expressive dys/aphasia**
   This man has expressive dysphasia and particularly dysnomia. He is unable to consistently find the correct words during normal speech and cannot name particular items such as a watch and pen. This speech defect may be quite subtle and patients may adequately cover with confabulation. Although this problem is often localised to the temporal region in the dominant hemisphere, lesions in several other regions may produce a similar picture and localisation in this case is questionable.

2. **C and I – Expressive dys/aphasia and receptive dys/aphasia**
   This man has had a severe left middle cerebral artery stroke leading to a dense right hemiparesis, receptive and expressive aphasia. This sort of stroke carries a very poor prognosis with over 50% dying within six months of their stroke and less than 5% regaining independence.

3. **F – Hoarseness**
   This man has a left-sided bronchial carcinoma causing a recurrent laryngeal nerve palsy and hoarseness.

4. **C and G – Expressive dys/aphasia and jargon speech**
   This patient has 'jargon' speech secondary to a stroke, usually in the left temporo-parietal region. Patients who have recovered from such events describe how other people's speech sounds like a foreign language. Their own speech is often of a normal rhythm but is completely nonsensical.

5. **E and H – Glossal dysarthria and pharyngeal dysarthria**
   This man has developed motor neurone disease. He has brain stem or bulbar problems causing pharyngeal and glossal weakness. This in turn leads to dysarthria, an inability to articulate his speech correctly. The pharyngeal weakness leads to an inability to say 'K/C' or 'G' sounds and the hypoglossal lesion leads to loss of 'L' sounds.

15. PERIPHERAL SENSORY NEUROPATHY

1. **A – Alcohol**
   This patient has signs and investigations consistent with chronic alcoholic liver disease. The macrocytosis, thrombocytopenia, hyponatraemia and low serum urea are all due to the toxic effects of the alcohol. Alcohol and medications such as amiodarone, flecainide and isoniazid are relatively common toxic causes of a peripheral sensory neuropathy.

2. J – Vitamin B12 deficiency

This patient has a pancytopenia with a marked macrocytic anaemia due to vitamin B12 deficiency. B12 deficiency causes a peripheral sensory neuropathy due to subacute combined degeneration of the cord (SACD) which is characterised by demyelination of the dorsal and lateral spinal columns. It leads to a sensory neuropathy and then motor weakness, both affecting the lower more than upper limbs. It may also cause optic atrophy and cognitive impairment. The hypersegmented neutrophils are characteristic of B12 and folate deficiency.

3. D – Demyelination

This patient has features of demyelination secondary to multiple sclerosis. It is unusual for patients to present with an isolated sensory neuropathy and most will have evidence of other neurological deficit, such as motor weakness, optic neuritis, cerebellar or brain stem signs.

4. F – HIV infection

This man has two AIDS defining illnesses, Kaposi's sarcoma and CMV retinitis. As syphilis before it, HIV disease is the 'great impersonator' and may present with a huge diversity of signs and symptoms, including neurological problems. HIV may cause peripheral sensory, motor and mixed neuropathies. The sensory neuropathy is characteristically painful and occurs after the development of AIDS. The HIV associated Guillain-Barré, syndrome occurs earlier at the time of seroconversion.

5. C – Carcinoma

This man has signs and symptoms suggestive of a right-sided renal carcinoma. A peripheral sensory neuropathy may develop as part of a paraneoplastic syndrome, particularly associated with carcinoma of the bronchus and stomach, and lymphoproliferative disease. The cause of the neuropathy is unclear but the condition may improve on removal and treatment of the tumour.

On testing peripheral sensation it is important to remember that light touch, proprioception or joint position sense and vibration are carried by the dorsal columns and pain and temperature by the spinothalamic tracts.

Causes of a peripheral motor neuropathy include motor neurone disease, demyelination, Guillain-Barré, syndrome, paraneoplastic, lead toxicity, HIV infection, diphtheria, botulism and porphyria.

16. MOTOR-SENSORY NEUROPATHY

1.   G – Lyme disease

This gentleman has developed Lyme disease, a tick borne spirochaetal infection, caused by *Borrelia burgdorferi*. The infection is characterised by the rash, erythema chronicum migrans, which may be accompanied by 'flu-like symptoms and lymphadenopathy. The early symptoms are variable in nature and duration, lasting from a few days to several weeks. There then follows a latent second stage, marked by cardiac, neurological and arthritic symptoms. The neurological sequelae include cranial nerve palsies, meningitis and a peripheral radiculoneuropathy.

2.   C – Charcot-Marie-Tooth syndrome

This gentleman has hereditary sensory and motor neuropathy (HSMN) or peroneal muscular atrophy, eponymously known as Charcot-Marie-Tooth syndrome. HSMN type I and II present in early adolescence with walking problems. There is weakness and deformity of the distal lower limbs, sensory loss and hypo/areflexia. The associated distal wasting gives the lower limbs a characteristic 'inverted champagne bottle' appearance. Type I is due to diffuse demyelination, whereas type II is an axonal neuropathy. They may be clinically difficult to distinguish although type I tends to be earlier in onset and associated with greater sensory and upper limb signs. Both are inherited in an autosomal dominant manner. There is also a less common X-linked type, clinically similar to type I but female carriers are asymptomatic. There is a HSMN type III which occurs in children and is associated with ataxia. This is an autosomal recessive disorder.

3.   H – Multiple myeloma

This patient has signs and symptoms suggestive of bone marrow failure secondary to his multiple myeloma. The axonal motor-sensory neuropathy in myeloma is often painful and is more commonly associated with the sclerosing form of the condition. Monoclonal gammopathy of unknown significance (MGUS) has recently been recognised as a cause of a demyelinating neuropathy in later life. The paraproteins are found on the myelin sheath and probably act as autoantibodies.

4.   A – Beriberi

This gentleman has presented with 'wet' Beriberi. The associated features of a mixed neuropathy and cardiac failure (cardiomyopathy) are due to a deficiency of several members of the vitamin B group. It is more commonly found in areas of the third world where polished rice forms the staple diet but may be seen in cases of neglect and malnutrition, as in this case. Treatment includes vitamin supplements and diuretic therapy.

5. **F – Diabetes mellitus**

This diabetic man has a long-standing sensorineuropathy and has now developed diabetic amyotrophy. This is an ill understood motor neuropathy of the lower limbs which occurs principally in type II diabetic, middle aged to elderly, obese men. The symptoms are often asymmetrical and usually improve with insulin treatment.

17. MOTOR WEAKNESS

1. **B – Guillain-Barré syndrome**

This gentleman has developed Guillain-Barré syndrome following a viral respiratory tract infection. The disorder represents a polyneuropathy which is thought to be an autoimmune cellular response directed against the myelin sheath. Patients usually develop motor and sensory symptoms several weeks after the onset of an infection although up to 40% have no identifiable preceding event. Infective causes include mycoplasma, EBV, campylobacter and HIV. Most cases recover spontaneously and, although still widely used, steroids have not been shown to influence the course of the disease. In severe cases patients may require ventilatory support due to the involvement of the respiratory muscles and plasma exchange and intravenous human immunoglobulin may also be needed.

2. **D – Hypokalaemia**

This patient has developed severe hypokalaemia secondary to her diuretic therapy. The combination of frusemide and metolazone is extremely potent and commonly causes renal dysfunction and hypokalaemia. Patients may complain of non-specific symptoms including lethargy, malaise and weakness. This combination may also cause hypomagnesaemia which can present in a similar manner.

3. **E – Middle cerebral artery infarct**

This man has the features of a left middle cerebral artery stroke. The right hemiparesis is associated with a right homonymous hemianopia, visual and sensory inattention and expressive dysphasia. This sort of stroke has a poor prognosis and less than 5% of such patients manage to live independently again.

4. **J – Spinal cord compression**

Myelomatous deposits in the vertebrae may cause a cord compression syndrome by causing vertebral collapse or fracture. Bilateral limb weakness in the elderly or recurrent falls should alert one to the possibility of a cord syndrome. This patient has a spastic paraparesis, a definable sensory level at T10, constipation and a palpable bladder, all signs consistent with a cord lesion. Neurosurgery and/or radiotherapy may be required if the patient is well enough.

5.   H – Myasthenia gravis
This young woman has developed features of myasthenia gravis characterised by her 'fatiguability'. Her weakness is global and worsens with repetition of a movement such as chewing (hence the problems with a long Sunday lunch). Emotional stress or infection may precipitate the first episode of the disease. The diagnosis may be confirmed by the presence of acetylcholine receptor autoantibodies or using a test dose of an anticholinesterase, edrophonium (the tensilon test). The edrophonium is given intravenously and should produce a rapid improvement lasting a few minutes. The receptor antibodies in this condition are directed against the post-synaptic part of the neuromuscular junction. A similar condition, Lambert-Eaton myasthenic syndrome (LEMS), may be seen with small cell carcinoma of the lung. The autoantibodies in LEMS are directed presynaptically and anticholinesterases do not produce an improvement. LEMS may occur in isolation, without a malignancy, and may be associated with other autoimmune disorders such as thyroid disease and vitiligo.

Motor weakness is graded 0–5, as shown below.
Grade
0 – No movement at all
1 – Flicker of muscle response
2 – Movement of the muscle group but not against gravity
3 – Movement against gravity but easily overcome by examiner
4 – Movement against gravity but some demonstrable weakness
5 – Normal movement

18. PARKINSONISM

1.   D – Idiopathic Parkinson's disease
This patient has idiopathic Parkinson's disease. Clinically it is characterised by the triad of bradykinesia, rigidity and tremor, and pathologically by the loss of dopaminergic cells within the basal ganglia and the presence of Lewy bodies, eosinophilic inclusion bodies. Features of the disease (parkinsonism) may be seen in numerous other central nervous system disorders including diffuse, generalised degenerative disorders such as Alzheimer's and Lewy body dementia, and cerebrovascular disease. Other disorders such as multisystem atrophy and progressive supranuclear palsy show signs of Parkinson's and other very definite neurological features, hence their collective name of 'parkinsonism-plus'. Treatment with L-Dopa and a peripheral decarboxylase inhibitor (e.g. *Sinemet*) improves symptoms but does not change the progression of the disease.

2. **H – Prochlorperazine**

Drugs acting as central dopamine antagonists will cause parkinsonism, particularly when given over prolonged periods. Examples include the antiemetics prochlorperazine (which is often used as a vestibular sedative) and metoclopramide, and neuroleptic agents such as the phenothiazines and butyrophenones.

3. **I – Progressive supranuclear palsy**

This patient has progressive supranuclear palsy, eponymously known as Steele-Richardson-Olszewski syndrome. It is characterised by parkinsonism, supranuclear paralysis of upward and downward gaze, and cognitive impairment. Like Parkinson's disease it is progressive in nature but it responds poorly to L-Dopa therapy.

4. **F – Multisystem atrophy**

This patient has multisystem atrophy, another parkinsonism-plus syndrome. This is a generalised term for three conditions whose features often overlap. *Olivopontocerebellar degeneration* is characterised by parkinsonism plus features of cerebellar, pontine and inferior olive degeneration as well as autonomic failure. *Striatonigral degeneration* is characterised by cellular loss from the substantia nigra and striatum, but clinically may be difficult to distinguish from idiopathic Parkinson's disease. *Autonomic failure or Shy-Drager syndrome* is characterised by severe postural hypotension, and other autonomic features, akinesia and rigidity. As with progressive supranuclear palsy this group of disorders responds poorly to L-Dopa therapy.

5. **J – Wilson's disease**

This young man has Wilson's disease, an autosomal recessive disorder affecting copper metabolism. The copper is preferentially deposited in the liver, the lenticular nucleus (the putamen and globus pallidus) and the other basal ganglia structures, the cornea (causing the Kayser-Fleischer rings) and the kidneys. Patients may present with features of cirrhosis and chronic liver disease, and neurological problems including chorea, akinesia, rigidity and tremors. There may also be personality and behavioural problems and without treatment, severe cognitive impairment. Any young patients with features of liver disease or parkinsonism should be screened for Wilson's disease as it may be easily treated with penicillamine.

19. CEREBELLAR DISEASE

1. **D – Cerebellar infarction**

This patient has signs consistent with a right cerebellar infarct, as confirmed by the CT head scan. An infarction shows up as a low attenuation area, whereas a haemorrhage is seen as a dense, white area. Cerebellar strokes produce ipsilateral cerebellar signs which include dysdiadochokinesia (an inability to perform rapid, alternating movements), an intention tremor, past pointing and nystagmus towards the side of the lesion. Other ipsilateral signs may include hypotonia and hyporeflexia.

2. **A – Alcohol excess**
This gentleman has developed a cerebellar syndrome secondary to his alcohol abuse. A cerebellar syndrome includes bilateral cerebellar signs (as above) but also cerebellar speech (dysarthria with a staccato quality) and an ataxic gait. The syndrome is seen as a result of generalised toxic affects, (e.g. alcohol excess or drug toxicity), degenerative diseases (e.g. demyelination, paraneoplastic effect, posterior fossa tumours and hypothyroid disease).

3. **G – Friedreich's ataxia**
This young girl has features of Friedreich's ataxia, an autosomal recessive disorder which usually presents in early adulthood. The features are due to progressive degeneration of the dorsal root ganglia, spinocerebellar and corticospinal tracts as well as the Purkinje cells of the cerebellum. It is characterised by motor and sensory loss in the lower limbs associated with wasting and hyporeflexia. The feet have a pes cavus deformity. The patient may have truncal and lower limb ataxia, nystagmus and optic atrophy. They are often asymptomatic of the associated cardiomyopathy at presentation but have the ECG changes (as above). There is no cure for this disorder and patients usually die before the age of 40 of cardiac failure and respiratory infections.

4. **H – Hypothyroidism**
This woman has developed gross hypothyroidism and a subsequent cerebellar syndrome. This is a relatively rare cause of cerebellar disease but should always be excluded.

5. **F – Demyelinating disease**
This patient has signs consistent with demyelination within the brain stem and cerebellum. An internuclear ophthalmoplegia (INO) represents a lesion in the medial longitudinal fasciculus (MLF). This bundle of nerve fibres links ipsilateral IIIrd and VIth nerve nuclei, and through the parapontine reticular formation co-ordinates conjugate gaze (i.e. one eye ADducting as the other eye ABducts). Thus in the presence of a right INO, (i.e. a lesion in the right MLF), on looking to the left, the left eye IS able to abduct but the right eye can NOT adduct. Coarse nystagmus occurs in the abducting eye, in this case the left eye. Bilateral internuclear ophthalmoplegia is almost pathognomonic of demyelinating disease.

20. SEIZURES I

1. **B – Cerebral abscess**
   This patient has developed cerebral toxoplasmosis, which has formed a cerebral abscess. The differential of ring-enhancing lesions in HIV patients includes toxoplasmosis and other causes of abscess such as *Aspergillus, Nocardia, Candida* and *Cryptococcus*, non-Hodgkin's lymphoma, a syphilitic gumma, and primary and secondary malignant tumours.

2. **F – Hyponatraemia**
   This patient has iatrogenic induced hyponatraemia. Both bendrofluazide (and other diuretics) and the SSRIs are common causes of hyponatraemia in the elderly. This degree of hyponatraemia is rare but well recognised and is an indication to stop the medications. A serum sodium above 115 mmol/l rarely causes seizures but requires further investigation. Raised intracranial pressure will cause both SIADH and hyponatraemia, and seizures.

3. **H – Phenytoin toxicity**
   This gentleman was prophylactically placed on phenytoin after his neurosurgery. This has now caused a macrocytic anaemia (folate deficiency), hypocalcaemia (unlikely to have caused the seizure) and, through toxicity (as evidenced by the nystagmus), a seizure. Phenytoin has a narrow therapeutic window and serum levels should be regularly checked. Patients may suffer seizures due to toxic or subtherapeutic levels.

4. **C – Cerebral metastases**
   This patient has herpes simplex encephalitis which is invariably fatal if not treated early. Patients may present in a similar manner to those with meningitis but may have atypical features such as complex partial seizures, decreased level of consciousness and lesions suggestive of a herpes infection (as in this case). There should be a low threshold to treat with intravenous acyclovir. The virus forms lesions within the temporal lobe and this is the reason for the seizures.

5. **D – Hypocalcaemia**
   This patient has post-thyroidectomy hypocalcaemia, which commonly occurs as a transient feature but may be more permanent if the parathyroid glands have been removed. Chvostek's sign is the production of twitching in the facial muscles by gentle tapping on the cheek. Trousseau's sign is the production of tetanic spasm in the fingers and hand after blowing up a sphygmomanometer cuff for several minutes. Both are seen along with seizures in significant hypocalcaemia.

21. SEIZURES II

1. **G – Simple partial seizure**

This patient has developed simple partial seizures. Such seizures are characterised by the anatomical site of their abnormal epileptic focus. They may be motor (as in this case), sensory, visual, olfactory or aphasic. They are not associated with impairment of consciousness. Motor seizures such as these were previously termed 'Jacksonian fits'.

2. **E – Complex partial seizure**

This young girl has developed complex partial seizures. As in this case the commonest focus is the temporal lobe and this type of seizure was previously called temporal lobe epilepsy. Patients may describe a feeling of foreboding sweeping over them as the seizure begins. The patient has an impaired level of consciousness (hence the term 'complex') but is often able to respond to their environment and may be able to be guided through normal movements such as walking and sitting down into a chair. Motor components of such seizure are often stereotypical (i.e. always present) and can be quite elaborate (e.g. undressing).

3. **J – Typical absence**

Typical absence attacks are characterised by an abrupt onset associated with a decreased level of consciousness. There may also be myoclonic, tonic and autonomic components. They may be indistinguishable clinically from atypical absence attacks but have a characteristic pattern on the EEG of spikes and waves discharging at a frequency of 3 Hz. Such seizures were previously known as petit mal seizures.

4. **H – Tonic-clonic seizure**

Tonic-clonic seizures, previously known as grand mal seizures, are characterised by disorganised muscle contraction. The tonic phase lasts between a few seconds and minutes. The patient becomes rigid and if standing will drop to the floor. Contractions of various muscle groups lead to the characteristic appearances. The jaw and facial muscles contract causing the face to become deeply cyanosed. The tongue may be bitten and the patient may dribble saliva. The respiratory muscles contract, expelling air from the chest causing a cry or bellow. Abdominal and sphincter contraction leads to incontinence of urine and more rarely, faeces. The clonic or convulsive phase is characterised by the rhythmic contraction of the truncal and limb muscles. This too lasts between a few seconds and minutes. Following this phase the patient slowly awakens but may be drowsy and incoherent for several minutes. The patient on waking often complains of headache and of feeling battered and bruised.

5. **F – Partial with secondary generalisation**
Secondary generalisation of a partial seizure may occur with either simple or complex seizures. The initial partial seizure phase may be so brief that it may be missed clinically and only diagnosed on EEG recordings.

22. SEIZURES III

1. **D – Hypocalcaemia**
This woman has had her parathyroid glands removed along with the thyroid and has thus become hypocalcaemic. Routine postoperative care for thyroidectomy and parathyroidectomy should include daily serum calcium estimation, Chvostek test and six-hourly Trousseau test.

2. **G – Meningitis**
This patient could have had a further bleed or could be phenytoin toxic but the examination findings point towards sepsis. Given a history of recent intracranial surgery, meningitis is the most likely problem. Early microbiological advice is important since the causative organism is more likely to be a Gram-negative bacillus, such as *Klebsiella* or *E. coli,* rather than one of the typical causes of spontaneous, community-acquired meningitis.

3. **F – Hyponatraemia**
Elderly patients are particularly susceptible to the side-effects of antihypertensives and, indeed, most medications. In this case it is likely that the GP would have prescribed a thiazide diuretic as a first-line agent and hyponatraemia has occurred as a result. Whilst mild hyponatraemia is a common finding in patients on thiazides alone, it is uncommon for the serum sodium to fall to a level sufficient to provoke seizures. If, on the other hand, the patient is prescribed several medications, the potential for mishap is far greater.

4. **B – Cerebral abscess**
This man has developed staphylococcal endocarditis of the aortic valve resulting in rapidly progressive valve destruction with systemic embolisation and cerebral abscess formation. An isolated VIth cranial nerve palsy is likely to be a false localising sign caused by raised intracranial pressure but this gentleman may develop localising neurology later. In the A&E Department the most important thing to do is to ensure microbiological diagnosis by taking several sets of blood cultures and by swabbing the boil on the neck. With regard to further management, neurosurgical evacuation of the cerebral abscess and antimicrobial therapy will be important but the intervention that will save the patient's life is urgent aortic valve replacement.

5. **E – Hypomagnesaemia**
This girl has failed to (or refused to) recognise that she is pregnant. Hypomagnesaemia has resulted from hyperemesis gravidarum. Prolonged vomiting causes metabolic alkalosis, dehydration and hypokalaemia but a wide range of nutritional deficiencies are encountered less commonly, especially in the context of pregnancy, which exerts its own nutritional demands on the mother.

23. PSYCHIATRIC PRESENTATIONS

1. **E – Depression (severe)**
This woman has developed features of severe depression. She has no interest in her environment, has several somatic features including poor sleep and loss of appetite, severe psychomotor retardation. She expresses feelings of worthlessness and suicidal ideation. Severe depression may be accompanied by psychotic symptoms, and delusions of guilt and self-deprecation. Mild depression has fewer somatic features, the patient may still be able to function normally but only just.

2. **F – Mania**
This young man has features of mania. He has pressure of speech, flight of ideas and grandiose, delusional ideation. Other features include lack of sleep, seemingly endless energy and increased libido. Such patients have no insight into their condition. Patients with episodes of depression and mania are described as suffering from 'bipolar affective disorder'. Hypomania has features of mania but is not so destructive. It is claimed that patients with hypomania have increased energy and creativity but this is disputed. Mania and bipolar affective disorder may be treated with lithium.

3. **C – Generalised anxiety disorder**
This patient has developed a generalised anxiety disorder. This is characterised by apprehension, motor tension and autonomic activity. Unlike the phobic anxiety state it is not associated with anxiety inducing states or stimuli and symptoms are experienced for several weeks to months at a time.

4. **H – Phobic anxiety disorder**
This gentleman has developed agoraphobia, a phobic anxiety state. Phobias are an 'irrational fear' of an object, animal or situation leading to avoidance behaviour. They may develop at any age but are more common in the third to fourth decade. Patients may benefit from behavioural therapy but may require anxiolytics and /or antidepressants in the initial stages.

5. **J – Schizophrenia**

This young man has developed acute psychosis secondary to schizophrenia. This condition most commonly starts in the early twenties, it has an equal M:F incidence. It is characterised by the symptoms shown below.

Positive symptoms (Schneider's first rank symptoms)

A Thought disorder
   Associated with Word salad – nonsensical speech
   'Knights moves' – words in the wrong places and
   Neologisms – made up words
B Abnormal or inappropriate mood
C Delusional perceptions – paranoid, alienation (being externally controlled)
D Thought insertion, blockade, broadcasting, echoing and withdrawal
E Passivity – feeling of being unable to control one's emotions or thoughts
F Auditory and visual hallucinations

Negative symptoms include – Loss of initiation, psychomotor retardation, poverty of speech, social withdrawal.

24. PSYCHIATRIC MEDICATIONS

1. **A – Amitriptyline**

Amitriptyline is a relatively old-fashioned tricyclic antidepressant, principally used in severe depression where sedation is required. It has multiple side-effects including antimuscarinic effects – blurred vision, raised intra-ocular pressure, dry mouth, constipation and urinary retention. It may also cause metabolic derangement including hyponatraemia, abnormal liver function tests and jaundice. It may also cause leucopenia and thrombocytopenia. Lofepramine is a newer tricyclic which causes less antimuscarinic and general side-effects.

2. **G – Lithium**

Lithium is used in mania, bipolar affective disorder and depressive illness. Like phenytoin and digoxin it has a narrow therapeutic window and the serum levels should be closely monitored. It too has multiple side-effects and patients need to have serum levels monitored three monthly to avoid toxicity. Patients should be supplied with a lithium card (similar to a steroid card) which explains the potential hazards and interactions of the drug.

3. **B – Chlormethiazole**

Alcohol withdrawal is still principally managed with chlormethiazole in most general medical wards, although many specialist units would advocate the use of a diazepam withdrawal scale. It is a relatively short-acting hypnotic but does cause dependence and therefore should not be used for prolonged periods. In the elderly it is commonly used for night sedation. The side-effects of increased bronchial and nasal secretions and irritation of the eyes are rare.

4. **D – Fluoxetine**
    Hyponatraemia is a relatively common side-effect of many of the antidepressants, particularly the SSRIs. Elderly patients are often on several medications, particularly diuretics, which may also cause hyponatraemia, and this potentiates the drop in serum sodium. It is thought the hyponatraemia is due to an increased secretion of ADH.

5. **J – Thioridazine**
    This rather unbelievable scenario serves to illustrate why thioridazine has recently been withdrawn from routine use. The patient has been brought in with 'torsade de pointes' a ventricular tachyarrhythmia caused by prolongation of the QT interval. Prolongation of the QT interval may be caused by thioridazine, terfenadine, tricyclic antidepressants, class Ia and III anti-arrhythmics. Thioridazine was commonly used in the elderly, particularly in the cognitively impaired, with behavioural problems, requiring sedation. Other antipsychotics such as haloperidol and risperidone are now more commonly used.

25. DELIRIUM

1. **A – Diabetic ketoacidosis**
    This patient has presented with diabetic ketoacidosis, the first presentation of her diabetes mellitus. She has hyperglycaemia (glucose 34.9), a metabolic acidosis (pH 7.13, HCO_3^- 12.6), and urinalysis shows ketosis. Although she is dehydrated and is technically hyperosmolar, the clinical presentation and investigations show she has diabetic ketoacidosis, rather than hyperosmolar coma. HONK pre-coma is characterised by extreme hypernatraemia, hyperglycaemia and thus hyperosmolality, where serum osmolality = 2[Na$^+$ + K$^+$]+ urea + glucose. The third hyperglycaemic associated coma is lactic acidosis.

2. **D – Hypercalcaemia**
    This gentleman has signs and investigations consistent with a right-sided hilar mass causing collapse and consolidation of the right upper lobe. The hyponatraemia is probably secondary to SIADH caused by a bronchogenic carcinoma, but is not severe enough to cause the confusion. This is due to the hypercalcaemia which may be secondary to bony metastases or secretion of parathyroid-like peptide.

3. **E – Hypercapnia**
This gentleman has several possible causes of his acute confusion. He is septic and unwell, acidotic, hypoxic and hypercapnic. This combination is common in COPD. The raised serum bicarbonate indicates that this gentleman is a chronic CO_2 retainer and means he needs to be treated with 24–28% oxygen. The severity of his hypoxia and hypercapnia indicates he may need ventilatory support.

4. **I – Subdural haemorrhage**
This patient has features suggestive of a right-sided acute subdural haemorrhage leading to her confusion and focal left-sided neurological deficit. She requires urgent neurosurgical intervention to remove the clot.

5. **B – Encephalitis**
This woman has developed herpes simplex encephalitis, a condition which is invariably fatal if untreated. It is principally a clinical diagnosis which should carry a high index of suspicion. Patients present with features of raised intracranial pressure, pyrexia, meningism and temporal lobe seizures. The encephalitis particularly affects the temporal lobes although the reasons for this are uncertain. The presence of 'cold sores' is a rare finding. Patients suspected of the condition should be treated with intravenous acyclovir. The diagnosis may be confirmed on CT head scan with typical changes in the temporal lobes. It is rarely necessary to perform a lumbar puncture and may often be contraindicated due to raised intracranial pressure.

26. DEMENTIA

1. **J – Vascular dementia**
This gentleman is an arteriopath having evidence of both cerebrovascular and cardiovascular disease. His stepwise loss of cognitive function is characteristic of a vascular dementia, previously called multi-infarct disease. This is a common condition which often co-exists with Alzheimer's type dementia. Such patients should be on aspirin, if not contraindicated.

2. **B – Alzheimer's disease**
Alzheimer's disease is the commonest of all dementias. It is characterised by an insidious deterioration (at least six months) in cognitive function associated with dyspraxia, visuospatial and speech problems. The initial phase is associated with short-term memory loss, and personality and social skills may be well preserved. Pathologically it is characterised by neurofibrillary tangles, which have at their core the microtubule protein, tau, and senile plaques of amyloid protein. The principal risk factor for developing this condition is increasing age and it is estimated that 1:5 of the over 80 population has Alzheimer's disease. The new anticholinesterases have recently been shown to slow the cognitive decline.

3. **G – Normal pressure hydrocephalus**
    Normal pressure hydrocephalus is characterised by the triad of cognitive impairment, gait dyspraxia and falls, and urinary incontinence. It is a subcortical dementia and leads to psychomotor retardation. It is largely a clinical diagnosis which may be aided by CT head scanning but can be confirmed by CSF pressure measurement. The title 'normal pressure' is in fact a misnomer as such patients actually have rises and falls in the CSF pressure. Ventriculo-peritoneal shunting may produce quite a marked improvement, particularly for those with all three features of the triad.

4. **D – Hypothyroidism**
    This woman has developed cognitive impairment secondary to her hypothyroidism. The macrocytosis and hyponatraemia both give an indication to the diagnosis. The cognitive deficit may improve quite dramatically providing there is no other underlying dementia.

5. **H – Pick's disease**
    This patient has developed a frontal dementia, also known as focal lobar dementia or Pick's disease. Frontal disease is characterised by personality changes, loss of judgement, inertia and difficulty planning. They may become socially and sexually disinhibited. In the initial phases their cognitive function is relatively well preserved. This condition may also affect the temporal lobes, either in isolation or in association with the frontal atrophy. Such patients have particular problems with speech and have progressive dysphasia, anomia and confuse everyday objects. This condition is therefore known as the 'semantic dementia'.

    The Folstein test is a cognitive test commonly used in psychiatry for old age and medicine for the elderly. It combines the testing of short-term memory, long-term memory and cognitive skills, such as concentration, literacy and interpretation of information. It is scored out of 30 points and is used as an objective guide to the degree of cognitive impairment. A score of 23–26 is considered mild impairment, 22–16, moderate to severe, and 15 and below, severe. The introduction of the new anticholinesterases for dementia has meant the Folstein test being used to set the limits by which these medications can be prescribed, with patients being excluded from receiving treatment if their Folstein score is less than 10.

    In the acute medical setting patients are often assessed using the abridged mental test score (AMTS) which is scored out of 10.

Common questions used in this test are:

1   Full name
2   Address for recall,
     e.g. 45, Westfield Road
3   Date of birth
4   Place
5   Year
6   Name of the Prime Minister
7   Name of the monarch
8   Dates of World War II
9   Recognition of two people
10   Count backwards from 20 -1

ANSWERS TO CHAPTER – CARDIOVASCULAR AND HAEMATOLOGY

1. SURFACE MARKINGS OF THE HEART

1. **A – Left costoxiphoid angle**
   The needle is directed 45° cranially in the sagittal plain into the pericardial sac.

2. **C – Left fifth intercostal space in the mid-clavicular line**
   This is the site for palpation of the cardiac impulse and for auscultation of the mitral valve. Murmurs from the valve may radiate to the axilla and an opening snap may be heard more prominently over the fourth left costal cartilage.

3. **F – Medial end of the second right intercostal space**
   An aortic murmur may radiate into the right side of the neck or towards the apex of the heart. The aortic valve is sited medial to the third left intercostal space.

4. **J – Right sternal border, in line with the fourth intercostal space**
   The surface marking of the tricuspid valve is in the midline at the level of the fourth intercostal space.

5. **D – Left third costosternal junction**
   The pulmonary valve sounds are heard best at the medial end of the second left intercostal space.

2. BLOOD SUPPLY OF THE HEART

1. **F – Left coronary artery**
   The left coronary artery lies between the left auricular appendage and the pulmonary trunk. It gives off the anterior interventricular branch to become the circumflex artery.

2. **C – Coronary sinus**
   The coronary sinus lies in the posterior atrioventricular groove. The opening lies between the inferior vena cava and the right atrioventricular valve. The sinus is the continuation of the great cardiac vein and receives most of the venous drainage of the heart.

3. **I – Right coronary artery**
    The right coronary artery originates in the anterior aortic sinus and lies between the right auricular appendage and pulmonary trunk, before descending in the anterior atrioventricular groove. It passes around the inferior margin of the heart to become the posterior interventricular artery.

4. **H – Posterior interventricular artery**
    The first septal branch of the posterior interventricular artery supplies the AV node in 80 to 90% of individuals: the SA node is usually supplied by a branch of the circumflex artery.

5. **A – Anterior interventricular artery**
    The anterior interventricular artery passes to the apex of the heart and often passes on to the posterior surface. Its 2–9 branches supply the anterior surface of the left ventricle, and usually include a prominent diagonal artery.

3. CHEST PAIN

1. **F – Pericarditis**
    Pericarditis tends to cause a sharp pain which is variable in site and intensity. Its hallmark is that it is positional, with the pain being worse on lying flat and relieved by sitting forward. Inflammation of the pericardium may occur as a result of a wide range of processes including viral, bacterial and fungal infections; acute rheumatic fever; systemic lupus erythematosus; rheumatoid disease; Dressler's syndrome; metastatic neoplasia; radiotherapy and hypothyroidism. The most important complication is pericardial effusion causing tamponade, so it is important to record the jugular venous pressure at presentation, request an echocardiogram if the pressure starts to rise and consider this diagnosis if the patient deteriorates.

2. **D – Myocardial infarction**
    The pain of myocardial infarction does not always fit classical descriptions. In this case the patient's relative youth makes the diagnosis unusual but the quality and severity of the pain, along with its gradual onset, are typical. The bradycardia indicates that the patient is likely to be suffering an inferior myocardial infarction since the inferior myocardium shares its blood supply (from the right coronary artery) with the sinoatrial and atrioventricular nodes.

3. **B – Dissecting thoracic aortic aneurysm**
    Dissection of a thoracic aortic aneurysm causes severe tearing chest and back pain and a variety of signs and symptoms depending on which branches of the aorta are involved in the dissection. A difference in pulse pressure between the arms is thus a common, but not invariable, sign. Other complications include hemiplegia, acute limb ischaemia and myocardial infarction which may occur if the coronary arteries are involved at the aortic root.

4. J – Unstable angina

Angina occurring at rest is known as unstable angina and is a condition associated with significant mortality. It affects known angina sufferers most commonly but may rarely be the presenting symptom of new-onset ischaemic heart disease. Once the pain has been settled using medical treatment, it is usual to arrange an exercise electrocardiogram or a stress thallium myocardial perfusion scan with a view to proceeding to coronary angiography and revascularisation if indicated.

5. G – Pulmonary embolism

This woman has antiphospholipid syndrome which, in conjunction with a short period of immobility and stress, has caused a left lower limb deep venous thrombosis (DVT) with subsequent pulmonary embolism. The presentation of pulmonary embolism is extremely variable. Chest pain is commonly sharp and pleuritic. Dyspnoea is a feature of larger or multiple emboli but is more prominent in older patients and those with pre-existing lung disease. Massive pulmonary embolism may result in sudden death, often immediately preceded by an urge to defecate.

4. SHORTNESS OF BREATH

1. C – Aortic stenosis

Aortic stenosis in adults occurs most commonly as a result of calcification of a congenital bicuspid valve but may also be caused by senile calcification of a normal tricuspid valve, rheumatic heart disease or, rarely, by gross atheroma in severe hypercholesterolaemia. It presents with dyspnoea, angina, syncope, palpitation or sudden death. Importantly, since the ejection systolic murmur is caused by turbulent flow across the valve, it may be quiet or even absent when the stenosis is very severe.

2. H – Left ventricular failure

Shortness of breath and fatigue are the commonest symptoms of left ventricular failure. As dyspnoea worsens, it may make simple actions requiring minimal exertion, such as washing or dressing, impossible. Many patients are affected by orthopnoea (dyspnoea caused by lying flat) and so the number of pillows required in bed is a useful guide to the severity of failure. Left ventricular ejection fraction is another commonly-quoted guide; values can be derived from both echocardiography and from a ventriculogram performed during coronary angiography. The normal resting value is 67% ± 8%. Current anti-failure treatment includes a loop diuretic (e.g. frusemide); an angiotensin converting enzyme inhibitor (e.g. lisinopril); a beta-blocker (e.g. metoprolol) and spironolactone. Many cardiologists would also advocate digoxin, which relieves symptoms but does not affect overall mortality, and warfarin, to try to prevent mural thrombosis. Despite these treatments the outlook is very poor in this group of patients, with an overall mortality of 50% at one year.

3. **G – Constrictive pericarditis**

   Constrictive pericarditis is an uncommon, chronic disorder that presents as congestive cardiac failure. The onset of symptoms may be gradual or sudden. The most important sign is the prominence of both x and y descents in the jugular venous pressure, the y descent occurring because of rapid early diastolic filling of the right ventricle. The third heart sound is caused by rapid early diastolic filling of both left and right ventricles and is known as a 'pericardial knock.' Causes of constrictive pericarditis include tuberculosis and other bacterial, viral and fungal infections; connective tissue diseases; malignancy and radiotherapy; chronic renal failure and post-surgical haemopericardium. Many cases remain unexplained. This lady may have developed pericarditis as a result of her rheumatoid disease but she should be investigated thoroughly for tuberculosis, bearing in mind that she may be chronically immunosuppressed by her usual medication.

4. **E – Cardiac tamponade**

   Cardiac tamponade presents acutely, usually as a result of a sudden accumulation of blood in the pericardial space, but may occasionally be a chronic process, when the effusion is more likely to be inflammatory or transudative in nature. Symptoms include dyspnoea and dull central chest pain but also fatigue and ankle swelling if the presentation is chronic. Signs include a raised jugular venous pressure (JVP) with prominent x descent (resulting from downward motion of the base of the heart during systole) but absent y descent (because the effusion prevents the right ventricle from filling when the tricuspid valve opens). Kussmaul's sign (rise in jugular venous pressure with inspiration) may be present if the pressure is low enough in the neck to see it. There is usually tachycardia with hypotension and pulsus paradoxus (palpable decrease in pulse pressure during inspiration). The effusion causes heart sounds to be faint on auscultation and voltages to be reduced on electrocardiogram. Management involves pericardial aspiration, correction of the cause and supportive treatment. In this case, the most likely cause is failure of an arterial anastomosis.

5. **D – Atrial fibrillation**

   Thyrotoxicosis frequently causes atrial fibrillation. The bruit occurs as a result of hypervascularity of the thyroid gland. Treatment in this case should combine a beta-blocker (e.g. propranolol) and an antithyroid drug (e.g. carbimazole) and many physicians would also digitalise and anticoagulate. As the patient becomes euthyroid, the propranolol can be stopped, and the atrial fibrillation often reverts spontaneously to sinus rhythm. Carbimazole should be gradually weaned down over 18 months before attempting to withdraw it completely.

5. MURMURS AND ADDED SOUNDS

1. C – Ejection systolic murmur
Angina is often a presenting feature of aortic stenosis, which in this case may be diagnosed from the character of the carotid pulse. Ejection systolic murmurs also occur in aortic sclerosis, hypertrophic obstructive cardiomyopathy and high output states in normal hearts.

2. I – Pan-systolic murmur
This gentleman has developed a dilated cardiomyopathy as a result of his alcoholism. Left ventricular dilatation is often accompanied by mitral regurgitation, which produces a pan-systolic murmur.

3. A – Atrial 'plop'
This woman has an atrial myxoma from which a fragment has embolised to the right cerebral cortex. In addition to the atrial 'plop' which is heard in early diastole, there may be a variable murmur of mitral stenosis and signs of constitutional upset.

4. B – Early diastolic murmur
The history of constitutional upset along with splinter haemorrhages and Quincke's sign suggests aortic regurgitation secondary to endocarditis. The early diastolic murmur of aortic regurgitation, which is often difficult to hear, may be accentuated by sitting the patient forward and asking them to hold their breath in expiration. In addition, the mid-diastolic Austin Flint murmur, caused by the regurgitant jet vibrating the anterior leaflet of the mitral valve, may be audible.

5. E – Machinery murmur
Patent ductus arteriosus causes a continuous machinery murmur which is loudest during systole. If the duct is small it may be asymptomatic, coming to attention only incidentally. Larger ducts causing left-to-right shunt result in circulatory compromise, and occasionally in development of Eisenmenger syndrome (where pulmonary hypertension causes shunt reversal).

6. ST SEGMENT CHANGES ON ECG

1. B – Digoxin effect
Digoxin causes a 'reversed-tick' sloping depression of the ST segment which may resemble the changes occurring in myocardial ischaemia.

2. **H – Pericarditis**

ECG changes in pericarditis may be limited to T-wave inversion. If ST elevation occurs, it may be differentiated from myocardial infarction by the saddle-shaped appearance with a concave rather than convex upper surface. In addition, whilst the changes associated with infarction are usually confined to one or more territories, those in pericarditis are widespread.

3. **I – Posterior myocardial infarction**

The changes in posterior infarction are the mirror image of those occurring in other territories. Thus tall R waves are the equivalent of Q waves and ST depression occurs instead of elevation. Tall R waves in V1 also occur in type A Wolff-Parkinson-White syndrome and right bundle branch block.

4. **D – Inferior myocardial infarction**

The inferior leads are II, III, and aVF. ST elevation in these leads during inferior myocardial infarction is often accompanied by reciprocal ST depression in the anterolateral leads (V1–V6).

5. **A – Anterior myocardial infarction**

The presence of Q waves implies full-thickness infarction as may be caused by a proximal thrombosis of the anterior descending branch of the left coronary artery.

7. COMPLICATIONS OF MYOCARDIAL INFARCTION

1. **G – Pericarditis**

Fibrinous pericarditis occurs at about the second or third day after a transmural myocardial infarct as an inflammatory response to the necrotic heart muscle. It is usually localised to the area of infarction. Fibrin on the pericardial surfaces manifests clinically as acute onset of pain and fever. The 'rubbing together' of the inflamed visceral and parietal pericardia leads to a pericardial friction rub on auscultation, though this tends to disappear if a pericardial effusion develops. This type of pericarditis usually resolves spontaneously.

2. **F – Mural thrombus**

Myocardial infarction leads to akinetic (non-moving) segments of ventricular wall. The resulting stasis promotes the formation of mural thrombi on the inflamed endocardium. The larger the infarct, the greater the risk of such thrombi occurring. Fragments of thrombus can break off and embolize to various organs, particularly the brain, spleen, gut, kidney and lower limbs, producing infarction. This patient has symptoms of an infarct in the left middle cerebral artery territory.

3. **L – Ventricular wall rupture**
   Rupture of the left ventricular free wall usually occurs 5–10 days after the infarct when the damaged myocardium is particularly soft. Blood bursts through the ruptured wall into the pericardial cavity leading to haemoperi-cardium. The sudden rise in intrapericardial cavity pressure prevents cardiac filling, so-called cardiac tamponade. This classically presents with electro-mechanical dissociation – a normal rhythm on ECG with no pulse or cardiac output. Resuscitation measures are almost always unsuccessful.

4. **J – Ventricular aneurysm**
   Ventricular aneurysm is a late complication of transmural myocardial infarc-tion. It results from replacement of the infarcted muscle by a thin layer of collagenous scar tissue that progressively stretches and bulges as the intraven-tricular pressure rises during systole. Complications of ventricular aneurysms include arrhythmias, left ventricular failure and mural thrombosis with systemic embolisation; rupture of the aneurysm itself is rare.

5. **C – Dressler's syndrome**
   Dressler's syndrome is a rare type of pericarditis that presents weeks or months after a myocardial infarct. Patients present with chest pain, pyrexia, a pericardial effusion and a high ESR. It is caused by an immune-mediated response to damaged cardiac tissue. Anti-inflammatory medication, including systemic corticosteroids, may be necessary.

6. **E – Mitral valve incompetence**
   The patient's symptoms and signs suggest the development of mitral valve incompetence. This is a common complication caused by ischaemic damage to the papillary muscle, particularly when the infarct is posterior. In a small number of patients, the papillary muscle can rupture completely leading to sudden and torrential mitral valve incompetence. In the late stages after an infarct, post-ischaemic fibrosis and atrophy can lead to shortening of the papillary muscle and varying grades of mitral valve incompetence.

8. ARRHYTHMIA AND CONDUCTION DISTURBANCES

1. **J – Ventricular tachycardia**
   Broad complex tachycardia is a potentially life-threatening condition which requires diagnosis before the correct treatment can be given. The underlying arrhythmia may be supraventricular in origin with co-existing bundle branch block or it may be ventricular. ECG findings favouring a diagnosis of ventricu-lar tachycardia include QRS concordance in the chest leads, left axis devia-tion, fusion and capture beats. In this case, as long as the BP holds up, the treatment of choice is IV lignocaine followed, if necessary, by amiodarone.

Electrolyte abnormalities (e.g. hypokalaemia, hypomagnesaemia) should be corrected urgently. If the drugs are ineffective or the BP falls, synchronised DC shock should be administered.

2. **B – Atrial flutter with 2:1 block**
Atrial flutter is a co-ordinated but ineffective electrical state in which atrial depolarisation occurs approximately 300 times/min. Fortunately, the atrio-ventricular node is rarely able to conduct that fast and a block results which may be variable but which is often 2:1. Thus a narrow complex (i.e. supraventricular or nodal) tachycardia with a rate of approximately 150 bpm is atrial flutter until proven otherwise. 'Sawtooth' pattern flutter waves may be visible on ECG, especially in V1, or may be revealed when atrioventricular node conduction is slowed temporarily by Valsalva manoeuvre, carotid sinus massage or an intravenous bolus of adenosine. Cardioversion is often achieved by one of the above methods but, if necessary, intravenous vera-pamil, amiodarone and DC cardioversion are all useful.

3. **A – Atrial fibrillation**
Atrial fibrillation is common, especially in the elderly. Chaotic, rapid electri-cal activity in the atria results in an irregular ventricular rhythm. It occurs in all types of heart disease and also as a result of infection, thyrotoxicosis, neopla-sia and excessive alcohol ingestion. Treatment in chronic atrial fibrillation is aimed at controlling the ventricular rate, usually with digoxin. Warfarin is used to prevent thrombus formation since, without anticoagulation, the risk of embolic stroke is 5% per year. In acute presentations, sinus rhythm will often be restored spontaneously once the underlying cause has been treated. If rate control is necessary, digoxin or amiodarone is effective but, as with all tach-yarrhythmias, if atrial fibrillation is poorly tolerated, DC cardioversion may be necessary.

4. **C – Complete heart block**
Acute inferior myocardial infarction frequently results in conduction abnor-malities. In this case, the rate is typical of a ventricular escape rhythm, indi-cating that complete heart block is present. If it is asymptomatic, it would be reasonable to attempt to manage the bradycardia conservatively since many cases resolve spontaneously within a few days. If however, hypotension develops, pacing using a temporary wire, or external cardiac pacemaker may be required. In anterior infarction, temporary pacing is mandatory even if complete heart block is asymptomatic.

5. **H – Mobitz type 2 block**
Atrio-ventricular block may be first, second or third degree. In first degree heart block the PR interval is prolonged (> 0.22 seconds) but conduction of every atrial depolarisation occurs, resulting in a QRS complex after every P wave. In third degree block there is complete dissociation with QRS complexes occurring entirely independently from atrial activity. In second

degree block there is failure of conduction of some but not all P waves. The classification of second degree block is divided into two types: Mobitz type 1 block (the Wenckebach phenomenon), where the PR interval lengthens over successive beats until QRS complex is dropped, and Mobitz type 2 block, where the PR interval is fixed but QRS complexes are dropped intermittently. Asymptomatic Mobitz type 2 second degree block should be treated with temporary pacing in the context of acute anterior myocardial infarction but this is not necessary for inferior infarction.

9. SIDE-EFFECTS OF ANTI-ARRHYTHMIC DRUGS

1. J – Verapamil
Verapamil injection is useful in the termination of supraventricular tachycardias but it has a marked hypotensive and bradycardic effect. This makes it unsafe to use in patients taking beta-blockers and in those with pre-existing hypotension, conductive disorders, bradycardia or heart failure.

2. A – Adenosine
A transient sensation of chest tightness is almost invariable during use of adenosine. Bronchospasm is also common so the drug should be used with caution in patients with asthma. Both side-effects and the therapeutic effect of AV nodal blockade are prolonged if the patient is taking dipyridamole so in these circumstances, if it is absolutely necessary to use adenosine, the starting dose should be greatly reduced.

3. B – Amiodarone
Amiodarone commonly causes both hypothyroidism and hyperthyroidism as a result of its high iodine content. Prolonged administration can result in formation of corneal microdeposits, phototoxicity, slate-grey discoloration of the skin and a diffuse pneumonitis, which may progress to pulmonary fibrosis if the drug is not stopped.

4. I – Sotalol
Torsade de pointes, a form of ventricular tachycardia, occurs in conditions associated with a prolonged QT interval. There are several inherited syndromes causing prolonged QT but drugs are a far more common cause. Amongst the most frequently used drugs are sotalol, amiodarone, quinine, chlorpromazine, haloperidol, erythromycin, terfenadine and astemizole.

5. **H – Propranolol**
    Sleep disturbance, vivid dreams and nightmares are a class effect of beta-blockers but occur mostly with the lipid-soluble drugs. Water-soluble beta-blockers, such as atenolol, are less well absorbed across the blood–brain barrier, and so cause less of a problem.

10. LEFT VENTRICULAR FAILURE

1. **E – Hypertrophic obstructive cardiomyopathy**
    Hypertrophic obstructive cardiomyopathy (HOCM) causes symptoms similar to those of aortic stenosis. In contrast to aortic stenosis, however, the haemo-dynamic derangement in HOCM arises beneath the aortic valve as a result of the hypertrophied septum partially occluding the left ventricular outflow tract. Signs include a prominent apex beat, jerky carotid pulse and harsh ejection systolic murmur. The severity of obstruction, and thus loudness of the murmur, varies according to the degree of ventricular filling in diastole. This feature may be used to differentiate HOCM from aortic stenosis and is most easily demonstrated by asking the patient to perform the Valsalva manoeuvre. During the Valsalva, raised intrathoracic pressure reduces ventricular filling, thus worsening both the outflow obstruction and the murmur. After release of the Valsalva, the sudden increase in ventricular filling relieves the obstruction and the murmur becomes less audible.

2. **G – Mitral stenosis**
    Mitral stenosis is almost always a result of rheumatic fever. It usually presents insidiously with fatigue and dyspnoea although, occasionally, flash pulmonary oedema may occur, either spontaneously or as a result of new onset atrial fibrillation. Signs include malar flush, 'tapping' apex beat (which represents a palpable first heart sound), loud first heart sound, opening snap and a rumbling mid-diastolic murmur heard at the apex and radiating into the axilla. The opening snap becomes earlier and the murmur becomes longer as the degree of stenosis worsens but the opening snap disappears altogether if the valve becomes immobile. Atrial fibrillation is usual in advanced disease but if the patient is still in sinus rhythm, the murmur becomes louder at the end of diastole as the atrium contracts – so-called 'pre-systolic accentuation.' Management is medical, with diuretics and digoxin, until symptoms necessi-tate balloon valvuloplasty, surgical valvotomy or valve replacement. Antibiotic prophylaxis against infective endocarditis is advisable.

3. **F – Mitral regurgitation**
This man has developed acute mitral regurgitation secondary to papillary muscle rupture. The outlook is grave unless urgent mitral valve replacement is possible. In contrast, chronic mitral regurgitation may cause few or no symptoms as long as the left ventricle functions well. It may be caused by rheumatic fever, cardiomyopathy, papillary muscle dysfunction, endocarditis or a number of connective tissue diseases. Principal presenting features include fatigue and dyspnoea but mild cases may be picked up incidentally. The majority of patients are in atrial fibrillation. Other signs include parasternal heave (caused by expansion during systole of the left atrium and also by right ventricular hypertrophy if pulmonary hypertension is present), displacement of the apex beat laterally, and an apical pansystolic murmur radiating to the axilla. As with mitral stenosis, management is medical unless symptoms become intolerable, but surgery is safer and more efficacious if left ventricular function has not deteriorated. Antibiotic prophylaxis against infective endocarditis is mandatory.

4. **A – Aortic regurgitation**
Causes of aortic regurgitation include infective endocarditis, rheumatic fever and severe hypertension, although it is associated with a wide range of diseases and congenital disorders. Many patients with chronic aortic regurgitation are asymptomatic but fatigue and dyspnoea become apparent with worsening regurgitation as the left ventricle progressively dilates and fails. Signs include collapsing pulse, visible capillary pulsation (Quincke's sign), visible pulsation in the neck (Corrigan's sign), head-nodding in time with the pulse (de Musset's sign), pistol-shot sound on auscultation of the femoral pulses (Traube's sign), to-and-fro murmur on compression of the femoral artery with the stethoscope (Duroziez's sign), laterally-displaced and heaving apex beat, an early diastolic murmur at the left sternal edge, an ejection systolic 'flow' murmur (not necessarily as a result of aortic stenosis) and a rumbling mid-diastolic murmur heard at the apex (Austin-Flint murmur) which is caused by the anterior leaflet of the mitral valve vibrating in the regurgitant jet. The aim of treatment is to replace the valve before left ventricular function deteriorates. Antibiotic prophylaxis against infective endocarditis is mandatory.

5. **D – Complete heart block**
The ECG findings demonstrate failure of the atrio-ventricular node to conduct atrial depolarisation to the bundle of His. Where there is complete dissociation, as in this case, the condition is termed complete or third degree heart block. Verapamil and diltiazem (but not the dihydropyridine subgroup of calcium channel blockers) are well-recognised causes of first, second and third degree heart block, especially when given to patients receiving beta-blockers.

11. SECONDARY CAUSES OF HYPERTENSION

1. **J – Renal artery stenosis**
    Renal artery stenosis may arise from fibromuscular dysplasia or atherosclerosis, as is most likely in this case. Since ACE inhibitors may drastically reduce the glomerular filtration rate of a patient with occult renal artery stenosis, and thus cause acute renal failure, urea and electrolytes should always be checked before and one to two weeks after starting them.

2. **C – Conn's syndrome**
    This woman has a hypokalaemic alkalosis which, in the context of undetectable renin, is strongly suggestive of aldosterone excess. Liquorice ingestion gives the same picture. Cushing's syndrome may result in a similar metabolic derangement, especially when caused by ectopic ACTH production, but the possibility of Cushing's syndrome resulting from autonomous secretion of cortisol from the adrenal tumour is excluded by the detectable plasma ACTH. The most likely diagnosis is therefore Conn's syndrome.

3. **B – Coarctation of the aorta**
    When coarctation of the aorta presents in adult life, it is often an incidental finding on routine medical examination. Obstruction to the flow in the aorta results in a difference in BP between the arms, a diminution in pulse pressure in the femoral arteries, radio-femoral delay, left ventricular hypertrophy and an ejection systolic murmur, emanating both from the coarctation and the bicuspid aortic valve with which it is commonly associated. Rib notching, caused by dilatation of the posterior intercostal arteries, is seen on chest X-ray. Without surgery, the prognosis is poor, with stroke, subarachnoid haemorrhage, aortic rupture and infective endocarditis being common before the age of 40 years.

4. **G – Polyarteritis nodosa**
    Polyarteritis nodosa is a vasculitis affecting medium size arteries throughout the body which occurs most commonly in men. There is an association with chronic hepatitis B infection. Initial symptoms include lethargy, malaise, fever and weight loss but organ-specific features subsequently develop. Renal involvement is characterised by infra-renal arterial aneurysms, focal segmental glomerulonephritis, haematuria and hypertension. p-ANCA (anti-myeloperoxidase) antibodies are often detectable but the diagnosis is confirmed by biopsy of an affected organ. Treatment is with high dose corticosteroids and cyclophosphamide, adding azathioprine and using plasmapheresis if necessary.

5. **F – Phaeochromocytoma**
    10% of phaeochromocytomas are extra-adrenal and 10% of patients have multiple phaeochromocytomas. Furthermore, a minority of adrenal phaeochromocytomas are too small to be visualised by CT or MRI scanning. Further investigations in this case would therefore include a scan using MIBG tracer, which is taken up by phaeochromocytomas, and whole body venous

catheter sampling, in which blood samples from around the body are assayed for catecholamines. Pre-operative management requires treatment with an alpha-blocker, such as phenoxybenzamine and a beta-blocker, such as propranolol. When treatment is started, alpha-blockade must be instituted before beta-blockade in order to avoid a hypertensive crisis.

12. SIDE-EFFECTS OF ANTIHYPERTENSIVE DRUGS

1. A – Atenolol

Bronchial and bronchiolar smooth muscle express beta-2-adrenoceptors whilst the myocardium expresses beta-1-adrenoceptors. The cardioselective beta-blockers, which have a greater effect at beta-1 than beta-2 receptors, thus cause less bronchoconstriction than non-selective agents such as propranolol. Nonetheless, the risk of precipitating bronchospasm is still high and all beta-blockers are contraindicated in asthma.

2. J – Nifedipine

Gum hyperplasia is a well-recognised but uncommon side-effect of several of the dihydropyridine group of calcium channel blockers.

3. E – Enalapril

Dry cough is a class effect of ACE inhibitors which is probably caused by elevated bradykinin levels. Angiotensin II receptor antagonists do not share the problem so, if the cough is troublesome and dose reduction is not possible, it is often useful to change to one of the latter group.

4. H – Minoxidil

Minoxidil is an extremely effective antihypertensive and is similar to hydralazine in causing tachycardia and peripheral oedema. It is very rarely used in women because of its side-effect of hypertrichosis; this quality is made use of in the treatment of male-pattern baldness, where it is applied topically to the scalp in the form of a lotion.

5. F – Hydralazine

Hydralazine is a very effective vasodilator antihypertensive drug. It is usually given in combination with a beta-blocker and a diuretic in order to avoid reflex tachycardia and peripheral oedema. Unfortunately, prolonged treatment at higher doses is associated with development of a systemic lupus erythematosus-like syndrome.

13. TYPES OF ANAEMIA

1. **F – Iron deficiency anaemia**
   This patient has a microcytic hypochromic anaemia, the most common cause of which is iron deficiency. Most iron deficiency is due to blood loss, usually from the gastrointestinal tract or uterus. In this patient, the findings at colonoscopy strongly suggest a carcinoma of the proximal colon. Such tumours often bleed from their ulcerated surface and while this may not be obvious as overt rectal bleeding, a faecal occult blood test is usually positive. Over several months this insidious bleeding leads to iron deficiency anaemia.

2. **H – Megaloblastic anaemia**
   This patient has a macrocytic normochromic anaemia. Anaemia is common in coeliac disease due to malabsorption of iron and/or folic acid. The dietary iron supplements have probably prevented significant iron deficiency and the most likely cause of this patient's anaemia is therefore folate deficiency. Lack of folic acid causes defective DNA synthesis and results in large erythroblasts with immature nuclei (megaloblasts) in the bone marrow. Hypersegmented neutrophils in the peripheral blood are a characteristic feature of megaloblastic anaemia.

3. **C – Aplastic anaemia**
   This patient has a severe anaemia and pancytopenia. Pancytopenia can be caused by a number of different conditions, but the absence of reticulocytes and the hypocellular bone marrow indicate bone marrow failure. The anaemia is therefore an aplastic anaemia. About half the cases of acquired aplastic anaemia are idiopathic, though immune mechanisms almost certainly play a role.

4. **G – Macrocytic anaemia**
   This patient has a macrocytic normochromic anaemia. The absence of megaloblastic change in the bone marrow rules out megaloblastic anaemia, which can occur due to the toxic effect of alcohol on erythropoiesis or to dietary folate deficiency, and also excludes pernicious anaemia. Alcohol excess is a common cause of macrocytosis in an otherwise normal individual. The exact mechanism is uncertain but may be due to incorporation of excess lipids into red cells which leads to an increase in cell size.

5. **A – Anaemia of chronic disease**
   This patient has a normocytic normochromic anaemia. This type of anaemia is seen in association with chronic diseases, with endocrine hypofunction and in some haematological disorders such as aplastic anaemia and some haemolytic anaemias. It is also seen acutely following blood loss. This patient has long-standing chronic osteomyelitis, which is almost certainly the cause

of her anaemia. Patients with painful chronic diseases who take non-steroidal anti-inflammatory drugs can also develop microcytic hypochromic anaemia from chronic blood loss associated with gastritis.

6. **D – Autoimmune haemolytic anaemia**
   This patient has a normocytic normochromic anaemia. The presence of unconjugated hyperbilirubinaemia and spherocytes in the blood film strongly support a diagnosis of haemolytic anaemia. The direct antiglobulin test (Coombs' test) detects autoantibody on the surface of red cells and when positive indicates an autoimmune haemolytic anaemia (AIHA). These anaemias can be divided into 'warm' and 'cold' types depending on whether the antibody attaches better to the red cells at 37°C or at a lower temperature. SLE is a recognised cause of 'warm' AIHA.

14. MACROCYTOSIS

1. **F – Liver disease**
   This patient has primary biliary cirrhosis (PBC) as evidenced by her auto-antibodies. This condition is characterised by the presence of anti-mitochondrial antibodies but anti-smooth muscle antibodies are often present as well. The patients are classically middle-aged women (the sex ratio being 6:1 F:M) and they may suffer episodes of pruritus years before they are ever clinically jaundiced. PBC is classically associated with peri-orbital xanthelasma.

2. **J – Reticulocytosis**
   This West African patient has an acute right lower lobe pneumonia which has precipitated an acute haemolytic process. This could be an auto-immune haemolytic anaemia associated with a mycoplasma infection but in this case it may well be due to a commonly inherited disorder, G6PD deficiency. This disorder is common in West Africans and may be precipitated by acute stressors such as infection, severe illness or more commonly medications. The African variety of this disorder is usually self limiting but the Mediterranean variety may prove more malignant.

3. **E – Hypothyroidism**
   This patient has signs and symptoms suggestive of hypothyroidism. Such patients may have a macrocytosis as a direct result of their thyroid disease but may also have an associated pernicious anaemia. It is therefore important to check their auto-antibody screen.

4. **H – Myeloma**
    This patient has signs, symptoms and investigations suggestive of myeloma.
    Other investigations may include a serum calcium, plasma electrophoresis
    and a blood film and bone marrow aspirate looking for the presence of
    plasma cells.

15. HAEMOLYTIC ANAEMIA

1. **C – CLL induced AIHA**
    This patient has a warm type Coombs' positive AIHA associated with chronic
    lymphocytic leukaemia. This disorder is principally seen in the elderly and is
    extremely rare before the age of 45. It often runs a relatively benign course
    and treatment (hydroxyurea) is reserved for more fulminant cases such as the
    patient described.

2. **J – Sickle cell disease**
    This patient is having an acute sickle cell crisis. The bony pain and oxygen
    desaturation is caused by sickling of red cells causing bony infarcts and pneu-
    monitis. A precipitating cause should be sought and treated and supportive
    therapy including opiate analgesia, fluids, blood transfusion and high flow
    oxygen should be given. In severe cases exchange transfusion and assisted
    ventilation may also be required.

3. **H – Methyldopa induced AIHA**
    This is another warm type AIHA associated with methyldopa. This anti-hyper-
    tensive is rarely used as a first-line therapy except in pregnancy induced
    hypertension. The mechanism of antibody induction remains unclear but
    immediate withdrawal of the drug is necessary. The antibodies however may
    persist for several months.

4. **G – Hereditary spherocytosis**
    This patient has hereditary spherocytosis which is the commonest hereditary
    haemolytic anaemia in Northern Europeans. The disorder is caused by a
    defective gene for the erythrocyte membrane protein, spectrin. Anaemia may
    present at any age and is associated with acute jaundice due to haemolysis.
    Other clinical features include splenomegaly and pigmented gallstones. The
    blood film may show a reticulocytosis, between 5–20%, and spherocytes. The
    osmotic fragility test is positive.

5. **B – Beta-thalassaemia**
    This young boy has features suggestive of β-thalassaemia major. The radi-
    ographic changes of the skull X-ray are characteristic and are a result of the
    expansion of the marrow into the bone cortex. Patients often present in the
    first year after birth with severe anaemia. They commonly get

hepatosplenomegaly but most of their problems arise due to repeated blood transfusions with resultant iron overload. Iron deposition in the various organs leads to cardiac failure, hypothyroidism, diabetes mellitus and cirrhosis. The problem is avoided by giving concomitant desferrioxamine infusions with each blood transfusion which chelates the iron.

Haemolysis, the increased rate of breakdown of circulating red cells has many causes including congenital abnormalities of the red cell structure, enzyme deficiencies and the haemoglobinopathies. It may also arise due to secondary acquired factors such as prosthetic valve fragmentation, infection, drugs and malignancy.

Haemolysis is characterised by increased red cell breakdown, red cell production and damaged red cells. These features are evidenced by

- Raised unconjugated serum bilirubin
- Raised urinary urinobilinogen
- Reduced or absent serum haptoglobins
- Reticulocytosis
- Changes in red cell morphology
- Decreased red cell survival time

16. APLASTIC ANAEMIA

1. **B – Chlorpromazine**
    This patient has been started on chlorpromazine which has numerous side-effects including aplastic anaemia. Other psychiatric drugs causing aplastic anaemia include mianserin and promazine.

2. **E – Gold**
    The aplastic anaemia in this case is a result of gold therapy. Unlike the other disease modifying agents (DMARDs – see EMQs Volume 2 – Musculoskeletal chapter question 14) it may be given by intramuscular injection. It may also cause a nephrotic syndrome, severe skin reactions, peripheral neuropathy and pulmonary fibrosis.

3. **H – Phenytoin**
    After neurosurgical procedures it is common practice to place patients on prophylactic anti-epileptics such as phenytoin.

4. **I – Propylthiouracil**
    Carbimazole is the first-line treatment in most areas of the UK for thyrotoxicosis. It has several common side-effects including aplastic anaemia and skin rashes. Propylthiouracil is substituted where patients are unable to tolerate the carbimazole as in this case. However, it too may cause an aplastic anaemia and patients starting antithyroid treatment should be warned about this relatively common side-effect.

5. **J – Tolbutamide**
    Older diabetic patients should not be started on any of the longer acting sulphonylureas, such as chlorpropamide, as they commonly cause hypoglycaemia in this group. Gliclazide and tolbutamide are therefore used.

    Aplastic anaemia, a pancytopenia resulting from aplasia of the bone marrow, may present with features of the anaemia, neutropenia or thrombocytopenia or a combination of the three. Drug therapies are a relatively common cause and patients being placed on any of these medications should be told to see a doctor immediately if they develop pharyngitis (the upper respiratory tract is a common site of initial infection), bruising, overt bleeding or feel extremely lethargic and unwell. A simple way to remember the groups of drugs that cause aplastic anaemia is to be suspicious of any 'ANTI' medication – anti-biotic, –inflammatory, –thyroid, –epileptic, –psychotic, –cancer, –histamine and –hyperglycaemia. Remember drugs can cause everything!

17. WHITE CELL DISORDERS

1. **G – Hodgkin's disease**
    The presence of Reed-Sternberg cells in the right cellular background is pathognomonic of Hodgkin's disease. In this case, the mixed inflammatory cell infiltrate accompanying the Reed-Sternberg cells, together with the lack of nodule formation and lymphocyte depletion, is diagnostic of the 'mixed cellularity' subtype of Hodgkin's disease. Fever and night sweats are common 'B' symptoms. The restriction of the disease to one nodal site thus indicates stage 1B disease.

2. **L – Plasma cell myeloma**
    The presence of large numbers of cytologically abnormal plasma cells in the bone marrow, a monoclonal band and lytic bone lesions are diagnostic of plasma cell myeloma. Deposits of multiple myeloma are most commonly found in the vertebrae, ribs and skull. When marrow infiltration is heavy, there is suppression of normal haemopoiesis resulting in varying degrees of pancytopenia. The neoplastic plasma cells produce a paraprotein, most often IgG, which can be detected as a monoclonal band on protein electrophoresis. In 75% of patients, the paraprotein is associated with excretion of light chains in the urine; these are known as Bence-Jones protein.

3. **E – Chronic myeloid leukaemia**

Chronic myeloid leukemia is a neoplasm of multipotent haemopoietic stem cells that show granulocytic differentiation. In 90% of patients, the leukaemic cells bear the Philadelphia chromosome, a reciprocal translocation between chromosomes 9 and 22 resulting in the fusion of the bcr gene and abl proto-oncogene. Replacement of the bone marrow by leukaemic cells causes anaemia and thrombocytopenia while involvement of the spleen results in splenomegaly.

4. **D – Burkitt's lymphoma**

Burkitt's lymphoma is a high grade B-cell lymphoma that is endemic in parts of sub-Saharan Africa where falciparum malaria has a high prevalence. Throughout the rest of the world it occurs sporadically. The endemic form is common in children, particularly in extranodal sites such as the jaw, ovary and retroperitoneum. The tumour cells invariably exhibit a translocation involving the c-myc gene on chromosome 8, usually with chromosome 14. There is a strong association between the endemic form of Burkitt's lymphoma and Epstein-Barr virus; in most patients, viral RNA is demonstrable in the tumour cells by in-situ hybridisation.

5. **B – Acute myeloid leukaemia**

The diagnosis of acute myeloid leukaemia (AML) is made by finding myeloblasts in the bone marrow and peripheral blood. This patient has extensive marrow involvement resulting in profound pancytopenia. The anaemia is responsible for the symptoms of tiredness and dyspnoea on exercise, while the thrombocytopenia leads to easy bruising. In the WHO classification, AML is subdivided into prognostic groups on the basis of cytogenetic and morphological features.

6. **C – B-cell chronic lymphocytic leukaemia**

B-cell chronic lymphocytic leukaemia (B-CLL) is the most common leukaemia of adults in the Western world. It is characterized by peripheral blood lymphocytosis and an uncontrolled monoclonal proliferation of small, mature lymphocytes in the bone marrow, lymph nodes and spleen. The appropriate immunophenotype on flow cytometry is important in confirming the diagnosis. Patients with CLL are often asymptomatic and when symptoms do develop they tend to be non-specific. Generalised lymphadenopathy and hepatosplenomegaly are seen in 50–60% of cases. The bone marrow involvement takes the form of interstitial or nodular infiltrates of small lymphocytes without blasts.

18. COMPLICATIONS OF BLOOD TRANSFUSION

1. **F – Immediate haemolytic transfusion reaction**

   Immediate haemolytic transfusion reaction is evidenced by the short timescale in relation to blood administration and the severity of the reaction. This is almost always caused by ABO incompatibility between donor and recipient blood, leading to complement activation and red cell haemolysis (hence haemoglobinuria was detected). The transfusion must be stopped and hydrocortisone 100 mg and chlorpheniramine 10 mg administered i.v. immediately. Fluid resuscitation will also be required to maintain blood volume. 90% of cases are due to clerical error, and all documentation should therefore be rechecked, and donor and recipient blood re-grouped. Diagnosis is based on finding the clerical error. Renal failure and DIC are serious consequences of an acute haemolytic transfusion reaction, and may lead to death.

2. **D – Fluid overload**

   These are the cardinal signs of fluid overload. The normal fluid requirement of a healthy 70 kg man is 2–3 litres/24 hrs. In an elderly patient such as this, with poor renal and possibly cardiac function, fluid, especially blood products should be administered slowly, and the patient clinically monitored for signs of heart failure. Fluid overload, as in this case, is managed in the same way as acute left ventricular failure (i.e. sit the patient up, administer high concentration oxygen and i.v. frusemide +/- diamorphine).

3. **H – Non-haemolytic febrile transfusion reaction**

   Non-haemolytic febrile transfusion reactions are a relatively common adverse consequence of blood transfusion. They typically occur within hours of the start of transfusion in patients who have been previously exposed to allogenic leucocytes either by a previous transfusion or through pregnancy. The reaction is caused by the presence of anti-HLA antibodies against donor leucocytes with subsequent pyrogen release from damaged white cells. The transfusion should be slowed or stopped, and an antipyretic such as paracetamol administered. Leucocyte-depleted blood or a white cell filter can be used if the problem is recurrent. In contrast, delayed haemolytic transfusion reaction refers to haemolysis of transfused red cells one to three weeks after transfusion caused usually by antibodies to rhesus antigens.

4. **G – Iron overload**

   Iron overload is an inevitable consequence of repeated blood transfusions, and causes damage to endocrine glands, the myocardium, liver and pancreas. It can be prevented with nightly parenteral desferrioxamine, but compliance can be a problem in teenagers. Untreated, patients typically die of cardiac failure in their early twenties.

5   B – Bacterial contamination

A rapid fever spike of > 40°C shortly after the start of a transfusion may be indicative of haemolysis. However, once ABO incompatibility has been excluded, the most likely cause is bacterial contamination of transfused blood. *Yersinia enterocolitica*, a Gram-negative Coccobacillus, is commonly implicated. In contrast, non-haemolytic febrile transfusion reactions produce a slower, less marked rise in temperature (< 40°C).

19. VASCULAR ANATOMY OF THE HEAD AND NECK

1.   A – Abdominal aorta

The abdominal aorta lies on the bodies of the upper four lumbar vertebrae, dividing just to the left of the midline. The inferior vena cava is on its right side, separated at its origin by the right crus of the diaphragm and the cisterna chyli. To the left are the left crus of the diaphragm and left sympathetic trunk. Anteriorly, the aorta is covered by the lesser sac, pancreas, splenic vein, left renal vein, third part of the duodenum and the root of the small gut mesentery. Further anteriorly are the stomach, transverse colon and coils of small intestine.

2.   D – Descending thoracic aorta

The descending thoracic aorta is continuous with the aortic arch at the upper border of the fourth thoracic vertebra. It passes through the posterior mediastinum to pass between the crura of the diaphragm and become the abdominal aorta over the body of the twelfth thoracic vertebra. It passes behind the hilum of the lung and the pericardium separates it from the left atrium.

3.   C – Coeliac trunk

The coeliac plexus is the largest of the autonomic nervous plexuses: it is made up of the right and left coeliac ganglia. It surrounds the origin of the coeliac trunk, lying across the crura of the diaphragm between the suprarenal glands. It receives the greater and lesser splanchnic nerves, and branches from both vagi and phrenic nerves.

4.   J – Superior mesenteric artery

The superior mesenteric artery supplies the gut from the inferior duodenum to the junction of its proximal two-thirds and distal third of the transverse colon. It arises from the aorta 1 cm distal to the coeliac trunk and is crossed by the body of the pancreas and splenic vein before passing downwards to the right iliac fossa within the root of the mesentery. It crosses the inferior vena cava, right ureter and the psoas muscle.

5. **G – Right common iliac artery**
    The right common iliac artery passes obliquely across the bodies of the fourth and fifth lumbar vertebrae separated from them by the termination of the left common iliac vein and the formation of the inferior vena cava. Other posterior relations are the sympathetic trunk, the obturator nerve and the lumbosacral trunk.

20. VENOUS ANATOMY OF THE LOWER LIMB

1. **B – Anterior to the medial malleolus**
    I – Subcutaneously, posteromedial to the knee joint
    E – Medial to the femoral artery in the femoral triangle
    The great saphenous vein originates from the medial end of the dorsal venous arch. It ascends 1 cm anterior to the medial malleolus, along the medial calf, posteromedial to the knee joint, and along the medial thigh to the saphenofemoral junction. The surface marking of the latter is in the groin crease medial to the palpable femoral artery. The great saphenous vein receives the posterior arch vein just below the knee, which itself receives three or four perforators within 10 cm of the medial malleolus. Another constant perforator is at the mid-thigh level directly to the great saphenous vein.

2. **F – Posterior to the lateral malleolus**
    The small saphenous vein originates from the lateral end of the dorsal venous arch. It ascends behind the lateral malleolus along the back of the calf and ends by piercing the fascial roof of the popliteal fossa to enter the popliteal vein. The saphenopopliteal junction is variable in its site, and may be 4–5 cm above the line of the knee joint.

3. **J – Superficial to the popliteal artery at the level of the knee joint**
    The popliteal vein lies superficial to the popliteal artery as it passes through the popliteal fossa from its origin, between the heads of the gastrocnemeus muscle, to the adductor hiatus, where it becomes the femoral vein.

21. LIMB ISCHAEMIA

1. **B – Aortic dissection**
    Acute non-traumatic limb ischaemia in young people raises the possibility of intra-arterial injection of recreational drugs, emboli from abnormal heart valves and dissections of abnormal vessels, such as in Marfan's syndrome. The back pain in this lady suggests an acute dissection, the early death of her mother being a supportive feature of a familial disorder.

2. **G – Post-catheter femoral artery false aneurysm**
This patient has a false aneurysm of the femoral artery, that has produced compression and thrombosis of the parent vessel. Emergency femoral thrombectomy and closure of the aneurysmal opening are required.

3. **A – Acute on chronic lower limb ischaemia**
This patient has acute on chronic occlusive arterial disease of the right leg requiring urgent angiography and treatment, possibly with thrombolysis and dilation, or if this is not effective, surgical reconstruction. This is an important differential diagnosis in acute limb ischaemia, as management is more complex than with an acute embolic episode.

4. **J – Thrombosis of a popliteal aneurysm**
This patient has occluded his second popliteal aneurysm, on this occasion with severe ischaemia due to lack of adequate collateral flow. The popliteal arteries are deeply placed in the popliteal fossa and small aneurysms may go unnoted. Other possible diagnoses are popliteal entrapment and cystic degenerative disease at this site: these conditions usually present with claudication. Emergency revascularisation, bypassing the aneurysm or diseased segment, is required for acute ischaemia.

5. **C – Embolism**
The acute left leg ischaemia with normal vessels on the right, and no history of trauma, is suggestive of acute embolism. A common source is the left side of the heart, either related to valvular disease or from thrombus secondary to myocardial infarction. The latter may produce a large enough embolus to block the aortic bifurcation (saddle embolus) producing bilateral leg ischaemia. The likely diagnosis in this patient is a tumour embolus, from tumour extension along a pulmonary vein: emergency embolectomy is required.

22. VENOUS THROMBOSIS

1. **H – Superficial venous thrombosis**
Superficial venous thrombosis is very tender to palpation and produces a local inflammatory response in surrounding tissues as it becomes established. This may occur in clotting of an arteriovenous fistula, or varicosites of the leg, perianal region or an arteriovenous malformation. Spontaneous thrombosis unrelated to trauma or other precipitating factors can be associated with underlying neoplasia (Trousseau's sign). As in this patient, there may be no symptoms related to the precipitating disease, common sites being pancreas, stomach and lung.

2. **G – Superior vena caval obstruction**

This lady has acute on chronic respiratory problems, accompanied by upper extremity oedema from superior vena caval obstruction. The probable diagnosis is squamous carcinoma of the lung, with direct spread or secondary lymph node involvement compressing the superior vena cava. There may be added signs of T1 root involvement, (i.e. Horner's syndrome) and weakness of the small muscles of the hand.

3. **E – Postphlebitic syndrome**

This lady has a recurrent venous ulcer, the most common cause being the postphlebitic syndrome. This is typically due to postpartum venous thrombosis producing incompetence of the deep and superficial venous systems.

4. **F – Pulmonary embolism**

This patient has symptoms of pulmonary embolism. This is secondary to perioperative immobilisation and changes in clotting factors, and linked with neoplastic disease. Emboli originate from the lower limbs, but there may be minimal signs of venous thrombosis and a pulmonary infarct may not be demonstrated radiologically. The infarct may produce an alteration in the ventilation perfusion ratio and be demonstrable on spiral CT.

5. **B – Deep venous thrombosis**

This lady has a postpartum iliofemoral venous thrombosis. The condition is more common on the left side where the common iliac vein can be compressed by the overlying right common iliac artery. Active anticoagulation is required to reduce the chances of pulmonary embolism and also reduce the instance of the postphlebitic syndrome.

23. LEG PAIN

1. **H – Torn fibres of the soleus muscle**

The site of pain suggests a muscle tear resulting from the unaccustomed exercise. Common tendon injuries include partial or complete rupture of the tendo calcaneus, but calf muscle tears are usually fibres of the soleus, with accompanying haemorrhage. The popular diagnosis of a torn plantaris tendon is a rarity.

2. **J – Venous thrombosis**

Hospitalisation increases the incidence of venous thrombosis, this being more common on the left side as the right common iliac artery lies across the left common iliac vein. Another important differential diagnosis is an acute embolus from thrombus developing adjacent to the myocardial infarction. Acute ischaemia typically presents with the six Ps (pain, paraesthesia, paralysis, pulseless, pale and perishingly cold). Swelling is not a feature but both conditions may produce white or blue discoloration: swelling may be accompanied by mild sensory changes in venous as well as arterial thrombosis.

3.   **A – Bone tumour**
Children are prone to leg pains and bruises, 'growing pains' usually occur between 5 and 15, particularly 'shin splints' of the lower tibia: they can be severe, lasting for many hours. In the absence of injury, a progressive pain must be thoroughly investigated. Infection of a bone or joint must be excluded and a malignant bone tumour may present in this way. This boy has an osteogenic sarcoma of his lower femur. Clinical examination usually shows diffuse swelling and deep tenderness by the time of presentation. Radiographs show replacement of the bone with dense radiating 'sunray spicules' and calcification beneath the peripherally raised periosteum (Codman's triangle).

4.   **G – Torn cartilage**
Acute injuries include fractures, dislocations, and tears of ligaments and cartilages. Torn cartilages, as in this patient, become interposed between the femoral and tibial condyles, preventing full extension. The tissue may return to its original position, subsequently producing locking and 'giving way' of the knee joint in certain movements. McMurray's Test, in which the knee is straightened with the tibia held in medial or lateral rotation, produces pain or locking as the damaged cartilage comes between the adjacent condyles.

5.   **E – Osteochondritis**
This patient has osteochondritis of the medial femoral condyle and an associated loose body which has produced the episode of locking. The bony abnormality may be demonstrated by MRI and the loose body by radiographs in certain joint positions. The condition may follow trauma or be a local area of defective ossification. Stress injuries may also affect the tibial tubercle (Osgood-Schlatter's disease) and distal pole of the patella (Sinding-Larsen's disease).

24. PAIN AND SWELLING IN THE LOWER LIMB

1.   **H – Secondary lymphoedema**
The cause is malignant infiltration of the inguinal/iliac lymph nodes leading to obstructed lymphatic flow from the lower limb and subsequent swelling. Although deep vein thrombosis may also complicate pelvic carcinomatosis, the clinical presentation usually also includes pain and tenderness (see vignette 2).

2. **D – Deep vein thrombosis**

This patient has a deep vein thrombosis which has probably occurred as a result of prolonged immobility during her long haul flight (the venous stasis of Virchow's triad). Swelling is the main sign but tenderness and a firmness of the muscles on palpation, and ankle oedema are often also present. Homan's dorsiflexion test is inaccurate and should be abandoned. Venous imaging using B-mode ultrasound is the diagnostic test of choice (replacing bipedal ascending contrast phlebography).

3. **F – Primary lymphoedema**

This condition affects about 1:6000 and has a 3:1 F:M predominance. The diagnosis is made after all other causes of oedema have been excluded as in this case. There is an accumulation of tissue fluid as a result of a defect within the lymphatic system. The cause is not known but a genetic defect is possible on the basis that 30% of patients (as in this case) have a family history of swollen legs.

4. **A – Atherosclerosis**

The clinical syndrome is one of rest pain, which is caused by severe chronic arterial insufficiency, usually as a result of atherosclerotic disease. The pain is usually experienced in the dorsum of the foot and toes, being worse at night. The pain is severe, usually requiring opiate analgesia for symptomatic relief. The patient commonly relieves the pain by hanging the foot over the side of the bed or as in this case taking to sleeping in a chair. The findings of a positive Buerger's test, and of dependent rubor support a diagnosis of critical ischaemia and severe arterial insufficiency is confirmed by the very low ABPI.

5. **I – Spinal stenosis**

This is an important differential diagnosis of intermittent claudication. The spinal canal is narrowed usually by lumbar degenerative spondylosis and pain/weakness and tiredness occur in the lower limbs on walking. The two diagnoses may usually be distinguished by the resolution time of symptoms which is much longer in spinal stenosis. Root tension signs are rarely present and neurological examination may be normal or demonstrate neurological signs in both lower limbs. Foot pulses may be present in intermittent (vascular) claudication, but the APBI of 1.0 after exercise excludes any vascular cause of this patient's symptoms (the situation is difficult when the two problems co-exist).

25. LEG SWELLING

1. C – Filariasis
This lady is suffering from filariasis, a tropical disease caused by a nematode worm. The larvae of the organism obstruct the lymphatics, producing secondary lymphoedema. Although there are no other clinical features of the disease, the eosinophilia points to a parasite infection. The lymphoedema is markedly improved with medication.

2. I – Primary lymphoedema
Primary lymphoedema may present at birth (lymphoedema congenitalia), at puberty (lymphoedema praecox) or later in life (lymphoedema tarda). A familial form is termed Milroy's disease. It is often precipitated by minor trauma or an insect bite, becoming bilateral at a late date. In the early stages the oedema pits, but as the condition progresses and bouts of cellulitis occur, tissues become more rigid; also, the skin becomes keratinised, particularly over the anterior aspect of the ankle.

3. E – Malignancy
Enlarged nodes are usually inflammatory or neoplastic in origin, and there is no sign of an infective focus in this lady. The previous wide excision of a foot lesion is suggestive of malignancy, and the late lymph node recurrence and secondary lymphoedema is probably indicative of recurrent malignant melanoma.

4. J – Venous thrombosis
This lady has a post-operative left iliofemoral venous thrombosis. Precipitating factors are immobilisation, perioperative changes of clotting factors and peroperative pelvic venous trauma. The left leg is more commonly affected due to compression of the left common iliac vein by the right common iliac artery

5. G – Nephrotic syndrome
Hypoprotinaemia could be due to hepatic and alimentary causes, but there are no clinical manifestations suggestive of these diseases in this patient: quantification of proteinuria of greater than 5 g per 24 hrs would confirm the presence of the nephrotic syndrome. In this age group, the most likely causes are the glomerular nephrites, SLE, hypertensive renal disease and diabetes.

26. LEG ULCERS I

1. **J – Venous**
   This patient has lipodermatosclerosis, which are the chronic skin changes seen after venous thrombosis or varicose veins. The 'eczema' surrounding the ulcer is varicose eczema. This patient has now developed a venous ulcer, classically arising above the medial malleolus and extending around the lower calf or 'gaitor' region. This patient would benefit from compression bandaging and later compression stockings to avoid further ulceration. The normal Doppler ratios indicate that compression would not compromise the arterial supply to the lower limbs.

2. **A – Arterial**
   This gentleman has developed an arterial ulcer secondary to peripheral vascular disease. It is important with diabetic patients to exclude a peripheral sensory neuropathy which may be contributing to the ulceration. Doppler ratios in diabetic patients are usually falsely high due to the rigid vessels. However, in this case the readings indicate severe peripheral vascular disease and this ulcer will heal poorly unless some form of intervention is undertaken; he may end up with a below knee amputation.

3. **D – Neuropathic**
   This patient has developed a peripheral sensory neuropathy secondary to his alcohol abuse. Neuropathic ulcers occur at sites of trauma such as the distal toes and the heels. Such ulcers are often quite difficult to heal.

4. **F – Pyoderma gangrenosum**
   This lesion is pyoderma gangrenosum which may be mistaken for a venous ulcer, particularly in the early stages. Other lesions commonly mistaken for simple venous ulcers include basal and squamous cell carcinomas.

5. **G – Sickle cell disease**
   This patient has sickle cell disease which may cause ulceration of the lower limbs. The patients have normal Doppler ratios and are treated with compression bandaging as with venous ulceration.

   All patients presenting with lower limb ulceration should have Doppler ratios measured. A ratio > 0.80 is usually taken as the safe cut-off for compression bandaging to be applied. Below this point compression will lead to worsening ischaemia and healing will be impaired. Patients who benefit from compression bandaging should be fitted with compression stockings to avoid future ulceration.

27. LEG ULCERS II

1. **A – Artefactual**
Artefactual ulcers can be difficult to diagnose and impossible to treat. Patients deny involvement, even when this is demonstrated to them. Features suggestive of this diagnosis are: straight edges, unusual grooves, normal surrounding skin and nutrition of the remainder of the leg, faecal organisms and failure to respond to every treatment. Although other forms of ulcer commonly recur, they do respond to appropriate therapy.

2. **D – Neuropathic**
Neuropathic ulcers are common in diabetic patients and, more rarely, are seen with peripheral nerve and spinal cord disorders. Diabetic patients are also prone to ulcers from arterial disease and infectious complications. The arterial pressure measurement may be misleadingly high because of calcified vessels. The lack of pain means that every diabetic and their carer must be taught to examine the feet, if necessary using a mirror, so that ulcers can be identified and treated, before the onset of severe secondary infection.

3. **G – Squamous cell carcinoma**
This is a malignant leg ulcer as evidenced by the progressive enlargement, the raised edge and the contact bleeding. The diagnosis should be confirmed histologically, and followed by adequate excision and grafting. Malignant ulcers can also develop in long-standing infective lesions, this lesion being termed a Marjolin's ulcer.

4. **F – Scleroderma**
Scleroderma progresses at a variable rate and with variable involvement of systemic tissues, such as the alimentary tract. Ulcers and ischaemic gangrene of the tips of the fingers can be very painful and difficult to manage, often requiring distal amputation: there may be improvement with digital sympathectomy. Ulcers of the lower leg and ankle are equally difficult to manage, and in spite of analgesics, vasodilators and a range of medications, including antimitotic agents, conservative amputation may be necessary.

5. **J – Venous**
The recurrent ulcers could be due to chronic osteomyelitis, however they are situated away from the original injury and are more likely to be venous in origin. The initial injury and subsequent episodes of venous thrombosis, due to tissue injury and prolonged immobilisation, having resulted in long-term incompetence of the deep system. The associated venous hypertension has given rise to skin ulceration, around the lower shin.

ANSWERS TO CHAPTER – RESPIRATORY

1. SURFACE MARKINGS OF THE LUNG AND PLEURA

1. **J – 12th rib**
   This relationship is important in posterior surgical approaches to the kidney and adrenal gland.

2. **H – 10th rib**
   This is the marking of the costodiaphragmatic recess. The base of the lung is usually two rib spaces (5 cm) above this level.

3. **F – 8th rib**
   The oblique fissure of the lung follows the line of the 6th rib. The transverse fissure of the right lung is at the level of the 4th costal cartilage.

4. **D – 4th rib**
   The pleura on the left side is reflected away from the midline and a needle may be inserted into the heart, through the medial end of the 5th and 6th intercostal spaces, without passing through the pleural cavity.

5. **B – 2nd rib**
   The cervical dome of pleura on each side is 2.5 cm above the clavicle, in line with the junction of its medial and middle thirds.

2. RELATIONSHIPS OF THE LUNG

1. **C – Body of the 5th thoracic vertebra**
   The tracheal bifurcation is just to the left of the midline. The 3 cm long right principal bronchus lies more vertical than the 5 cm left. The pulmonary roots extend from the 5th to the 7th thoracic vertebrae.

2. **J – Superior vena cava**
   The superior vena cava, right atrium and inferior vena cava are in line and are related to the mediastinal surface of the right lung anterior to the hilum.

3. **A – Aortic arch**
   The aortic arch lies in the superior mediastinum. It continues as the descending aorta that passes behind the hilum and remains a medial relation of the left lung.

4. **H – Left ventricle**
   The impression is mainly of the left ventricle but also the infundibulum passing to the pulmonary trunk, both overlain by the phrenic and vagus nerves.

5. **B – Azygos vein**
   The azygos vein passes anteriorly to enter the superior vena cava.

3. CHEST PAIN

1. **I – Tietze's syndrome**
   Tietze's syndrome is a benign condition of unknown aetiology consisting of non-specific inflammation and swelling of one or more costal cartilages. The resulting discomfort may be similar to pleuritic pain but local tenderness is elicited on palpation of the lump. Treatment is conservative, with local corticosteroid injection if necessary.

2. **C – Pancoast's tumour**
   This lady has a right apical bronchogenic carcinoma (Pancoast's tumour). Horner's syndrome (ptosis, meiosis, anhydrosis and enophthalmos) has occurred as a result of neoplastic infiltration of the sympathetic outflow.

3. **E – Pulmonary embolism**
   Clinical examination suggests deep venous thrombosis (DVT) of the right leg and pulmonary embolism has occurred as a result. Whilst the risk of developing a DVT is increased by oral contraceptive use, the current consensus holds that this risk is acceptable because pregnancy results in a far higher incidence, even in normal, healthy women. However, the risk becomes less acceptable in the presence of other factors, such as inherited thrombophilias, smoking, obesity and increasing age.

4. **D – Pneumothorax**
   Tall, young men are more prone to spontaneous pneumothorax than the general population. If tension pneumothorax develops, a needle should be inserted immediately into the pleural space on the side of the pneumothorax in the second intercostal space, in the mid-clavicular line. A formal chest drain with an underwater seal should then be inserted. In the absence of tension, however, and if respiration is not otherwise compromised, it is safe to allow the air to be resorbed naturally.

5. **G – Sarcoidosis**
   The clinical diagnosis of sarcoidosis in this case is based on the chronic nature of the presentation, the suggestions of a multi-system disorder, and on the recognition of the shin rash being erythema nodosum. Subsequent investi-

gations would include chest X-ray, looking for bilateral hilar lymphadenopathy, serum calcium and serum angiotensin converting enzyme (ACE). Serum ACE is not a specific test but, when elevated, it is a useful marker of disease activity. In this patient especially, an electrocardiogram and 24-hour ECG are necessary in view of the possibility of cardiac involvement. A definitive diagnosis requires histological evidence of non-caseating granulomata and this is often obtained by trans-bronchial biopsy at bronchoscopy.

4. SHORTNESS OF BREATH

1. F – Mycoplasma pneumonia
Mycoplasma pneumoniae is one of the principal causes of atypical pneumonia. Non-specific symptoms, such as headache, diarrhoea and fatigue, tend to precede chest symptoms and, at presentation, chest X-ray often shows consolidation before auscultatory signs become apparent. *M. pneumoniae* is notable for causing a wide range of extra-pulmonary conditions, including erythema multiforme and cold agglutinin production leading to haemolytic anaemia. There is also a strong association with Guillain-Barré, syndrome.

2. I – Pulmonary embolism
This man has a history suggestive of a colorectal tumour. He is therefore at risk of developing deep venous thrombosis, both as a result of direct venous compression by the tumour and also because of the pro-coagulant effect associated with carcinomatosis. The history of sudden onset dyspnoea strongly suggests pulmonary embolism but it is equally common for the dyspnoea to be of insidious onset, often associated with several episodes of niggling, pleuritic chest pain, if emboli are multiple and small. Frequently there are no radiographic changes on plain chest X-ray but if a wedge infarct is apparent, haemoptysis is likely to feature in the presentation. In this case, either a VQ scan or a CT pulmonary angiogram is necessary to prove the diagnosis but anticoagulation should be started before the test results are available in order to reduce the risk of further life-threatening embolisation.

3. B – Asthma
Wheeze results from turbulence in air flow through constricted airways. In acute severe asthma, polyphonic wheeze is heard throughout the chest but, if the patient tires and is less able to move air in and out, the wheeze may reduce despite there being no relief of bronchoconstriction. Under these circumstances, intubation and ventilation on ITU is almost always necessary.

4.   J – Sarcoidosis

The diagnosis of sarcoidosis in this case is based on the non-specific symptoms of weight loss and malaise coupled with a history of polyuria which is suggestive of hypercalcaemia, a common feature of active sarcoid. A maculopapular or vesicular rash on the face occurs frequently and, if it becomes chronic and granulomatous, is termed 'lupus pernio.' Sarcoidosis is a multi-system granulomatous disease and in cases of insidious onset the presentation may therefore reflect involvement of any organ. More commonly, however, the onset is acute and is characterised by erythema nodosum and bilateral hilar lymphadenopathy on chest X-ray, which is often associated with varying degrees of dyspnoea and non-productive cough.

5.   C – Cryptogenic fibrosing alveolitis

Cryptogenic fibrosing alveolitis (known as idiopathic pulmonary fibrosis in the USA) generally presents in the sixth decade of life. Respiratory symptoms, other than progressive dyspnoea and dry cough, are uncommon. The classic examination findings are digital clubbing and fine end-inspiratory bibasal crackles. As the disease advances, the crackles become prominent throughout inspiration, the patient becomes centrally cyanosed, and cor pulmonale develops (see note below). Pulmonary function tests demonstrate a restrictive defect and are important in assessing progression of disease. High resolution CT scanning of the thorax usually confirms the diagnosis, showing changes starting in the periphery of the lungs and ranging from a ground-glass opacification to a reticular, fibrotic honeycomb pattern.

NB. Cor pulmonale is the term used to describe the process of adaptation and failure that the right side of the heart undergoes as a result of lung disease. The pulmonary vasculature responds to local hypoxia by arteriolar constriction. Thus, in lobar pneumonia, blood flow to the affected lobe is reduced, so minimising the amount of poorly oxygenated blood reaching the systemic circulation. When the pneumonia resolves, the vasoconstriction ceases and flow normalises. On the other hand, if pulmonary hypoxia is widespread and irreversible, as occurs in cryptogenic fibrosing alveolitis, severe chronic obstructive pulmonary disease and many other chronic lung diseases, the resulting arteriolar constriction is equally widespread and irreversible. The direct consequence is pulmonary hypertension. Over time this results in right atrial and right ventricular hypertrophy. Eventually the limit of the heart's ability to adapt to the increased pressure is reached and right ventricular failure then becomes apparent clinically. The principal signs are a raised jugular venous pressure, a third heart sound causing gallop rhythm and ankle oedema. In addition, the pulmonary hypertension results in a loud pulmonary component to the second heart sound and the right ventricular hypertrophy causes a parasternal heave.

5. HAEMOPTYSIS

1. **G – Small cell carcinoma**
   Diplopia and bilateral ptosis are suggestive of a complicated disorder of the central nervous system such as multiple sclerosis or myasthenia gravis. In myasthenia gravis, weakness worsens with exercise but the opposite is true of Lambert-Eaton syndrome, which occurs in 3% of patients with small cell bronchial carcinoma. Other paraneoplastic conditions associated with small cell tumours include syndrome of inappropriate anti-diuretic hormone secretion (SIADH) and ectopic adrenocorticotrophic hormone (ACTH) secretion.

2. **D – Pulmonary abscess**
   Young people with cystic fibrosis may do well for many years with regular vigorous physiotherapy and prompt antibiotic treatment at the first sign of respiratory tract infection. However, there usually comes a time when chest infections become more frequent. Antibiotic resistance develops and, as different treatment regimens are used, the types of colonising and pathogenic organisms gradually change. The usual progression is from 'normal' respiratory pathogens, such as *Streptococcus pneumoniae*, towards *Staphylococcus aureus* and, eventually, *Pseudomonas*. The Gram stain in this case suggests *Staphylococcus*, which is often responsible for cavitating lung disease, resulting in lung abscess, empyema and pneumothorax.

3. **E – Pulmonary embolism**
   This lady's unfortunate history suggests pulmonary metastases as well as pulmonary embolism but the chest X-ray findings point to the correct diagnosis. Pulmonary embolism frequently causes no changes on plain chest X-ray but infarction, which is difficult to differentiate from infective consolidation, occasionally occurs following large emboli.

4. **J – Tuberculosis**
   Primary infection by *Mycobacterium tuberculosis* in healthy adults is usually asymptomatic. An immune response is mounted, resulting in inactivation (but not complete destruction) of mycobacteria, usually within a peripheral pulmonary calcified nodule known as a 'Ghon focus.' Reactivation may occur in the context of relative immunosuppression, such as with corticosteroid use, diabetes mellitus, HIV disease or any severe intercurrent illness. Symptoms are insidious in onset with weight loss, malaise and fever being prominent. Night sweats may also occur. A productive cough with purulent or blood-stained sputum is usual but presentation is often with dyspnoea secondary to lobar collapse or consolidation. The chest X-ray generally shows evidence of apical consolidation, fibrosis and cavitation.

5. **A – Goodpasture's disease**
Goodpasture's disease usually presents as a respiratory tract infection for which no infectious cause can be found. The chest X-ray shows patchy shadowing throughout the lungs. Renal involvement is often missed initially and only becomes apparent as the patient deteriorates. The severity of haemoptysis ranges from flecks in the sputum to life-threatening haemorrhage and is usually worst in young, male smokers. Renal biopsy demonstrates a crescentic, necrotising, rapidly progressive glomerulonephritis. For a diagnosis of Goodpasture's syndrome to be made, antiglomerular basement membrane (anti-GBM) antibodies must be found, either in serum or deposited along the basement membrane. The combination of pulmonary haemorrhage and rapidly progressive glomerulonephritis occurs in a number of immune mediated disorders including the vasculitides such as microscopic polyarteritis. In contrast to Goodpasture's syndrome, however, microscopic polyarteritis is often preceded by a period of constitutional upset, with malaise, weight loss and fever being prominent. Both illnesses are associated with development of anti-myeloperoxidase (p-ANCA) antibodies but anti-GBM antibodies do not occur in microscopic polyarteritis. Thus the term Goodpasture's disease or antiglomerular basement membrane disease is now used for cases where the antiglomerular basement membrane is shown to be present.

6. AUSCULTATORY FINDINGS

1. **C – Bronchial breathing right base**
This lady has aspirated her tea. The most common site for aspirational pneumonia is the right lower lobe because of the anatomy of the bronchial tree. Bronchial breathing occurs because consolidation of the alveoli allows superior transmission of sounds through the bronchi and bronchioles to the periphery of the lung.

2. **B – Absent breath sounds right hemithorax**
This man has a right pneumothorax. If the pneumothorax is small, breath sounds may be audible but reduced. In this case, however, total collapse has occurred. Percussion is hyper-resonant over a pneumothorax.

3. **G – Monophonic wheeze**
Monophonic (i.e. at one pitch) wheeze occurs where a single mass is partially obstructing an airway. Typical lesions include bronchial tumours, as in this case, or inhaled foreign bodies.

4. **F – Fine inspiratory bibasal crackles**
As the illness progresses, the fine crackles heard in cryptogenic fibrosing alveolitis become more prominent and are heard throughout inspiration. For a description of cryptogenic alveolitis, see question 5.4, *Theme: Shortness of breath* page 234.

5.   **A – Absent breath sounds left base**
A left haemothorax presents with the same signs as a left pleural effusion: stony dullness to percussion and absent breath sounds at the left base. If the amount of blood is massive, it may push the mediastinum over to the right, resulting in a displaced trachea and apex beat.

7.   ABNORMAL RESPIRATORY CLINICAL FINDINGS

1.   **A, E, I, J**
Large pneumothoraces cause reduced expansion on the side of the lesion, tracheal deviation away from the lesion with reduced or absent breath sounds, tactile vocal fremitus and vocal fremitus. The percussion note is normal or hyper-resonant.

2.   **A, E, G, H, J**
Large pleural effusions cause reduced expansion on the side of the lesion. Tracheal deviation only occurs with huge effusions and is away from the lesion, percussion note is classically describes as 'stony dull' and breath sounds, tactile vocal fremitus and vocal fremitus are reduced or absent. In smaller effusions bronchial breathing may be heard at the fluid/air interface just above the effusion.

3.   **B, C, F**
Right middle lobe pneumonia may be missed clinically if one forgets to examine the right axillary region. As with all areas of consolidation there may be reduced expansion, bronchial breathing and coarse crackles heard with inspiration.

4.   **A, E, F, H, J**
Lobar collapse produces tracheal deviation towards the area of collapse. Expansion may be reduced and breath sounds, percussion note and vocal fremitus will be also be reduced. Causes of lobar collapse include pneumonia and proximal obstructing lesions such as hilar lymphadenopathy, a foreign body lodged in a main bronchus and obstructing tumours.

5.   **B, D, F, I, J**
Apical fibrosis pulls the trachea towards the side of the lesion, expansion may be reduced as may percussion note. The breath sounds will be bronchial with fine inspiratory crepitations and vocal fremitus and tactile vocal fremitus will be largely unaffected.

8. FINGER CLUBBING

1. J – Tuberculosis
Finger clubbing in pulmonary tuberculosis most commonly occurs when there has been chronic production of purulent sputum. This may occur both in post-primary pulmonary tuberculosis and in Brock's syndrome, where hilar lymphadenopathy during primary tuberculosis causes lobar collapse and subsequent bronchiectasis.

2. G – Mesothelioma
Asbestos exposure results in a number of different conditions including asbestosis, pleural plaque formation and bilateral diffuse pleural thickening. It also predisposes to malignant mesothelioma and bronchial carcinoma. The CT scan in this case suggests mesothelioma, although confirmation of the diagnosis requires tissue biopsy and is notoriously difficult *ante mortem.* Prognosis is uniformly poor and no treatment has been shown to prolong life.

3. E – Infective endocarditis
The signs in this case indicate infective endocarditis with tricuspid regurgitation. In intravenous drug abusers, the commonest site of vegetations is the tricuspid valve. The diagnosis is confirmed by serial blood cultures and trans-oesophageal echocardiography.

4. I – Squamous cell carcinoma
This lady was exposed to asbestos during the war. Her symptoms suggest hypercalcaemia with a primary lung lesion. Squamous cell carcinomas secrete parathormone-related peptide in a minority of cases but hypercalcaemia is more often associated with bony metastases. Treatment of severe hypercalcaemia involves rapid intravenous rehydration and administration of intravenous bisphosphonates. In approximately 3% of patients with bronchial or pleural tumours, hypertrophic pulmonary osteopathy follows the development of clubbing.

5. C – Cryptogenic fibrosing alveolitis
See question 5.4, *Theme: Shortness of Breath,* page 234 for a description of cryptogenic fibrosing alveolitis.

9. RESPIRATORY INVESTIGATIONS

1. B – Bronchoscopy and bronchial aspirate
The social history suggests the possibility of HIV infection and thus of *Pneumocystis carinii* pneumonia (PCP). PCP tends to cause hypoxia, out of proportion to X-ray changes, which is accentuated by mild exercise. The

organism is detected best in washings taken at bronchoscopy.

2. **G – Pleural biopsy and aspiration**

The history of illness in this woman suggests a differential diagnosis of pulmonary tuberculosis with Pott's disease (tuberculous infection of the spine) or disseminated malignancy. The pleural effusion is thus an ideal target for investigation since it is easily accessible and, furthermore, drainage will relieve the patient's breathlessness. Pleural biopsies should be sent in normal saline to microbiology for culture, and in formalin for histology.

3. **C – Chest X-ray**

This woman's erythema nodosum, anterior uveitis and systemic symptoms suggest a diagnosis of sarcoidosis. Chest X-ray looking for bilateral hilar lymphadenopathy is the most appropriate first step but the test with greatest sensitivity is transbronchial biopsy during bronchoscopy.

4. **F – Peak expiratory flow rate diary**

This boy has symptoms typical of asthma but examination findings are unhelpful. In this situation, a peak flow diary demonstrating diurnal variation in airways resistance (worst on waking, best in evening) is useful in establishing the diagnosis and later, monitoring the response to treatment.

5. **H – Spirometry**

Spirometry is an extremely useful test for monitoring chronic obstructive pulmonary disease. Both the forced expiratory volume in one second (FEV_1) and the forced vital capacity (FVC) are measured. The ratio of FEV_1/FVC, the normal value for which is approximately 0.75, falls in obstructive lung disease and rises again in response to treatment. In contrast, restrictive lung disease results in a normal or raised FEV_1/FVC ratio.

10. ARTERIAL BLOOD GASES

1. **B**

Severe pulmonary embolism in a previously healthy person causes type I respiratory failure, which is the term used to describe hypoxia ($P_aO_2 < 8$ kPa) with normal or low P_aCO_2. Other causes of type I respiratory failure include pneumonia and pulmonary oedema. Hypoxia, resulting from ventilation-perfusion mismatch, leads to increased respiratory drive. CO_2 is therefore blown off, causing a fall in P_aCO_2 and a rise in pH.

2. **E**

This woman has developed infective exacerbation of chronic obstructive pulmonary disease. She may well have a right lower lobe pneumonia but her underlying chronic condition means that she will develop type II, not type I, respiratory failure. Type II respiratory failure describes hypoxia with a high P_aCO_2. Other causes of type II respiratory failure include respiratory muscle weakness (e.g. Guillain-Barré syndrome) and depression of the respiratory centre (e.g. opiate overdose). In this woman's case chronic obstructive pulmonary disease causes alveolar hypoventilation. This results in hypoxia, a high P_aCO_2 and, hence, respiratory acidosis, even when she is relatively well. In steady state, the kidneys excrete H^+ ions and conserve HCO_3^- ions, thus creating a compensatory metabolic alkalosis and keeping the pH in the normal range. When a chest infection is superimposed, hypoxia worsens and the P_aCO_2 rises further. Acutely, the kidneys cannot compensate fast enough to prevent the pH falling.

3. **C**
Hysterical hyperventilation is not an example of respiratory failure and there is no hypoxia. CO_2 is blown off, resulting in respiratory alkalosis. This in turn causes a temporary decrease in plasma ionised calcium concentration, which accounts for the sensory symptoms. Rebreathing allows the P_aCO_2 to rise, correcting the alkalosis and thus achieving resolution of the tingling.

4. **D**
Chronic diarrhoea causes loss of HCO_3^- and K^+ ions from the gut. The kidneys compensate in part by conserving K^+ at the expense of H^+ ions. This process generates HCO_3^- ions but, if the diarrhoea continues for long enough, a metabolic acidosis eventually predominates. A compensatory respiratory alkalosis with Kussmaul respiration ensues, resulting in a low P_aCO_2. The pH usually remains low until the diarrhoea is stopped or HCO_3^- supplements are given.

5. **A**
Diabetic ketoacidosis is characterised by a metabolic acidosis resulting from accumulation of ketones. Dehydration arises both from vomiting and osmotic diuresis as a result of hyperglycaemia. The metabolic acidosis causes a compensatory respiratory alkalosis (Kussmaul respiration – a deep, sighing hyperventilation) so the P_aCO_2 falls. The pH does not normalise, however, until intravenous fluids and insulin are administered. In contrast to the situation in chronic diarrhoea, the base excess in diabetic ketoacidosis becomes very negative owing to the presence of the organic ketoacids.

11. CHEST INJURY

1. **I – Tension pneumothorax**
This develops when a 'one-way valve' air leak occurs either from the lung or the chest wall. Air is forced into the thoracic cavity without any means of escape, completely collapsing the affected lung. The mediastinum is displaced to the opposite side, decreasing venous return and compressing the opposite lung. The commonest cause of tension pneumothorax is mechanical (positive pressure) ventilation in the patient with a visceral pleural injury (as in this case). Rapid decompression is required (needle then chest drain) to

prevent rapid death.

2. **B – Cardiac tamponade**

The pericardium can fill with blood from the heart, especially following pene-trating injuries. Only a small amount of pericardial blood is required to restrict cardiac activity and prevent filling. The diagnosis of cardiac tampon-ade can be difficult. The classic diagnostic Beck's triad consists of increased CVP, decreased BP and muffled heart sounds, but muffled heart sounds are difficult to assess in a trauma care scenario. In general, marked hypotension or cardiac arrest with pulseless electrical activity in the absence of hypo-volaemia or tension pneumothorax should prompt consideration of this diag-nosis. Treatment is with needle pericardiocentesis and/or thoracotomy.

3. **E – Massive haemothorax**

This is defined as a rapid accumulation of more than 1.5 l blood in the chest cavity. A build up of such fluid in a hemithorax can significantly compromise respiratory efforts by compressing the lung and preventing adequate ventila-tion. The patient therefore presents with signs of hypovolaemic shock and respiratory distress. It can be caused by penetrating or blunt chest trauma. Treatment is initially managed by restoration of blood volume and decom-pression of the affected hemithorax by chest drainage.

4. **H – Simple pneumothorax**

Pneumothorax results from air entering the pleural space and can be caused by penetrating and blunt trauma. Air in the pleural space collapses lung tissue causing a ventilation/perfusion mismatch because the blood perfusing the nonventilated area is not oxygenated. Clinically, symptoms are those of mild respiratory distress and signs include decreased breath sounds and hyper-resonance on the affected side. The diagnosis will be confirmed by an upright, expiratory X-ray and treatment is by chest drain insertion (unlike spontaneous pneumothorax, NEVER manage even a small traumatic pneumothorax conservatively).

5. **D – Flail segment with pulmonary contusion**

This is the most common potentially lethal chest injury and commonly occurs with overlying multiple rib fractures/flail chest secondary to blunt trauma, as in this case. The rib fractures are themselves not sufficient to restrict adequate ventilation, but respiratory failure develops over time rather than sponta-neously due to underlying lung injury. Mechanical ventilation is required if significant hypoxia develops and is more likely in patients with chronic lung disease.

12. LUNG DISEASES ASSOCIATED WITH COUGH

1. **I – Pertussis (whooping cough)**
    The white cell count is considerably raised above normal and shows a lymphocytosis. A raised white cell count is a feature of pneumococcal pneumonia, but neutrophilia rather than lymphocytosis would be expected. In Legionnaire's disease and mycoplasma pneumonia, the white cell count is usually normal. In the early stages of pertussis, however, a high white cell count with lymphocytosis is a characteristic feature.

2. **K – Sarcoidosis**
    Sarcoidosis and tuberculosis are both granulomatous diseases. Distinction between the two on purely histological grounds is often difficult though the appearance of the granulomas can be helpful. In tuberculosis the granulomas are typically caseating (i.e. show central caseous necrosis) while in sarcoidosis, necrosis is rare. In addition, the granulomas of tuberculosis are commonly associated with a lymphocytic infiltrate but this is much less frequent in sarcoidosis where the granulomas are often described as being 'naked'.

3. **J – Pneumococcal pneumonia**
    Neutrophils in the sputum implies bronchopulmonary infection with pyogenic bacteria. This is a feature of bronchiectasis and pneumococcal pneumonia, but not of Mycoplasma pneumonia and Legionnaire's disease. In bronchiectasis, the major pathogens are *Staphylococcus aureus*, *Pseudomonas aeruginosa*, *Haemophilus influenzae* and anaerobes. In pneumococcal pneumonia, the pathogenic organism is *Streptococcus pneumoniae*, a Gram-positive diplococcus.

4. **D – Cystic fibrosis**
    Pulmonary infection is a major and recurrent problem in patients with cystic fibrosis. In early childhood, infections with *Staphylococcus aureus* predominate but with repeated courses of antibiotic therapy, subsequent infections with multiple antibiotic resistant organisms develop. These latter organisms include *Pseudomonas aeruginosa*, often 'mucoid' strains.

5. **F – Fibrosing alveolitis**
    An open lung biopsy showing interstitial fibrosis is characteristic of the fibrosing lung diseases, a broad spectrum of conditions with differing aetiologies. Though sarcoidosis and tuberculosis can both cause fibrosis, granulomas would also be expected in these diseases. Fibrosing alveolitis is a rare disorder of unknown aetiology that causes diffuse fibrosis throughout both lung fields, usually in late middle age. In common with all the other fibrosing lung diseases, the end stage of fibrosing alveolitis is the so-called 'honeycomb' lung.

13. CAUSATIVE ORGANISMS IN PNEUMONIA

4. **F –** *Mycobacterium tuberculosis*
    Löwenstein-Jensen (LJ) medium is a specialised medium for the culture of mycobacteria. *Mycobacterium tuberculosis* and *Mycobacterium bovis* characteristically grow on L-J medium at 35–37°C after six weeks' incubation, though this figure varies from 2–12 weeks depending on the number of organisms present. *M. tuberculosis* often grows best when the L-J medium contains appropriate concentrates of glycerol while the growth of *M. bovis* is stimulated by pyruvate in the medium.

2. **H –** *Pseudomonas aeruginosa*
    Pseudomonas is a common cause of nosocomial respiratory tract infection, especially in intensive care. It is also associated with advanced cystic fibrosis. Treatment is with a quinolone, such as ciprofloxacin, or a third-generation cephalosporin, such as ceftazidime. Unfortunately, resistance quickly develops in cystic fibrosis patients.

3. **J –** *Streptococcus pneumoniae (pneumococcus)*
    Streptococcus pneumoniae (pneumococcus) is the most common organism to cause pneumonia. There is usually a rapid onset of fever with dyspnoea and cough, which becomes productive of rust-coloured sputum after one or two days. It usually responds quickly to amoxycillin, erythromycin, cefuroxime or a newer quinolone, such as levofloxacin.

4. **E – Legionella pneumonia**
    Legionella pneumonia presents with a dry cough, dyspnoea, diarrhoea and confusion following a short history of malaise, headache and myalgia. The organism does not Gram stain and culture is slow so diagnosis is generally made by serology. Erythromycin is the drug of choice.

5. **G –** *Mycoplasma pneumoniae*
    See question 5.4, *Theme: Shortness of Breath* page 234 for a description of *Mycoplasma pneumoniae*. It responds well to erythromycin.

14. PLEURAL EFFUSION

1. **A – Cannonball metastases**
    This young man has signs consistent with a left testicular carcinoma with distal metastases in the liver and lungs. Urogenital tumours (i.e. renal, gynaecological and testicular) classically cause multiple large pulmonary metastases known as 'cannonball metastases'.

2. **E – Mesothelioma**
    This gentleman's occupational history gives the clue to his underlying pathology. People working with asbestos such as painters and decorators, plumbers, dockworkers and builders are all at risk of developing pulmonary complications, including fibrosis and mesothelioma. Both disorders are still eligible for compensation and need to be notified. Signs of asbestos exposure on chest radiograph include pleural, diaphragmatic and pericardial calcification, lower zone fibrosis (asbestosis) and mesothelioma (which may also occur within the peritoneum).

3. **H – Squamous cell carcinoma**
    This gentleman has developed squamous cell carcinoma of the lung. The hyponatraemia and hypercalcaemia are suggestive of a pulmonary malignancy but the diagnosis may be confirmed by sputum cytology and/or bronchoscopic biopsy. Depending on the position and stage of the tumour patients may be offered operative resection, radiotherapy, and occasionally chemotherapy. For advanced cases radiotherapy is reserved for problematic haemoptysis and the bony pain of metastases.

4. **J – Tuberculosis**
    This patient has pulmonary tuberculosis as evidenced by the presence of acid and alcohol fast bacilli in the sputum and pleural aspirate cultures. Treatment should include contact tracing, isolation of the patient if coughing and antituberculous therapy for a minimum of six months. Initial therapy for two months includes rifampicin and isoniazid (usually given as a combination tablet), pyrazinamide and more rarely ethambutol. If sensitivities of the mycobacterium strain are confirmed within the first two months the rifampicin and isoniazid are continued for a further four months with regular follow up and monitoring of LFTs.

5. **I – Streptococcal pneumonia**
    This old woman has developed a right middle lobe pneumonia caused by streptococcal infection. Patients with a history suggestive of a pneumonia should always be covered for possible streptococcal infection as it is by far the commonest cause and may be rapidly fatal if untreated, particularly in the elderly. Antibiotic regimes should therefore include amoxycillin, Co-amoxyclav or cefuroxime.

15. RESPIRATORY FAILURE

1. **D – Guillain-Barré syndrome**
    This gentleman has developed type II respiratory failure as evidenced by his hypoxia, hypercapnia and respiratory acidosis. The underlying cause is Guillain-Barré, syndrome secondary to his respiratory tract infection. Patients

admitted with distal limb weakness and sensory loss following respiratory tract infection must be carefully monitored. They should have serial (4–6 hourly) spirometry performed, with any significant reduction in FEV_1 indicating a possible need for assisted ventilation.

2. **B – Chronic bronchitis**

This gentleman has also developed type II respiratory failure secondary to his chronic obstructive pulmonary disease. The respiratory acidosis is partially compensated by a rise in serum bicarbonate, indicating chronic CO_2 retention. Such patients require 24–28% (maximum) oxygen. This patient should be encouraged to stop smoking and may require home oxygen in the future.

3. **I – Pulmonary embolism**

This young woman has developed type I respiratory failure as evidenced by her hypoxia and hypocapnia. Her hyperventilation has lead to a respiratory alkalosis which is common in hypoxic patients. Patients with hypoxia and a respiratory alkalosis are not 'hysterical' and should not be treated with a rebreathing bag and reassurance! If obvious risk factors for her pulmonary embolism have been excluded this patient needs to have a full coagulation screen including proteins C and S, antithrombin III anticardiolipin antibodies and factor V Leiden levels.

4. **G – Mycoplasma pneumonia**

This elderly gentleman has developed an atypical pneumonia as evidenced by the history of confusion, dry cough and wheeze, the type I respiratory failure, the hyponatraemia and the unremarkable chest radiograph. The most likely cause is a Mycoplasma infection, although in younger patients, particularly those who may have risk factors for HIV disease, *Pneumocystis carinii* may present in a similar manner. Treatment may include amoxycillin, erythromycin or cefuroxime until the diagnosis is confirmed.

5. **C – Fibrosing alveolitis**

This woman has developed fibrosing alveolitis as evidenced by her finger clubbing, the fine respiratory crepitations at the lung bases on auscultation and the type respiratory failure. The associated hypoxia classically worsens with exertion. The diagnosis may be confirmed by formal respiratory function tests, high resolution CT scanning of the thorax, and bronchoscopy and broncho-alveolar lavage.

16. COMPLICATIONS OF RESPIRATORY THERAPIES

1. **A – Beclomethasone inhaler**
This patient has oral candidiasis secondary to localised mucosal immunosuppression, which has been caused by excessive corticosteroid deposition in the mouth. It usually responds to nystatin lozenges and occurs much less commonly if the patient uses a spacer device with the inhaler and rinses his or her mouth out with water after taking a dose.

2. **H – Salbutamol inhaler**
Hand tremor is the most common side-effect of salbutamol. In common with corticosteroids and theophylline, high dose salbutamol can cause hypokalaemia, which may predispose to cardiac arrhythmia.

3. **D – Ipratropium bromide inhaler**
Ipratropium bromide acts as an antagonist at muscarinic receptors but, despite this, antimuscarinic side-effects, (which include dry mouth, blurred vision, constipation and urinary retention), are not commonly associated with its use. The most important, though thankfully rare, adverse effect is acute angle closure glaucoma, which may be precipitated when the nebulised drug leaks from around the mask into the patient's eyes.

4. **G – Prednisolone**
Osteoporosis is such a common side-effect of prolonged supraphysiological corticosteroid use that it is now virtually mandatory for patients to be given additional medication, such as a bisphosphonate, to reduce the risk of fracture. Other important corticosteroid side-effects include hypertension, hyperglycaemia, proximal myopathy, peptic ulceration, psychological disturbance and adrenal suppression.

5. **J – Theophylline**
Theophylline is an effective bronchodilator and may also have an immunomodulatory role in the treatment of bronchial hypersensitivity. It has a narrow therapeutic window and may predispose to cardiac arrhythmia even at therapeutic levels.

17. COMPLICATIONS OF TUBERCULOSIS

1. **G – Pericardial effusion**
This gentleman has symptoms and signs consistent with a large pericardial effusion. He has a positive Kussmaul's sign which is the paradoxical rise of the JVP with inspiration (the JVP should fall with inspiration due to a lowering of intrathoracic pressure and increased venous return to the heart). He has an

impalpable apex beat and poorly heard heart sounds with low voltage QRS complexes on the ECG. The CXR classically shows a large 'globular' heart, as well as evidence of pulmonary tuberculous infection. Patients require anti-tuberculous therapy and drainage of the effusion via a pericardial drain. The pericardial fluid should be sent for microscopy and culture.

2. C – Lobar collapse

This patient has signs of left lower lobe collapse as evidenced by the decreased breath sounds and dullness to percussion and the 'double left heart border' on the chest radiograph. Lobar collapse is principally caused by mucous plugging of the larger airways but may also be a result of hilar lymphadenopathy secondary to the infection.

3. D – Lupus vulgaris

Lupus vulgaris is the commonest skin condition caused directly by tuberculous infection. It appears as a raised, eczematous plaque-like lesion commonly on the face, upper limbs and truncal region. The condition most commonly occurs due to haematogenous spread from a primary lesion, although direct spread may occur from local infected tissue, primarily lymph nodes. Skin biopsy may confirm the diagnosis and a standard 6–9 month anti-tuberculous regime should be given.

4. A – Cerebral abscess

The rise of HIV disease has seen an increased incidence of tuberculous infections. HIV positive patients are at risk of both *Mycobacterium tuberculosis* and the atypical mycobacteria, such as *Mycobacterium avium intracellulare*. Patients may present with central nervous infections including meningitis and tuberculomas. The differential diagnosis of a ring enhancing lesion on a CT head scan in this case includes cerebral toxoplasmosis, lymphoma, primary and secondary brain tumours and an abscess, including aspergillosis and Nocardia.

5. E – Meningitis

This child has tuberculous meningitis (TBM). Patients often have a prodromal illness several weeks prior to a second, 'meningitic' phase. The prodrome may include a mild headache and 'flu-like' symptoms, and is therefore often mistaken for seasonal childhood illnesses. The second phase presents with signs of raised intracranial pressure, meningism, fever, febrile convulsions and is rapidly fatal if left untreated. TBM may affect any age group and is more common in third world populations and the immunosuppressed. Despite patients having clinical and radiographic evidence of raised intracranial pressure lumbar puncture may be both therapeutic (relieving some of the pressure) and diagnostic. The CSF classically shows raised protein and low glucose concentrations, the low glucose concentration differentiating it from viral meningitis. AAFB may be seen on microscopy but CSF should also be sent for polymerase chain reaction testing, as this confirms the diagnosis far more rapidly than culture.

18. ANTI-TUBERCULOSIS THERAPY

1.   A – Ciprofloxacin
Ciprofloxacin, a quinolone antibiotic more commonly used to treat non-pneumococcal respiratory tract infections, urinary tract and gastro-intestinal infections, is active against *Mycobacterium tuberculosis* and is used in cases resistant to first-line agents. There have been isolated reports of tendon inflammation and damage following its use, especially in the elderly.

2.   E – Isoniazid
Pyrazinamide, rifampicin and isoniazid may all cause hepatotoxicity. The other main adverse effect associated with isoniazid use is peripheral neuropathy, the risk of which is increased in slow acetylators and in those with other risk factors for peripheral neuropathy, such as malnutrition, alcoholism, diabetes and HIV infection. Pyridoxine (vitamin B_6) is given both prophylactically and, at higher dose, to treat established neuropathy.

3.   H – Rifampicin
Rifampicin is a potent hepatic enzyme inducer which increases metabolism of many drugs, including all the steroid hormones. Detailed advice regarding oral contraceptive dose and variation in administration is available in the British National Formulary but, in addition, barrier contraceptives should be used for four to eight weeks after a course of rifampicin is completed.

4.   D – Ethambutol
The main adverse effects of ethambutol are loss of visual acuity, restriction of visual fields and colour blindness. Their incidence is increased in renal impairment. Visual acuity should be tested prior to commencing treatment and the drug should be used with caution in children until they are old enough to perceive and report visual disturbance.

5.   I – Streptomycin
Streptomycin was one of the first antituberculous antibiotics but is now used only in cases resistant to first-line agents. In common with the other aminoglycosides, it causes ototoxicity and nephrotoxicity, especially in the elderly and in people with pre-existing renal impairment.

19. SARCOIDOSIS

1.   A – Anterior uveitis
This patient has developed acute anterior uveitis, which may (as in this case) be the presenting feature of sarcoidosis. It presents with blurring of vision, photophobia and watering of the eye, the eyes looking red and congested. Cases may resolve spontaneously but many require topical steroids. Other

ocular complications include chronic anterior uveitis, posterior uveitis, conjunctival deposits, dry eyes associated with lacrimal gland infiltration and a band keratopathy associated with hypercalcaemia. The retina may also suffer sarcoid deposits, there may be choroidoretinitis and retinal haemorrhages, as well as papilloedema.

2. H – Lupus pernio

Lupus pernio is due to granulomatous infiltration of the skin and has a predilection for the skin of the nose, cheeks and ears. It is a raised, violaceous lesion with papules centrally. The lesion is treated with systemic steroids but rarely, if ever completely resolves. The commonest skin condition associated with sarcoid is in fact erythema nodosum, and anyone presenting with this lesion needs to have sarcoid excluded. A relatively common combination of signs is erythema nodosum, acute anterior uveitis and bilateral hilar lymphadenopathy, termed Lofgren's syndrome.

3. E – Diabetes insipidus

Sarcoid tissue may infiltrate any of the major endocrine glands but as with most sites, this is largely asymptomatic. Infiltration of the hypothalamus and posterior pituitary gland may produce cranial diabetes insipidus, as in this case. Infiltration of the anterior pituitary may rarely cause panhypopituitarism. DDAVP is a synthetic ADH analogue and is administered nasally.

4. F – Erythema nodosum

This young woman has presented with respiratory symptoms and erythema nodosum. In the UK, sarcoidosis and tuberculosis are the commonest causes of erythema nodosum and it may be quite difficult to differentiate them in the early stages. Other causes include the oral contraceptive pill, infections including steptococcus, fungi and EBV, inflammatory bowel disease and haematological malignancies.

5. D – Conduction system disease

Infiltration of the heart is a relatively rare but significant presentation in sarcoidosis. Asymptomatic, granulomatous infiltration is common but significant myocardial disease causes cardiomyopathy and cardiac failure. Infiltration of the conduction system may produce various levels of atrioventricular node block, including complete heart block, as in this case, bundle branch block and ventricular arrhythmia.

20. INTRATHORACIC TUMOURS

1. J – Small cell carcinoma of the bronchus

A heavy smoker who presents with haemoptysis and dyspnoea is likely to have carcinoma of the bronchus unless proved otherwise. The fact that this

patient has a moon face, truncal obesity and hypokalaemia is strongly suggestive of Cushing's syndrome. Patients with carcinoma of the bronchus quite
often present with paraneoplastic endocrinopathies. Cushing's syndrome, in
which there is ectopic production of ACTH by the tumour cells, is one
example. The type of bronchial carcinoma most likely to cause paraneoplastic
Cushing's syndrome is small cell carcinoma as this is derived from neuroen-
docrine cells.

2.   E – Hodgkin's disease
The most common types of tumour presenting as an anterior mediastinal mass
are thymoma, Hodgkin's disease and germ cell tumours. In the posterior
mediastinum, neurofibroma also occurs. Biopsy of the mass shows Reed-
Sternberg cells, which are diagnostic of Hodgkin's disease. The patient's
symptoms, particularly night sweats and weight loss, are in keeping with the
diagnosis and indicate stage 'b'.

3.   A – Adenocarcinoma of the bronchus
Despite the fact this patient has never smoked, the lung tumour is undoubt-
edly malignant as liver metastases are present. Unlike squamous and small
cell carcinoma, adenocarcinoma of the bronchus does not show a strong
association with cigarette smoking. In addition, it is often located in the
peripheral part of the lung and is thus not visible at bronchoscopy. This type of
presentation, with a small primary tumour and widespread metastatic disease,
is not uncommon for adenocarcinoma of the bronchus.

4.   G – Malignant mesothelioma
Malignant mesothelioma is a pleural tumour that presents either as a pleural
mass or as diffuse pleural thickening. The tumour is strongly associated with
asbestos exposure and, as a docker, this patient would almost certainly have
been exposed to asbestos during his working life. The time interval between
exposure to asbestos and development of malignant mesothelioma is often
many years.

5.   K – Squamous cell carcinoma of the bronchus
As mentioned above, haemoptysis in a smoker is a sinister symptom and
should be considered as indicative of bronchial carcinoma unless proved
otherwise. This patient has Horner's syndrome, a common cause of which is
infiltration of the sympathetic chain in the neck by an apical lung carcinoma.
Highly keratinised cells in sputum are indicative of atypical squamous cells (it
is squamous cells that normally produce keratin), so the most likely diagnosis
in this case is squamous cell carcinoma of the bronchus.

6.   **L – Thymoma**

Myasthenia gravis is an autoimmune disease in which IgG antibodies to acetylcholine receptor protein are found. About 70% of patients with myasthenia gravis have thymic hyperplasia and about 10% have a thymoma. Thymomas are anterior mediastinal tumours composed of varying amounts of lymphocytes and thymic epithelial cells. They can be benign or malignant. Excision of the thymoma is necessary to remove a potentially malignant tumour but does not necessarily improve the myasthenic symptoms.

21. LUNG CANCER

1.   **J – Superior vena caval obstruction**

Direct invasion by bronchial carcinoma can cause a number of effects to the surrounding tissues. Invasion and obstruction of the superior vena cava typically leads to early morning headaches, facial congestion (hence a tightness around the collar), oedema in the arms, distended veins on the chest and neck and occasionally blackouts.

2.   **A – Bony metastasis**

This man has many of the symptoms of hypercalcaemia, most easily remembered by the rhyme 'bones (pain), stones (renal), abdominal groans (pain often secondary to peptic ulceration or constipation) and psychiatric moans'. His biochemistry shows he has high plasma calcium and is dehydrated, in this case due to the effect of hypercalcaemia on the renal tubules, impairing their ability to concentrate urine (a mild form of diabetes insipidus). There are two possible causes for hypercalcaemia associated with lung cancer: bony metastasis and ectopic PTH, however the former is much more common and the patient is complaining of severe back pain suggestive of metastasis to the spine.

3.   **E – Inappropriate ADH secretion**

There are many causes for SIADH of which the paraneoplastic (i.e. non-metastatic) syndrome associated with small cell carcinoma of the lung is one. Inappropriate levels of the hormone lead to hypervolaemic hyponatraemia with inability of the body to diurese in response to falling plasma osmolality. Severe hyponatraemia with $Na^+ < 110$ mmol/l can lead to generalised fits and coma.

4.   H – Pancoast's tumour

Pancoast's tumour describes a carcinoma of the apex of the lung. Invasion and mass effect in this region can involve the lower roots of the brachial plexus causing wasting and weakness in the intrinsic muscles of the hand. They may also invade the sympathetic ganglion leading to Horner's syndrome (this case however is not just Horner's!) with ptosis, meiosis and anhydrosis on the affected side.

5.   B – Eaton-Lambert syndrome

Eaton-Lambert myasthenic syndrome is a rare paraneoplastic syndrome associated with small cell carcinoma of the lung. There is impaired release of acetylcholine at the neuromuscular junction thought to be caused by autoantibodies directed to native calcium channels. The picture is therefore very similar to myasthenia gravis, typically with proximal weakness and often ocular or bulbar palsies. Unlike myasthenia gravis the weakness often improves with repeated muscle contraction.

Self-assessment EMQ Papers

Six practice examinations are listed below, drawing questions from across the syllabus: each is intended as a two-hour examination. Questions are taken from both texts. For those not yet fortunate enough to have bought or acquired both volumes, there is a clear distinction between the two halves of each examination, and they can be answered independently.

VOLUME 1

	Exam 1	Exam 2	Exam 3	Exam 4	Exam 5	Exam 6
1	1.2	1.3	1.5	1.6	1.7	1.8
2	1.9	1.11	1.17	1.14	1.12	1.15
3	2.1	2.2	2.3	2.5	2.7	2.9
4	2.10	2.11	2.12	3.2	3.4	3.6
5	3.8	3.10	3.11	3.18	3.12	3.15
6	3.19	3.17	3.16	3.20	3.23	3.26
7	3.25	3.26	3.21	4.3	4.6	4.7
8	4.8	4.10	4.1	4.13	4.14	4.15
9	4.18	4.16	4.11	4.21	4.22	4.23
10	4.24	4.19	4.26	5.3	5.1	5.4
11	5.5	5.7	5.8	5.13	5.10	5.17
12	5.14	5.21	5.15	5.20	5.12	5.19

VOLUME 2

	Exam 1	Exam 2	Exam 3	Exam 4	Exam 5	Exam 6
13	1.1	1.2	1.3	1.4	1.5	1.6
14	1.9	1.7	1.14	1.10	1.12	1.16
15	1.18	1.19	1.22	1.23	1.25	1.26
16	1.27	1.28	2.1	2.3	2.2	2.5
17	2.6	2.8	2.10	2.13	2.12	2.15
18	2.17	2.18	2.20	2.22	2.21	2.23
19	2.24	2.25	3.9	3.10	3.11	3.4
20	3.12	3.6	3.13	3.14	3.15	3.16
21	3.17	3.18	3.19	4.1	4.3	4.4
22	4.5	4.7	4.8	4.9	4.10	4.12
23	4.13	4.14	4.16	4.18	5.1	5.2
24	5.3	5.4	5.5	5.7	5.8	5.9

TB	Tuberculosis
Tbil	Total bilirubin
TBM	Tuberculous meningitis
TFTs	Thyroid function tests
TMRP	Transmembrane regulator protein
TSH	Thyroid stimulating hormone
TURP	Transurethral resection of prostate
U&Es	Urea and Electrolytes
USS	Ultrasound scan
UTI	Urinary tract infection
UV	Ultraviolet
VDRL	Venereal disease research laboratory
VER	Visual evoked responses
VQ	Ventilation/Perfusion scan
vWF	von Willebrand's factor
WCC	White cell count
WHO	World Health Organisation

Normal values

NB. These values may vary according to local populations

Haematology

Haemoglobin

Males	13.5—17.5 g/dl
Females	11.5—15.5 g/dl
MCV	76–98 fl
PCV	35–55%
WCC	4–11 × 10^9/l
Neutrophils	2.5–7.58 × 10^9/l
Lymphocyte	1.5–3.5 × 10^9/l
Platelets	150–400 × 10^9/l
ESR	0–10mm in the 1st hour
PT	10.6–14.9 s
PTT	23.0–35.0 s
TT	10.5–15.5 s
Fib	125–300 mg/dl
Vitamin B$_{12}$	160–900 pmol/l
Folate	1.5–10.0 μg/l

Ferritin

Males	20–250 μg/l
Females	10–120 μg/l

Immunoglobulins

IgM	0.5–2.0 g/l
IgG	5–16 g/l
IgA	1.0–4.0 g/l

Biochemistry

Na$^+$	135–145 mmol/l
K$^+$	3.5–5.0 mmol/l
Urea	2.5–6.5 mmol/l
Creatinine	50–120 μmol/l
ALT	5–30 iu/l
AST	10–40 iu/l
Bilirubin	2–17 μmol/l
Alkaline phosphatase	30–130 iu/l
Albumin	35–55 g/l
γGT	5–30 iu/l
αFP	<10 ku/l
CCa^{2+}	2.20–2.60 mmol/l
PO$_4^{3-}$	0.70–1.40 mmol/l
CK	23–175 iu/l
LDH	100–190 iu/l
Amylase	<200 u/l
Lactate	0.5–2.2 mmol/l
Mg^{2+}	0.75–1.00 mmol/l
Urate	0.1–0.4 mol/l
CRP	0–10 mg/l

Diabetes

Random glucose	3.5–5.5 mmol/l*
*If >5.5 then OGTT 2 hrs:	<7.8 = Normal
	7.8 –11 = IGT
	>11.1 = DM
HbA$_{1c}$	<7.0 %

Endocrinology

Prolactin	<400 mU/l
ACTH	<18 pmol/l
Cortisol	
0900	200–700 nmol/l
2400	<50 nmol/l
TSH	0.17–3.2 mu/l
T$_4$	11–22 pmol/l
FSH	
Prepubertal children	<5 u/l
Women	
Follicular phase	2.5–10 u/l
Mid-cycle	25–70 u/l
Luteal phase	0.3–2 u/l
Postmenopausal	>30 u/l

Men	1–8 u/l
LH	
Prepubertal children	< 5 u/l
Women	
Follicular phase	2.5–10 u/l
Mid-cycle	25–70 u/l
Luteal phase	0.5–13 u/l
Postmenopausal	> 30 u/l
Men	1–10 u/l

Cholesterol	< 5.2 mmol/l
Triglycerides	0–1.5 mmol/l
LDL	< 3.5 mmol/l
HDL	< 1.0 mmol/l
Total/HDL	< 5.0

Blood Gases

pH	7.35–7.45
P_aCO_2	4.6–6.0 kPa
P_aO_2	10.5–13.5 kPa
HCO_3^-	24–30 mmol/l
Base excess	2–2.0 mmol/l

CSF

Protein	< 0.45 g/l
Glucose	2.5 —3.9 mmol/l (two-thirds plasma)
Cells	< 5 (WCC)
Opening Pressure	6–20 cmH$_2$O

Index

PASTEST – DEDICATED TO YOUR SUCCESS

PasTest has been publishing books for doctors for medical students and doctors over 25 years. Our extensive experience means that we are always one step ahead when it comes to knowledge of current trends and undergraduate exams.

We use only the best authors, which enables us to tailor our books to meet your revision needs. We incorporate feedback from candidates to ensure that our books are continually improved.

This commitment to quality ensures that students who buy PasTest books achieve successful exam results.

100% Money Back Guarantee
We're sure you will find our study books invaluable, but in the unlikely event that you are not entirely happy, we will give you your money back – guaranteed.

Delivery to your Door
With a busy lifestyle, nobody enjoys walking to the shops for something that may or may not be in stock. Let us take the hassle and deliver direct to your door. We will despatch your book within 24 hours of receiving your order. We also offer free delivery on books for medical students to UK addresses.

How to Order:
www.pastest.co.uk
To order books safely and securely online, shop at our website.

Telephone: +44 (0)1565 752000
Fill out the order form as a helpful prompt and have your credit card to hand when you call.

PasTest Ltd, FREEPOST, Knutsford, WA16 7BR.
Send your completed order form with your cheque (made payable to **PasTest Ltd**) and debit or credit card details to the above address. (Please complete your ' address details on the reverse of the cheque.)

+44 (0)1565 650264
Fax your completed order form with your debit or credit card details.

PASTEST BOOKS FOR UNDERGRADUATES

PasTest are the specialists in study guides and revision courses for medical qualifications. For over 25 years we have been helping doctors to achieve their potential. The PasTest range of books for medical students includes:

Radiology Casebook for Medical Students
Wasan, Grundy & Beese
- Up to the minute cases relevant for final exams
- Contains X-rays, MR and CT scans
- Guidance on interpreting different types of X-ray
- Chapters on Abdomen, Chest, Bones, Neurology and Trauma
- Includes a 16 question test paper and answers

OSCES for Medical Undergraduates Volume 1
Feather, Visvanathan & Lumley
OSCES for Medical Undergraduates Volume 2
Visvanathan, Feather & Lumley
- Chapters covering history taking, examinations, investigations, practical techniques, making a diagnosis, prescribing treatment and other issues.
- Answers in a separate section so that students can assess their performance and identify areas needing further attention.
- Book 1 covers Neurology and Psychiatry, Ophthalmology and Otolaryngology, Cardiovascular diseases and Haematology, Respiratory medicine, Orthopaedics and Trauma, Ethics and Legal Medicine, including Consent and IV Procedures.
- Book 2 covers Endocrinology, Gastroenterology, Urology and Renal Medicine, Obstetrics and Gynaecology, Rheumatology and Dermatology.

Surgical Finals: Passing the Clinical
Kuperberg & Lumley
Medical Finals: Passing the Clinical
Moore & Richardson
- Over 90 examples of favourite long and short surgical cases
- Syllabus checklist for structured revision
- Detailed examination schemes with action tables
- Concise teaching notes highlight areas most relevant to finals
- Revision index for easy access to specific topics
- Vital tips on preparation and presentation

Surgical Finals: Structured Answer and Essay Questions – Second Edition
Visvanathan & Lumley
Medical Finals: Structured Answer and Essay Questions
Feather, Visvanathan & Lumley
- Prepare for the written examination with this unique combination of essay questions and the new structured answer questions
- Over 130 structured answer questions with detailed teaching notes
- Typical essay questions with sample essay plans and model essays
- Invaluable revision checklist to help you to track your progress
- Short textbook reviews enable you to select the best textbooks

150 Essential MCQs for Surgical Finals
Hassanally & Singh
150 Essential MCQs for Medical Finals
Singh & Hassanally
- The crucial material for your exam success
- Extended teaching notes, bullet points and mnemonics
- Revision indexes for easy access to specific topics

For priority mail order service, please contact PasTest on 01565 752000, or ORDER ONLINE AT OUR SECURE WEBSITE

PasTest, FREEPOST, Egerton Court, Parkgate Estate,
Knutsford, Cheshire WA16 7BR
Telephone: 01565 752000 Fax: 01565 650264
E-mail: books@pastest.co.uk Web site: www.pastest.co.uk

ORDER FORM

☐	Radiology Casebook for Medical Students	£14.95
☐	OSCES for Medical Undergraduates Volume 1	£16.95
☐	OSCES for Medical Undergraduates Volume 2	£16.95
☐	Surgical Finals: Passing the Clinical	£14.50
☐	Medical Finals: Passing the Clinical	£14.50
☐	Surgical Finals: Structured Answer and Essay Questions – 2nd ed	£14.50
☐	Medical Finals: Structured Answer and Essay Questions	£14.50
☐	150 Essential MCQs for Surgical Finals	£12.50
☐	150 Essential MCQs for Medical Finals	£12.50

FREE DELIVERY ON BOOKS FOR MEDICAL STUDENTS TO UK ADDRESSES

Name _____

Address _____

_____

_____

_____

Daytime telephone _____

I enclose a cheque for .... (made payable to **PasTest Ltd**)

Please charge my credit/debit card ☐VISA ☐Mastercard ☐ Switch ☐Solo

Issue number _____ (Switch cards only)

Card number _____

Expiry date _____ Date _____

Signature _____

Please print clearly and return your completed order form and payment to:

PasTest Ltd, FREEPOST, Knutsford, WA16 7BR
or Fax to **01565 650264**
Order online at **www.pastest.co.uk**